D1601366

From Erasmus to Tolstoy

FROM ERASMUS TO TOLSTOY

The Peace Literature of
Four Centuries;
Jacob ter Meulen's
Bibliographies of the
Peace Movement before 1899

EDITED, WITH AN INTRODUCTION, BY
PETER VAN DEN DUNGEN

FOREWORD BY
ARTHUR EYFFINGER

Bibliographies and Indexes in Law and Political Science,
Number 14

GREENWOOD PRESS
New York • Westport, Connecticut • London

Library of Congress Cataloging-in-Publication Data

ter Meulen, Jacob.
   From Erasmus to Tolstoy : the peace literature of four centuries :
Jacob ter Meulen's bibliographies of the peace movement before 1899
/ edited, with an introduction, by Peter van den Dungen ; foreword by Arthur Eyffinger.
     p. cm.—(Bibliographies and indexes in law and political
science, ISSN 0742-6909 ; no. 14)
   Includes bibliographical references and index.
   ISBN 0-313-26827-4 (lib. bdg. : alk. paper)
   1. Peace—Bibliography—Catalogs. 2. Peace Palace (Hague,
Netherlands). Library—Catalogs. 3. Meulen, Jacob ter, 1884-1962.
I. Title. II. Series.
Z6464.Z9V36 1990
[JX1963]
016.3271'72—dc20   90-3865

British Library Cataloguing in Publication Data is available.

Library of Congress Catalog Card Number: 90-3865
ISBN: 0-313-26827-4
ISSN: 0742-6909

First published in 1990

Greenwood Press, 88 Post Road West, Westport, CT 06881
An imprint of Greenwood Publishing Group, Inc.

Printed in the United States of America

The paper used in this book complies with the
Permanent Paper Standard issued by the National
Information Standards Organization (Z39.48-1984).

10 9 8 7 6 5 4 3 2 1

CONTENTS

FOREWORD

There was a time, nor indeed too long ago, when the Peace Palace Library was considered the best-equipped in the fields of both public and private international law. There have been days when its library system was unrivalled in Europe, when its printed catalogue, the impressive wine-red volumes, were called a "vollständige Bibliographie des Völkerrechts" ("complete bibliography of the Law of Nations") and when its acquisition lists, posted weekly to the entrance gates of the Palace, drew the keen attention of passing scholars. Those days have gone, and they have gone forever, it would seem.

There is nothing dramatic in this. Despite all the economizing of recent years, the staff of the Peace Palace Library may still justly boast a partly unique and at all times representative collection. Though no longer the world's centre for research in the international field, the library still serves many ends. The two Courts, the Hague Academy, numbers of scholars from home and abroad, men of law and university students invariably obtain (almost) all they need from the cosy reading room.

Still one cannot help looking back with something of nostalgia, if not envy at the heyday of the institution and the considerable production in those early days. In many ways, Jacob ter Meulen symbolizes that era. Even today, a quarter-century after his death, his name lingers in the ears of staff-members as the paragon of learned librarianship. Virtually every field of the library seems permeated by his labour. Not only did he reorganise the catalogues, expand the printed catalogue, assemble a mass of rare books (over three-quarters of this department, amounting to some 6,000 precious volumes, came in under his administration) and publish monographs and articles in a wide range of disciplines, but he also broke fresh ground for the library in many fields. Also in view of his character and the dramatic incidents over the years from 1940 to 45 his life and works make the subject of a most interesting thesis or monograph. The present reprint of the two bibliographies on early peace studies, one of the many collections ter Meulen had launched, is a fitting occasion to spend a few words on his life and activities.

Jacob ter Meulen (1884-1962): A Life Devoted to Peace and Study

Typically enough, not much has been written on ter Meulen's life and accomplishments. Indeed, most of his work was done "under the lee". Keen to promote his library whenever he could, he would never insist on his own part in the work. Still, some interesting details may be distilled from the *in memoriams* which his tried and trusted colleague in the field of Grotian studies, P.J.J. Diermanse, composed in 1962. From these emerges the picture of a steadfast and noble character, an orderly and systematic mind and an accurate and enthusiastic librarian. Though demanding for any of his subordinates, ter Meulen with his dignified appearance must have been a truly inspiring figure.

Jacob ter Meulen was born in The Hague on 3 December 1884, the only son of the landscape painter François Pieter ter Meulen and Augusta Wijnaendts. His father's family came from the northern part of Holland ("de Zaan") and had a firm Mennonite tradition. His first legal and international training was at Amsterdam University (1906-1909), where he studied municipal law, economics and international law. In 1910 he decided to change Amsterdam for Zurich and follow the courses of Max Huber, the internationalist and later president of the International Court of Justice, who had impressed him enormously during the debates of the Second Hague Peace Conference of 1907. The first in his long series of publications appeared in the *Grotius Internationaal Jaarboek* of 1913 (pp.19-53) and concerned an historical sketch in Dutch of the development of the community of states, which may be deemed a first step on the road he would go with so much ardour in later years.

It was in Zurich and under the guidance of Huber that, on 24 January 1914, he obtained his doctorate in public law *magna cum laude*. His thesis, *Beitrag zur Geschichte der internationalen Organisation 1300-1700* (The Hague, 1916) would serve as a basis for his impressive three-volume history of international organization which would appear in later years (*Der Gedanke der Internationalen Organisation in seiner Entwicklung*; The Hague, Nijhoff, 1917, 1929, 1940). The three volumes cover the period of, as ter Meulen himself liked to call it, the "independent Utopian thinkers" and discuss the history of pacifism from 1300 to 1889. After his doctorate he returned to Holland, where he was liable to military service due to the general mobilization. Apparently, at this juncture he did not yet object to the military system. His experiences over these years made him compile an exhaustive documentary system of the history of the Great War in the early years of his term at the Peace Palace Library. However, from the mid-twenties onwards, his Mennonite background, inborn nature and studies, as well as the turn of world politics would gradually change him into a fierce champion of Christian antimilitarism. Thus, he would serve some years as secretary to the International Mennonite Peace Committee and through numerous pamphlets zealously propagated the idea of conscientious objection to military service. It was thanks to these activities that he became acquainted with men such as the Rev. J.B. Th. Hugenholtz and the Austrian professor Johannes Ude.

On 1 November 1915 he married Wilhelmina ("Willy") Bosboom, who had outspoken musical tastes and contributed highly to the cultural and artistic atmosphere of their family life. They had no children. Contrary to what one would expect, ter Meulen did not opt for an academic career. In 1916 we find him teaching civics at secondary schools, but soon afterwards he left this sphere of action for the library field. In 1917 he was appointed assistant librarian at Utrecht University Library, in charge of the cataloguing of the legal department. Here he stayed for some five years and it is from these days that stem his reports on library cataloguing, being the reflection of prolonged visits to the Zurich and Frankfurt libraries. At last, in 1922, he was appointed librarian of the Netherlands School of Economics at Rotterdam (now Erasmus University), to replace P.C. Molhuysen, who had been asked to succeed Albéric Baron Rolin, the first director of the Carnegie Library in the Peace Palace. Within two years, however, Molhuysen was appointed librarian at the Hague Royal Library and ter Meulen was approached to replace him at the Hague Peace Palace. And so it happened that on 1 January 1924 he first entered the library which would remain his passion for the rest of his life.

The Peace Palace Librarian (1924-1952)

The Peace Palace Library, or Carnegie Library as it used to be called at the time, was opened in 1913, along with the inauguration of the Palace itself. The idea of the Palace was the outcome of the First Hague Peace Conference of 1899 and materialized largely through the personal sponsorship of Andrew Carnegie (1835-1912). Carnegie, the business tycoon, around 1900 withdrew from affairs to dispose gradually of his enormous wealth of an estimated $460 million in what he liked to call his "Gospel of Wealth", a philanthropic schedule with cultural and pacific overtones. In 1903, Carnegie voted $1.5 million to the constituting of a "Temple of Peace" at The Hague which was bound to become both the symbol of pacifism and a world centre of international studies. It would serve as a courthouse to the newly launched Permanent Court of Arbitration and also harbour a world library of international law to further the Court's proceedings and scholarly research in the rapidly expanding field. When ter Meulen took over, in 1924, some 50,000 volumes had been collected in the field of international law and the areas of political and diplomatic history and foreign municipal law. But something else had changed in the meantime. On 15 February 1922 the first official sitting of the newly installed judicial organ of the League of Nations, the Permanent Court of International Justice, took place. Again, one and a half years later, on 14 July 1923, the Hague Academy of International Law was inaugurated which was to organize summer courses in international law for hundreds of students from all over the world. It was, in other words, a hectic period of expansion -- the very thing to provoke the enthusiasm of ter Meulen: accordingly, from his very first day he proved himself the right man in the right place.

Ter Meulen's librarianship spans nearly three decades; at first though, there was nothing to indicate the long career. Indeed, his term was almost cut short at the very beginning when in 1926 he applied for the directorship of the library of the League of Nations in Geneva -- an indication of his international ambitions in those early years. Happily enough though, once settled down, he soon became too deeply involved in his numerous projects ever to consider a change, it would seem. From the beginning ter Meulen proved himself a consummate librarian, who was as well versed in academic spheres as in matters of management and finance. He took his province to be very wide indeed. To mention only three among the many catalogues he launched were, first, a portrait catalogue registering in endless files the alphabetically arranged names of men and women whose portraits were shown in the books collected in the library, second a genuine subject catalogue, which was indeed innovative in those days, and third a central catalogue of foreign legal periodicals in Dutch public libraries. He was also very involved with the national library world. And yet, despite all his organising and functioning in the sphere of management properly speaking, ter

Meulen's lasting repute in the library world has finally come to rest on two projects in the strictly scholarly domain. These concern the history of the peace movement and pacifism and the Grotian studies. Give or take a few years, these projects reflect the first and second half of his term of office.

Peace Studies

In all fairness, the cataloguing of Peace Studies at the Peace Palace Library had been instigated before ter Meulen's arrival by Dr. Molhuysen and Ms. Oppenheim and had almost grown into an integral part of the Library's domain. But it was ter Meulen who took the expansion of the collection into the sphere of pacifism as a matter of his personal concern -- it matched his character. Accordingly, large collections were purchased, while others were simply offered, such as parts of Alfred H. Fried's private collection in 1931 and in 1951 the collection of the former "Vredeshuis" built up by G.J. de Voogd. And not only did ter Meulen order books and pamphlets from whatever sources available, but along with his staff he also managed to lay open these often rare items to the interested public. Witness to this are the *Bibliographical Lists of the Peace Movement Before 1899* which are reproduced here. In his *Introduction* Peter van den Dungen has most competently discussed the genesis of these two lists. Let it suffice here to remind the reader that the idea was initiated in 1932 by the International Historical Commission which included prominent individuals such as Christian Lange, Hans Wehberg, Merle Curti and Rafael Altamira. The project was financed partly by the Oslo Nobel Committee and partly by ter Meulen himself, which incidentally was not the only time he drew on his personal means to further research! The first list was published in 1934 and recorded the period 1776-1898 in some 3,500 items, the second was published in 1936 and covered the period 1480-1776 in some 500 items.

However, ter Meulen did not content himself with bibliographical research only. Indeed by far his best-known and most penetrating study in the field is the massive three-volume *Der Gedanke der Internationalen Organisation in seiner Entwicklung* ("The Development of the Idea of International Organization") of which we spoke earlier and which was published between 1917 and 1940. In the first volume of this *magnum opus* which saw highly appreciative reviews in such publications as the *Times Literary Supplement* and Hans Wehberg's *Friedens-Warte*, ter Meulen discussed the period 1300-1800, including all major peace projects from Pierre Dubois to Immanuel Kant. The second volume covered the period from the French Revolution to the Franco-German War of 1870, featuring among other subjects the Anglo-American peace societies and French Socialism. The third bulky volume covered the years up to 1889, presenting an outline of "legal internationalism" and the arbitration movement. Together with the works of Christian Lange, the director of the Norwegian Nobel Institute (*Histoire de l'internationalisme*; 1919-1963) and of Théodore Ruyssen, the president of the French peace society "La Paix par le Droit" (*Les Sources doctrinales de l'internationalisme*, 1954-1961), ter Meulen's work helped form the thoughts of generations of international lawyers.

Grotian Studies

It is positively astounding that all the work we discussed above, done alongside the day to day cares of library management, is in fact only half of the scholarly work accomplished by ter Meulen during his 28 years of librarianship. The second half of his term, that is from 1940 onwards, was increasingly devoted to quite another field (though as innate to the Library's tradition as was pacifism) namely the life and works of Hugo Grotius. It goes without saying that, personal leanings set aside, the work of Holland's most renowned international lawyer, at the time almost universally looked upon as the "Father of International Law", had to be of special concern to any Peace Palace Librarian.

Instrumental in the Library's early focussing on Grotius was the gift made by the Hague publisher Martinus Nijhoff in 1913 of 55 editions of Grotius' precious book of 1625, *De Jure Belli ac Pacis* ("On the Law of War and Peace"), the book that was long held to be the most influential work in world literature except the Bible. Nijhoff's donation became the nucleus of what, particularly thanks to the efforts of ter Meulen and in later years of his collaborator Diermanse, has become the world's best-equipped Grotius collection. Of the 1,300 editions of works by Grotius, and these include all the reprints of scattered verse and the kind, the Peace Palace Library has more than a thousand, covering all major editions in any field.

However, again ter Meulen did not content himself with just collecting rare book editions. As early as 1925, on the tercentenary of Grotius' masterwork, he arranged a very successful exhibition in the Hague municipal reception rooms which then was continued on the premises on behalf of the Hague Academy and the *Institut de Droit International*. From these emanated a *Concise Bibliography of Hugo Grotius*, a bibliographical list of 76 editions and translations of *De Jure*

Belli and a fine collection of letters by Grotius in a bibliophile edition. On this occasion, too, a selection of Grotius' manuscripts from the famous Nijhoff auction of 1864 was donated to the library. It was indeed in this bibliographical area that the most gratifying work awaited him. During the war years and anticipating the tercentenary of Grotius' death in 1645, ter Meulen, along with his colleague Diermanse, set himself to the compilation of an exhaustive bibliography of Grotius' works. The commemoration itself, on account of war conditions, was restricted to the laying of a wreath by Foreign Minister Nicolaas van Kleffens and the Swedish ambassador. However, the *Bibliographie des écrits imprimés de Hugo Grotius* which appeared with Nijhoff's imprint in 1950, is definitive and will remain forever authoritative in the field, thanks to the authors' painstaking research, the work's completeness and its virtual faultlessness. The book was supplemented in 1961 by the *Bibliographie des écrits sur Hugo Grotius*, recording 17th century secondary literature on Grotius in a volume that covered 490 items. Also instrumental to ter Meulen's Grotian studies was his founding of a "Foundation to Promote the Study of the Life and Works of Grotius" in 1949.

Exhibitions

We have already spoken of ter Meulen's Grotius exhibitions. Ter Meulen, it seems, had a special leaning towards exhibitions and displays and was never at a loss to find an excuse for them. In February-March 1930 he helped organise a display of books and objects regarding the Peace Movement and the League of Nations at the Binnenhof in The Hague. In 1931, the First Congress of Comparative Law was supported with an exhibition and the following year the First International Conference on the Teaching of History, headed by Rafael Altamira again invited a large display. Still in the same year, with the departure of B.C.J. Loder, the first president of the Permanent Court of International Justice, the latter's room was reshaped into a permanent exhibition room and equipped with show-cases featuring Grotius' works, former projects of international leagues, the history of the laws of the seas and documents relating to the Peace Palace and the League of Nations. The room, incidentally, was unsuitable for this purpose and soon the idea was given up, but the exhibitions were continued in the corridors.

Typically, over the years, ter Meulen kept questioning the Board about a permanent exhibition room. To this end he also contacted J.A.G. van der Steur, the house architect who actually made some designs. Nothing came of it, nor for that matter of another dream of his, namely to have a documentary film produced on Carnegie and the Palace. Still, on 25 November 1935, Andrew Carnegie's hundredth birthday was commemorated by a wreath-laying ceremony and another successful exhibition on Carnegie and arbitration, held in four rooms of the Academy. On this occasion a reader's guide was produced, informing the visitors of the library's goals and treasures (which in subsequent years was published in four languages). With the winds of war abating, unrelentingly, a new series of exhibitions was started. Thus, in 1947, the fortieth anniversary of the stone-laying ceremony was commemorated; in 1948 the fiftieth anniversary of Czar Nicholas' Manifesto; in 1949 (ter Meulen's twenty-fifth year of office), the golden jubilee of the First Hague Conference; in 1950 the coming into effect of the Indian Constitution; finally, in 1951 an exhibition was put on by the International Baha'i Congress and the Conference of International Private Law.

Despite his chronically weak health (he was a diabetic) ter Meulen was a man of formidable energy and willpower. Numerous are the projects he launched, the contacts he made and the tokens of insight of which he gave proof. Thus, he initiated A. Lysen's well-known history of the Peace Palace. Again, in 1936, during the Spanish Civil War, he helped continue the Barcelona PATXOT prize competition by taking care of administrative affairs from The Hague. In the early forties, with typical foresight, he had his Grotius bibliographies microfilmed and the library's treasures stored away in the basements underneath the front façade. And another proof of his clear-mindedness: in the war years he collected masses of duplicates of valuable books and documents which afterwards served the less fortunate librarians of bombed-out collections. The collection was dispersed in 1951 when vans could be seen leaving the gates, transporting piles of books to Germany.

Ter Meulen invariably displayed a marked resourcefulness. In the months immediately following the liberation in 1945 he was the first to solve the problem of obtaining foreign currency through the "Deviezen Instituut" and tax and customs officials. Meanwhile, he managed to contact the Carnegie Endowment for International Peace and secure a loan of $2,000 in order to procure recent American literature. In September of that year, again mainly thanks to ter Meulen, an exhibition of the American and British book production for the years from 1939 to 1945 was opened in the Binnenhof. In that same month ter Meulen also concluded a contract with the Rockefeller Foundation stipulating a $30,000 donation from 1947 to 1951. When this contract had expired, he successfully approached the boards of British Petroleum, Unilever, and

Philips, for minor donations.

Apart from being competent, hard working, demanding and resource-ful, ter Meulen was an idealist with a warm heart for his employees. Being a man of ample means, he was always prepared to help less fortunate subordinates in a discreet and tactful manner. Several of his major works on the Peace Palace collection, among these the 1950 Grotius bibliography, were financed from his private means and the same holds good for the library's collection of maps, pictures and engravings. Even the book-case in which this collection was kept till 1987 came from his belongings. However, the most manifest testimonies to his steadfast character and resourcefulness are reflected in the vicissitudes of the Library during the years of German occupation. I will round off this sketch of ter Meulen by highlighting some of these events.

The War Years: 1940-1945

Probably the first indication of the Board's awareness of a storm brewing is found in the records for 1938, as van der Steur was ordered by ter Meulen to ensure that the new bookstorage areas he was designing would be bombproof and an adequate shelter for man and valuable objects of art in case of air-raids. Again, in the opening weeks of 1939, an urgent call was made for fire-extinguishers and either the sinking of a well or arrangements for conduit pipes to the lake "as in wartime the fire brigade is not to be depended on". Treasures were meanwhile carried into the vast basements, the Grotius collection was microcopied and a first aid team formed. During the summer courses at the Academy, in July and August, a certain uneasiness prevailed among the students and most American students hastened their departure. In subsequent months tension rapidly built up and from the moment the German armies invaded Poland an atmosphere of gloom and loneliness came over the place. The Judges and Registry of the Permanent Court of International Justice were frantically packing their bags, whereas the Dutch staff of the Foundation was virtually decimated as ever more clerks, gardeners and stokers enlisted.

On 10 May 1940, a delightful sunny day and with parks and lanes in spring foliage, the grim truth finally dawned upon Holland. Within twenty-four hours of the capitulation on 15 May, a German motor convoy drove up the entrance path with the clear intention of occupying the place. Oddly enough, at this juncture the exact legal status of the grounds and personnel were not perfectly clear, neither to the potential trespasser nor to the Board itself. The premises of course were Dutch property, the Courts, however, were international organizations. At length, being the outcome of informal dealings in which the Board maintained that the international standing of the Courts had never been questioned by the German Government, the Nazis, due mainly to the actual functioning of the Court of Arbitration, preferred to respect the status of the Palace if only for its symbolic stature, which pledge they maintained throughout. Meanwhile, library proceedings continued normally and the German military staff were among the most frequent borrowers, though they held the lending rules in perfect scorn, as ter Meulen observed somewhat morosely in his yearly reports. Naturally, all sorts of restrictions were ordered soon enough. Thus, "anti-German" books were to be listed and locked away and, predictably, Jewish scholars were to be struck from the users' files. Again, on 2 December 1940, the Carnegie Foundation, being a subsidized organization, was ordered to hand in a list of Jewish staff members. To this the Board and Librarian objected on formal grounds, arguing that the municipal grants (Dfl. 20,000 yearly at the time) were not essential to the Foundation's functioning. In the end it never handed in the names of the two staff members under consideration. Meanwhile, German officials showed a keen interest in the place all the time, perhaps only from a suspicion of irregularities. Similarly, German authorities paid regular visits to the Palace.

Generally speaking, the Germans never interfered with the daily proceedings at the Palace. Indeed, to the library officials the early war years in a way must have had a distinct charm of their own. As the "Nationale Bibliotheek" (as the Royal Library was renamed) and the "Rijksarchief" were closed down with increasing frequency, also due to the lack of fuel, prominent scholars from far and near, among them the "Rijksarchivaris" himself, frequented the cosy and centrally-heated reading room at the Peace Palace. From 1944 onwards, and notably during the "hongerwinter", there were many who found refuge in the warmth of the Palace. With communications with editors abroad disconnected, library officials spent much spare time in rearranging the collection. It was in these years also that ter Meulen and Diermanse launched their extensive Grotian studies.

The library cellars, for safety reasons, also welcomed extensive collections from the Ministries of Foreign Affairs, Colonies, Justice, and Education, as well as private collections from refugees. In 1944 things changed for the worse. The launching-pads of the experimental V-weapons nearby in the dunes formed a terrible risk. The frequent failures in launching operations held the population in constant fear as every now and then hideous projectiles flew over with high-pitched, whistling screams. Twice, in the dead of night of 2 November 1944 and 5 January 1945, the Foundation officials on nightwatch panicked as hundreds of windows were blown in and all over the place wooden panels came tumbling down with the shock of untimely exploding projectiles. Hastily, all valuable objects were assembled in the basements and the gaping windows were boarded up. On 25 January 1945, another V-weapon exploded and hit the house of ter Meulen in the nearby Archipelbuurt. Ironically, in the end more damage was done by the allied forces who constantly bombed the close surrounding areas of the Palace in order to eliminate the German launching installations. On 3 March 1945, the Bezuidenhout area was bombed with enormous casualties without damaging the installations in the least. The Palace was spared such a fate. All in all, the V-weapons and allied raids from 2 November 1944 to 30 April 1945 demolished some 210 square metres of windows, breaking 320 stained glass pieces. Fortunately, these could all be replaced and no serious damage was really done to the building.

Ter Meulen's resourcefulness must in fact have been inspiring, as witnessed by the following war-time incident. In the early days of May 1940, Ada Belinfante who had worked in the reading room since 1936, had disappeared without any previous notice. Not a word was heard of her until, shortly after the liberation in 1945, news of her whereabouts came in from London, where she proved to have been on the staff of the Department of Justice all those years, meanwhile contacting librarians and antiquarians and collecting stores of books on behalf of ter Meulen. On hearing this, he ordered her to stay in England till the end of the year and purchase whatever recent literature was available. There she proved extremely helpful indeed, if only in convincing the government officials whose duty it was to assemble books and periodicals for governmental institutions back in Holland, to put the Peace Palace Library on the distribution lists. Thus, in 1946, through the Royal Academy in Amsterdam, precious shipments of new acquisitions came in side by side with the many hundreds of books which Miss Belinfante had collected of her own accord.

I trust the foregoing will give the reader an overall impression of ter Meulen's significance for the Peace Palace Library and its collections. All in all, it is small wonder that in 1952, after a term of twenty-eight years, the advertisements for the succession of ter Meulen failed to evoke a satisfying response. First announced on 24 March 1951, it would take a full year and a half before the proper successor was found. And even then ter Meulen did not leave altogether. Along with

Diermanse he continued his peace studies and Grotian research for another full decade and was spotted almost daily in the reading room until finally his health gave in. On 15 August 1962, a small circle of intimates paid their last tribute to this man of principle at the Kerkhoflaan in The Hague.

The publication of the collection of peace literature references to be found in the stacks of the Peace Palace has been the wish of many staff members of the Library in the past years. It must be stated here that without the competent and generous help of Peter van den Dungen this wish would not have been fulfilled. It should be noted, incidentally, that the lists which are offered here are to be considered as the first part only of our project to have all references concerning the history of the Peace Movement printed and which were accumulated by ter Meulen after the present listings had appeared in their provisional form in the thirties. An additional listing of yet another 6,000 items is now in progress. I wish to thank Greenwood Press for publishing these time-honoured lists. I also thank Mr. Schalekamp, Director of the Peace Palace Library, for his kind assistance in realizing this project and Mr. Lugthart, Mr. de Man and Mr. Zonnevylle in helping me to collect the data for this introductory note on ter Meulen.

Arthur Eyffinger
Peace Palace, The Hague

PREFACE

This volume contains a reprint of the two 'provisional lists' of the *Bibliography of the Peace Movement Before 1899* compiled by Jacob ter Meulen and published by the Library of the Peace Palace in The Hague. It should be noted that they appear here in reverse order of their original publication: the bibliography for the period 1480-1776 was published in 1936, and that for the period 1776-1898 in 1934. Also reprinted, following each bibliography, is the corresponding alphabetical author index. (The index was published as a separate booklet for the 1934 bibliography, but formed an integral part of its 1936 sequel.) The numbers in the indexes refer to the year of publication, not the page numbers of the present volume. For the sake of clarity and convenience, new page numbers have been given to the bibliographies and their indexes, so that these (together with the new introduction and its index) now form one sequence.

Since the original index for the bibliography of the later period refers not only to year of publication but occasionally also to the bottom-of-the-page column numbers - in order to facilitate the looking up of an author - they have been retained. The system which ter Meulen used in his bibliography for the earlier period, namely to display at the top of each page the dates of the period covered on that page, has been applied also to the other bibliography (where such a display originally covered four columns, or two pages, at a time). Apart from these minor alterations affecting running heads and pagination, the bibliographies are reprinted intact.

For their generous help I owe a special debt of gratitude to Irwin Abrams, Antioch University, Wendy E. Chmielewski, Swarthmore

College Peace Collection, and Anne C. Kjelling, Norwegian Nobel Institute.

I am most grateful to Arthur Eyffinger for his interest and advice, and for making my research in the archives of the Peace Palace in The Hague so enjoyable and rewarding and to Angela Hicks for yet again turning my manuscript into readable English.

Lastly, I would like to express my appreciation to the British Academy for awarding me a grant which allowed me to pursue research on, among other projects, ter Meulen's bibliographies in the library and archives of the Peace Palace, the library of the Norwegian Nobel Institute in Oslo, and the University Library in Oslo.

From Erasmus
to Tolstoy

INTRODUCTION

On 25 May 1929 Jacob ter Meulen, the director of the library of the Peace Palace at The Hague, wrote to Christian L. Lange, the long-serving secretary-general of the Interparliamentary Union in Geneva, informing him that the second volume of his history of the idea of international organisation (*Der Gedanke der Internationalen Organisation in seiner Entwicklung*) had just appeared[1]. Since Lange was involved in a similar comprehensive study, the first volume of which had been published in 1919 (*Histoire de l'Internationalisme*), he was no doubt interested in this news. But the main reason for ter Meulen's letter was to propose a joint initiative to encourage the study of the history of pacifism. 'I would not wish to create a new, pompous association', he wrote, 'but my intention is to put into contact all those who are interested in the study of the history of pacifism by forming a group of historians and by seeking out an existing journal which would offer the opportunity of publishing important news in this area'. If Lange was willing to give advice and to countersign important documents, ter Meulen would be happy to take charge of the organisation of this group.

Lange replied: 'I must admit that I am extremely sceptical concerning the creation of new associations, even if they are very modest'. However, he agreed that a periodical which included articles and documents in this field would certainly be worthwhile, but he doubted whether this required the creation of an organisation. Lange requested ter Meulen's further views on the matter which were sent by return of post. Ter Meulen intended to ask the *Revue de Droit International et de Législation Comparée* (published in Brussels) to publish regularly a few pages devoted to important news in the area concerned and to produce offprints which could be sent to those interested in the study of the history of internationalism. If the *Revue* agreed to this, ter Meulen planned to send a circular to colleagues with the request to keep him informed of their work.

Lange found the choice of the *Revue* as 'rendez-vous' for historians of internationalism felicitous because it had a tradition in this field, particularly through the 'very valuable' contributions of Ernest Nys. Possible alternatives would be the *Revue d'Histoire Diplomatique*, which had published interesting contributions by de Beaufort and Vesnitch, and the *Friedens-Warte*. Lange also mentioned two young historians, A.C.F. Beales and Merle E. Curti, who had written to him with certain questions about the history of pacifism.

Ter Meulen was able to realise his plan with a minimum of delay through the *Revue de Droit International* (published in Paris, and established in 1927), and not the periodical he had in mind. It published three times a 'Special Bulletin devoted to the history of pacifism' in 1929-1930, and also an offprint combining the first two bulletins entitled *L'Histoire du Pacifisme*[2]. All three bulletins were written by ter Meulen who, in the first one, explained the need for this initiative. He deplored the absence of a detailed history of pacifism and the general lack of documentation for this subject. His survey of the existing literature revealed that, apart from the comprehensive studies by Lange and himself (both in progress), there were only a few monographs which dealt with aspects of the topic (he mentioned those by e.g. John Bassett Moore, J.B. Scott, Walther Schücking, Max Huber, the Academy of International Law in The Hague, and the Grotius Society in London). However, for a thorough history of pacifism a much greater number of specialised studies bearing on all countries and all times was required. In addition, researchers needed a centre where all questions and findings about the history of pacifism could be registered. In short, he envisaged a kind of encyclopedic bureau for the history of pacifism.

The second bulletin contained brief reviews of several publications on peace ideas and on the growth of international law in Russia. In the third bulletin an extensive summary of Merle Curti's *The American Peace Crusade 1815-1860* (which had just been published) appeared. Ter Meulen wrote: 'We hope not only that M. Curti will have the opportunity to continue his research, but that he will find followers in other countries[3]. It is desirable that more attention is given to the

development of the pacifist movement in the past, and to the difficulties
which the pioneers of the first associations had to overcome'. Ter
Meulen concluded his article: 'The crusade for peace is a history of
pioneers, full of beautiful examples, of sacrifices and of struggles. One
finds strong heads such as Dodge, practical spirits such as Richard,
sages such as Worcester, martyrs such as Ladd, prophets such as Burritt.
They were all heroes. Today, it is not easy to be a pacifist and still less
so to remain one in time of war. But in the past it was even more
difficult to be a crusader for peace. However, we are convinced that the
day will come when in school-textbooks the pacifists of the past will be
mentioned side by side with the great heroes of war'.

Committee for the Bibliography of the Peace Movement in History

The appearance of only three special bulletins in the *Revue de Droit
International* may be explained by ter Meulen's pre-occupation with a
new but not unrelated idea which seems to have ripened in his mind in
this period: a bibliography of the historical peace movement. Just as he
had chosen the *Revue* as a vehicle for providing an information
exchange for peace historians, so he pursued his new idea through the
International Committee of Historical Sciences (ICHS, founded in
Geneva in 1926) [4], and its progress can be followed through the pages of
the *Bulletin* of the ICHS from 1932 to 1937. In a report dated 12 May
1931, and published in the September 1932 issue of the *Bulletin* [5], ter
Meulen argued the need for such a bibliography and proposed that the
ICHS establish a small committee to direct the research required. Ter
Meulen volunteered to be nominated as its secretary and to undertake
most of the work. This proposal appeared on the agenda of the ICHS's
general assembly (meeting later in the same month) which forwarded it
to the publications committee for further discussion between its author
and the committee's president, the Danish historian Aage Friis [6].   In
March of the following year ter Meulen was able to send him the first
part of the provisional lists (printed) for the period 1856-1872, together
with further details concerning his conception of the bibliography.
Doubtlessly, ter Meulen was speaking from personal experience (gained
when writing the latest volume of his encyclopedic history) when he
wrote to Friis: 'One of the aims of this bibliography is to draw attention
to material which has largely become *very rare*. One searches often in
vain not only for books and pamphlets but also for the majority of the
older runs of periodicals'. He told Friis that as soon as the ICHS had
approved the continuation of this work (and its eventual publication), he
intended to involve colleagues and complete the work under the auspices

of the ICHS. In his reply of 3 May 1932 Friis suggested that Lange be included in the small group of experts which ter Meulen had proposed and indicated that the Nobel Committee might well provide financial assistance for the publication of such a bibliography[7].

Friis's encouraging reply led ter Meulen to resume his correspondence with Lange[8]. On 12 May 1932 he wrote: 'It is wholly superfluous to explain to you that books and collections on pacifism, especially before 1900, are on the whole extremely rare. The most important library in this field remains the Nobel Institute but even its collections still reveal many gaps ... In the Library of the Peace Palace pacifism constitutes only a secondary interest. I have nevertheless succeeded in acquiring a considerable number of works but the majority is still lacking. In a common effort we have therefore to preserve what exists, to rescue that which is in danger of being lost, and to publicise that which is available'. He suggested as a first step the publication of a bibliography of historical pacifism (with the location of each title) and informed Lange that he had prepared the first draft (of about 40 folio pages) of such a bibliography for the period 1856-1867. Ter Meulen enclosed copies of his recent correspondence with Friis and invited Lange to join the committee.

Lange congratulated ter Meulen on his initiative (which he had already learnt about from Friis)[9] which he thought would be realised with the help of the Nobel Institute[10]. Lange was pleased to become a member of the committee and suggested Curti as a third member because he was likely to be very useful considering the extensive literature in the United States. Ter Meulen followed up this suggestion and Curti enthusiastically accepted his invitation in a letter dated 1 June 1932, writing[11]: 'You deserve the greatest commendation for having taken the initiative in this important undertaking, and scholars the world over will thank you for it, both in our day, and later'. Referring to the 'very voluminous' Bajer papers in the Royal Library in Copenhagen, Curti suggested that 'the bibliography would be more useful, and certainly more complete, if we could include the chief manuscript materials'.

The letter by Curti -- who concluded by saying 'I shall be most interested in the response of the Historical Committee to your proposal' -- came at an opportune moment since the next assembly of the ICHS was to be held a few weeks later, in The Hague (4-6 July 1932). Ter Meulen consequently lost no time in sending copies of Curti's letter to Michel Lhéritier, the secretary-general of the ICHS, Friis, and Lange. At the assembly Friis, on behalf of the publications committee, supported Ter Meulen's proposal, pointing out, *inter alia*, that it would not entail large expenditures. In his general report Lhéritier commented: 'This project in no way commits us, or even its author, to a profession of pacifism. We are interested because we see in it, on the one hand, an opportunity to study the historical evolution of a movement of ideas which are difficult to define; and on the other hand, an example of a work [concerning] ... the history of international relations and its organisation'[12].

When the meeting in The Hague had duly authorised the formation of the committee that ter Meulen had proposed, Lange was invited to become its president. In the same month (July), Lange wrote to ter Meulen accepting his appointment, happy in the knowledge that his Dutch colleague was effectively to undertake the work with which 'our small committee of three' had been charged. Meanwhile ter Meulen had persuaded, in addition to Curti, Hans Wehberg (Geneva) and Rafael Altamira (Madrid and The Hague) to become members of the committee and on 14 October he was able to inform Lhéritier that it was fully constituted[13].

In the last months of 1932 ter Meulen was in touch with Lange concerning an approach to the Nobel Committee in Oslo for financial support. Ragnvald Moe, its secretary, could not give a personal opinion on the likelihood of ter Meulen obtaining a subsidy from the Committee and advised him to submit his request directly to the Committee instead. On 3 May 1933 ter Meulen and Lange jointly wrote to the Nobel Committee about the formation of the Committee for the Bibliography of the Peace Movement in History, whose work would be time-consuming and likely to involve considerable expense, some of which in the past few months had been born by ter Meulen privately. The first period to be treated would be from the declaration of American independence to the first Hague Peace Conference, i.e. 1776-1899. Provisional bibliographies for the period 1778-1853 were enclosed, and the rationale for printing and distributing parts of the bibliography as the work progressed was explained. Ter Meulen also enclosed a copy of the circular which accompanied the provisional lists (which were being sent to specialists) and which explained the purpose of the committee and the procedure to be followed by recipients. Ter Meulen wrote: 'We wish to collect the material here, in as far as the Library of the Peace Palace does not possess it, in order to catalogue the titles and to make annotations concerning the contents of the book or of the review article ... The Sub-Committee shall be greatly obliged to you, if you would kindly examine these lists and make a note of: 1. all the *omissions* that you can discover therein; 2. the *place* where each work etc., mentioned on the lists, is to be found' [14]. The budget submitted to the Nobel Committee amounted to 2,300 florins, most of which was for the employment of a secretary and typist, with the remainder for printing and postage (the latter including costs for receiving and returning literature missing in the Peace Palace library). Later that year the Nobel Committee granted the amount requested by awarding ter Meulen's committee 6,000 Norwegian Kroner, to be paid out over two years, in 1934 and 1935 [15].

In August 1933 ter Meulen, as secretary of the committee, prepared his first annual report for the meeting of the ICHS in Warsaw later that month. This report was presented to the conference by Lhéritier in ter Meulen's absence because of the latter's ill health [16] · Seven provisional lists had been sent to 70 individuals and institutions, and replies had been received from committee members Lange and Curti, A.C.F. Beales in London, the librarian of the Norwegian Nobel Institute, the secretary of the American Peace Society in Washington, and others. Institutional respondents included the Library and Museum of War in Vincennes, and the Information Bureau of German Libraries in Berlin (the latter was comparing the provisional lists with the union catalogue of the State Library and of the libraries of Prussian universities). Ter Meulen further reported that work on the preliminary lists for the period 1853-1899 was well advanced [17].

In February 1934 ter Meulen wrote to the members of his committee that he would be participating in the next meeting of the ICHS in Paris the following month. He informed them that the printing of the provisional lists for the entire period 1776-1899 was almost completed. 'We can have the satisfaction', he wrote, 'of having drawn attention to rare documents and we have already motivated more than one institution to bring a little bit of order in collections which have been too much neglected (confidential communication!)'. He also conveyed the good news of the subvention made by the Nobel Committee in Oslo. This information was the basis for his second report to the Paris meeting of the ICHS [18] . There he formally presented to the Bureau of the ICHS his provisional bibliography for the whole of the period 1776-1898, containing 3,500 titles of books, journals and articles (together with an index listing the names of 1,400 authors) [19].

In a letter to Lange in June ter Meulen raised various important issues concerning the bibliography. He wrote that he was pursuing work on the definitive version, and was maintaining a large correspondence with colleagues and experts in various countries: 'Mr. Beales is taking a lot of trouble in London. The Information Bureau of German Libraries is doing the work very thoroughly. I have promises from Eastern Europe. France and Italy do not show too much enthusiasm, etc. etc.' Ter Meulen also indicated for the first time that there was a need, as he saw it, to expand the period of the bibliography, and that therefore details for the period 1500-1776 were also being collected, starting with Erasmus. He raised the question of finding a publisher who would be willing to produce a volume large enough to contain the extensive annotations which he had planned. Martinus Nijhoff, the publisher in The Hague, was willing only to consider a small publication. Since ter Meulen would be disappointed if the bibliography was published without annotations, he wanted to know if Lange thought that the Nobel Committee might consider publishing it. A related issue was which language should be used for the editorial material in the bibliography. Ter Meulen and Nijhoff had come to the conclusion that English was preferable to French since the Anglo-Saxon countries showed the greatest interest in the development of pacifism, and French would be a great inconvenience for them. Did Lange agree that an extensive work, i.e. with many annotations, and covering the period 1500-1900 (from Erasmus to the First Hague Peace Conference), and in English, would be preferable? And did Lange expect the Nobel Committee to provide a further subsidy? (His letter also provided details of how the first part of the subsidy had been spent).

Lange did not reply for four months, until 20 October. In the meantime ter Meulen became impatient and at the end of August he wrote again to Lange saying: 'I very well understand that the various questions which I have raised are causing you some reflection. I even believe that sooner or later a meeting will be indispensable'[20]. In this letter ter Meulen also complained about the behaviour of two of his colleagues. He wrote: 'You know that I am fairly satisfied with the collaboration which I receive from colleagues in various countries. Only my compatriot and colleague at the League of Nations, Mr. Sevensma, has shown himself a bit disturbed by me competing with his "ideas"! This is a bit strange since it is addressed to someone who has been dealing with this material since 1910! But I believe that Mr. Sevensma will not refuse his indispensable help'[21]. Ter Meulen had not yet found a contact in Sweden (so necessary in view of the importance of the Scandinavian countries for the development of pacifism) and commented that 'the librarian of the Royal Library in Stockholm, a great figure in the field of incunabula, does not reply to me although we know each other'. Could Lange suggest the names of some Scandinavians who were interested in pacifism?

Still without a reply from Lange on 19 October, ter Meulen wrote again: 'I know your punctuality so well that the delay in your replies surprises me a little'. Lange's reply dated 20 October is inferred from ter Meulen's letter of 16 November but there is no copy of it in the Lange papers consulted. This is especially regrettable because it is likely that it contained Lange's appraisal of the provisional bibliography for the entire period 1776-1898. Ter Meulen's reply of 16 November 1934 reveals Lange's surprise that his supplementary list of titles sent to ter Meulen in May 1933 had not been incorporated into the bibliography published in March 1934. Apparently ter Meulen was keeping the information, received as a result of sending out the partial listings, for the definitive bibliography. He reassured his correspondent that 'it goes without saying that everything will be inserted in the definitive bibliography'. Lange also queried ter Meulen's idea of starting the second bibliography with Erasmus and apparently wanted to include even the Middle Ages. Ter Meulen's reply is interesting: 'I believe that the name of Erasmus is an excellent beginning for a bibliography of pacifism. The teachings of this author have, for a large part, a modern flavour. The pacifism of Erasmus is not too much linked to political goals such as the war against the Turks. As soon as one deals with the Middle Ages it will be difficult to establish a starting point. In principle our bibliography does not want to ignore manuscripts entirely. In that case it will be necessary to undertake research in this direction for the period, say, 1300-1500. Could you agree that we begin with the great European Dutchman?'[22].

Ter Meulen again raised the question of whether the Nobel Committee would publish the definitive bibliography in its publications series or whether he should approach Nijhoff again. 'I'm sure', he wrote, 'that it will not be possible to redo in the next twenty years the work that I have started. The manner of its publication is therefore a question of the first importance. In my view it will sometimes be indispensable to clarify titles by means of an annotation'[23]. Ter Meulen agreed with Lange's suggestion that English and French should both be used for the general headings (as in the provisional lists) but argued that a choice had to be made for the annotations. 'For us who do the annotations', he said, 'it will at times be convenient to use the language of the work concerned, and in that case the language will not be uniform, but even so there must be one language which prevails'[24]. In his concluding paragraph ter Meulen assured Lange: 'I will be able to prepare shortly the definitive publication of a bibliography of pacifism for the period 1500-1900, which may be an inexhaustible source for the subject in question. However, by providing annotations and comments this bibliography will assume much greater importance'[25]. A final thought was that it might be published in the form of fasciculi. Obviously, ter Meulen was willing to consider any alternative as long as it could safeguard his cherished goal.

We do not know whether Lange replied to ter Meulen's November letter; in any case, ter Meulen made no further progress with his project, either in attracting additional funds from the Nobel Institute or in securing a publisher. Ter Meulen's third report, which was extensive and informative, was issued on 1 March 1936 and a copy was sent to Lange. First of all he reported on the outcome of the distribution of the printed lists for the period 1776-1898. He received substantial information from about half of the individuals and libraries (i.e. 35) to which copies were sent[26]. He recorded the decision to extend the bibliography so as to cover the period 1480-1776. 'It was decided', he wrote, 'to produce a bibliography of pacifism also for the literature from the end of the Middle Ages up to 1776'[27]. He explained his decision as follows: 'It is true that for those centuries it is not possible to speak of a peace movement in the way these words are presently understood, but there exists without any doubt a relationship between later currents of peace and the pacifist ideas of the ancient authors'. The literature used in ter Meulen's and Lange's respective works on the history of internationalism (cf. supra) provided the basis for the bibliography covering the early period. From among the great number of other sources he singled out for their usefulness Bart de Ligt's *La Paix Créatrice* and the manuscript of Hermann Hetzel's *Die Humanisierung des Krieges* [28].

The decision to include a title was not always easy and ter Meulen elaborated the procedure adopted. The following quotation helps to explain the nature of the bibliography covering the earlier period: 'In the first place we have retained works which, either in their entirety or predominantly, have a pacifist content or tendency, followed by those which deal with projects for a federation of states or with general plans for peace. These can be normal [prose] writings as well as poems, plays, speeches or satires. We have excluded works which deal with religious, personal or familial peace, or with a particular peace treaty. Difficulties frequently arose with writers who preached peace among Christian princes and at the same time counselled them to combine in combat against the Turks. Writings which expressed only a few opinions against war also proved problematical as did a large category of works by religious sects which profess non-resistance. In all these cases the name of the author or the influence of the work on later currents may occasionally determine the decision to be taken. However, it was not always possible to avoid inconsistencies'. Ter Meulen indicates that of the 470 titles gathered together 136 belong to the period 1470-1600, 183 to the 17th century, and 151 to the period 1700-1776. As in the bibliography for the later period, different editions and translations of the same work have been listed, so that, for instance, the name of Erasmus is mentioned 138 times, of Saint-Pierre 25 times and of Robert Barclay 23 times.

Ter Meulen acknowledged the devotion and ability of two collaborators, Miss G. Berlage and J. Huizinga, whose names also appear on the cover of this bibliography. In his report ter Meulen also briefly discussed the financial position: the Nobel subsidy had been spent, and the rapporteur himself was bearing most of the cost of extending the bibliography. Although the Library of the Peace Palace might pay for the printing of the lists covering the early period, it would not be able to reimburse the considerable expenses involved in their preparation. Despite these financial difficulties ter Meulen concluded that the preparation of the definitive bibliography would be undertaken as soon as the lists for the earlier period had been distributed (and returned with amendments): 'By doing so we hope not only to produce a useful instrument of study, but also to assist with the preservation of material which for a large part has been neglected for too long. We are aware of more than one important collection in the world which is in danger of being lost forever if the necessary measures are not undertaken soon'[29].

Hans Wehberg proposed to publish the list for the earlier period in the *Friedens-Warte*, an offer which ter Meulen immediately accepted, and later that same year (1936) it appeared in two issues of this leading journal[30]. This procedure had the great advantage that it allowed ter Meulen to obtain a large number of offprints at relatively modest cost. Ter Meulen wrote to Lange on 27 October, enclosing two copies of the journal offprint, requesting that Lange return one with his comments: this is the last letter in the Lange file[31]. The last document in the file is a copy of ter Meulen's fourth (and apparently last) report, dated April 1937. Compared with the previous one, it is very brief, revealing that copies of the second list were again sent to some 70 individuals and institutions, and details were given of the 10 replies received which provided much important information. He reported that work towards the completion of the lists for the period 1776-1898 was proceeding apace, so much so that he hoped to be able to start work on the definitive bibliography soon[32].

Fate of ter Meulen's Bibliographies

It is ironic that ter Meulen's two bibliographies of the historical peace movement, whose purpose was to record the extant literature and also to provide details of its location, have themselves undergone the fate of many of the listed works. During the period of more than fifty years since their publication, these bibliographies have largely been forgotten or ignored and become a rarity in their own right. One reason for this is undoubtedly the fact that we are dealing with a provisional publication, a working document only, of which ter Meulen distributed worldwide not more than 70 copies. Moreover, the 1934 bibliography was printed in an awkward format (measuring 25 x 41 cm) and without a title-page[33]. Since the chief author of these bibliographies modestly asserted their provisional character, something which their physical appearance seemed to confirm, it is perhaps not surprising that only a few libraries which acquired them chose to catalogue them. A further consideration is that the period when they appeared was far from propitious: the prospect of another world conflagration became increasingly likely, and for many the idea of peace must have seemed as illusory or visionary as at any time in the past. What conceivable use was there for a bibliography of the historical peace movement when its failures were so manifest?[34].

Although no exhaustive effort has been made by the present author to trace the surviving copies of ter Meulen's bibliographies, the following details are suggestive of their rarity[35]. The *National Union Catalogue, Pre-1956 Imprints* (cf. infra) records only three copies of the 1934 bibliography in U.S. libraries: at the Library of Congress, the New York Public Library, and the Yale University Library. The only library recorded as possessing the 1936 bibliography is the Swarthmore College Peace Collection. (The entry refers puzzlingly to '2 parts' and transcribes incorrectly the name of J. Huizinga. This library also possesses, however, a copy of the 1934 bibliography)[36]. In the *National Union Catalogue* (NUC) both works are entered under the name of the library of the Peace Palace at The Hague and are not listed under the name of their author. Since, as was seen above, ter Meulen received the cooperation of several major libraries in the United States, their failure to catalogue his bibliographies is a surprising one. However, we can add a more pertinent explanation for this than the ones already offered: ter Meulen requested the return of the provisional lists after the receiving library had added to them items unknown to him and other amendments. (A small number of such amended lists have, indeed, been preserved at the Peace Palace library. The library of the Norwegian Nobel Institute also has two annotated copies of the 1934 bibliography.) In the United Kingdom only one of ter Meulen's bibliographies was found in those libraries which were consulted, namely in the British Library of Political and Economic Science (in the London School of Economics), which has a copy of the 1936 list [37].

If we pursue the search for references to ter Meulen's bibliographies in general and specialist bibliographies, a somewhat similar picture emerges. Theodore Besterman's *A World Bibliography of Bibliographies* mentions both works although it gives the date for the 1934 one erroneously as 'c. 1938' and does not indicate the period which it comprises; by contrast, it fully reports the details for the 1936 list[38]. Besterman cites the number of bibliographical references in each of the works as 2,500 and 400, respectively. Even on the basis of these figures (which, as regards the first list, are lower by a thousand when compared with ter Meulen's own estimate), the significance of ter Meulen's works in purely quantitative terms is evident when they are compared with the other bibliographies which Besterman includes under the heading of peace. He identifies 39 bibliographies on the subject of peace whose publication dates span the period 1888-1963. Only 11 contain 500 entries or more and of these only 5 contain over 1,000 entries. If, out of these 5 largest bibliographies, we leave aside an American periodical series which, in the period 1923-1932, indexed 5,000 articles on international relations (not specifically on peace), and also a Rumanian bibliography published in 1950 which comprises over 3,000 items, we are left with the following three bibliographies, each with approximately 2,500 entries: Henri La Fontaine's (published in 1904), the Norwegian Nobel Institute's library catalogue (published in 1912)[39] and ter Meulen's 1934 work. The first two bibliographies include publications which appeared up to 1903 and 1912, respectively, whereas ter Meulen's finishes at 1898, making his work by far the most complete for the period covered (since his two bibliographies together show, for a shorter and earlier period, 2,900 entries following Besterman's conservative estimate). These three major bibliographies are all in French even though they were compiled outside France. More than half of all the bibliographies on peace listed by Besterman are in English (24), and six are in Russian. The latter were all published in the early 1950s and are likely to refer to publications which are both partisan and contemporary.

Even today the bibliographies of ter Meulen, La Fontaine and the Nobel Institute are in a category of their own, not only on account of the number of entries they contain, but also because they survey the literature on peace comprehensively[40]. By contrast, about half of the peace bibliographies listed by Besterman either deal with a specific aspect of the subject only (e.g. conscientious objection to military service), or are the publications lists of specific peace organisations (e.g. the Carnegie Endowment for International Peace), or are the subject lists of certain libraries (e.g. Brooklyn Public Library, Library of Congress).

Ter Meulen's bibliographies are also mentioned in a recent work, Berenice A. Carroll et al.'s *Peace and War: A Guide to Bibliographies* [41]. The number of references contained in each bibliography is given as 3,536 (1934) and 466 (1936), and for the former the authors correctly note that 'the number of items is inflated by repetition of periodical titles for each year of publication'. (But this procedure had a rationale, as was made clear previously.) An earlier effort to record the historical peace literature, Blanche Wiesen Cook's *Bibliography on Peace Research in History* refers to the second (1936) bibliography alone. She only gives the general title with no indication of the period covered but adds, 'Indispensable for medieval and renaissance peace movements and ideas'[42].

Both of ter Meulen's works are absent from an ambitious effort to compile an international bibliography on peace science. Axel Swinne's *Bibliographia Irenica 1500-1970* [43] lists, in alphabetical order of author, 2,061 titles. Estimating roughly that half of them were published since 1899 (the cut off date for ter Meulen's 1934 work), it would be tempting to compare the remaining 1,000 or so entries in Swinne's bibliography with ter Meulen's 3,000 or 3,500 (for both works). However, because the figure assumed for the Swinne bibliography (for the same period as ter Meulen's, namely 1500-1898) is heavily inflated owing to the way he has defined peace, the numerical discrepancy is even greater than these figures suggest. As the sub-title of Swinne's book makes clear, for him peace comprises 'church and political efforts for unity and peace, ecumenism and international understanding'. It is true, of course, that religious divisions, not least within Christianity, have been an important cause of war. A vast contemporary literature exists on Christian theological disputations and divisions, and ways of resolving and healing them. The reestablishment of Christian unity, a subject close to the heart of such diverse figures as Erasmus and Leibniz, should not, however, be equated with the achievement of 'peace' as this notion is understood today. (As we have seen above, ter Meulen eliminated 'religious peace' writings from his bibliography.)

The wholly unsatisfactory nature of Swinne's definition of peace and also of the bibliography is demonstrated on every page of his book, where the reader is alternately confronted with references to, for instance, erudite studies on the persecution of witches in the Middle Ages and equally profound analyses of nuclear strategy[44]. Swinne and his assistants at the 'Institute for Scientific Irenology' of the Johan-Wolfgang-Goethe University in Frankfurt believe that irenology, which they define as 'a discipline which occupies itself exclusively with interfaith problems' (p. V), constitutes the foundations of a general science of peace. But the amalgamation of two disparate literatures, namely those of interchurch divisions and of world peace, is unlikely to succeed in establishing this science. In any case, such an attempt should have given primacy of place to the literature on peace in general, rather than to that on religious peace. Ter Meulen's bibliographies furnished precisely the kind of literature Swinne was looking for, *vide* his references to the emergence in the 19th century of a specific Anglo-Saxon peace tradition, the literature of which he says 'is widely dispersed and partly accessible with great difficulty only' (pp. V-VI). He mistakenly believed, however, that this literature 'has up to the present nowhere been systematically examined' (ibid.). His attempt to do this is most unsatisfactory since what he offers can be described only as haphazard. This misguided bibliography would not have come about, we daresay, if the author had been familiar with ter Meulen's which in all aspects (conception, comprehension, exactitude) is superior.

Likewise, other writers might have reconsidered some of their opinions had they known of ter Meulen's bibliographies. For instance, Gerardo Zampaglione writes in his valuable study, *The Idea of Peace in Antiquity*, 'One of my difficulties arose from the fact that discourses devoted wholly to this problem were rare in early antiquity and only a little commoner at later periods. Exceptions are Book XIX of *De civitate Dei* of St. Augustine and Kant's essay *Zum ewigen Frieden*. Generally contributions to the subject [of peace] are inorganic in form and are part ... of more comprehensive doctrinal or literary works'[45]. However, ter Meulen's 1936 bibliography, which covers the period from the end of the 15th century up to the last quarter of the 18th century, suggests that Zampaglione's 'exceptions' are not so rare or infrequent after all.

It is not surprising that among the very few scholars who refer to ter Meulen's bibliographies are his fellow 'peace encyclopedists', August Schou and Théodore Ruyssen. Both make use of the bibliography for the earlier period (1480-1776) only, in the similar second volumes of their respective histories of internationalism. Schou describes this bibliography as 'a precious means of verification', and in his preface thanks ter

Meulen for his inestimable help in putting at the author's disposal his 'abundant and considerable bibliographical documentation'[46]. Ruyssen refers to 'this precious documentation' and, writing of the 18th century peace ideas which flourished in the wake of Saint-Pierre, comments: 'To an erudite Dutchman ... belongs the merit of having explored that *terra incognita* ... he has discovered an impressive number of peace projects which emanated most often from mediocre writers, now forgotten'[47].

1480-1776

The definitive bibliography never materialised, but the library of the Peace Palace possesses a unique interleaved copy of the bibliography for the period 1480-1776 which, although without annotations, provides the location of many items not found in the Peace Palace library itself. In this copy all items have been numbered consecutively, the last one bearing the number 457. The provisional bibliography for this period identifies, through the indication 'P.P.', 113 items (or 25% of the total) present in The Hague. The location of a further 257 titles is indicated by ter Meulen or his assistants on the interleaved copy as a result of information received following the distribution of the provisional list. Less than 20% of the total (i.e. 87 works) are still without a location in the interleaved copy. This demonstrates the extent of the cooperation that ter Meulen received from the 45 libraries which are listed. The major libraries worldwide are included with the exception of the university libraries of Oxford and Cambridge; France is represented only by the Bibliothèque Nationale[48] and Italy and Spain by none. The information collated must therefore be regarded as being far from complete. Even so, this copy is most useful as the following example illustrates. In her scholarly introduction to a new German translation of Erasmus's 'Dulce bellum inexpertis', Brigitte Hannemann reports that she failed to trace in German libraries (through the university inter-library loan system) the two German translations of 1607 and 1659[49]. However, ter Meulen's interleaved bibliography suggests that, although the 1607 work has not been located, a copy of the 1659 edition is in the Jena university library[50].

The rarity of the majority of the items listed in ter Meulen's bibliography for the early period (this rarity is bound to be exaggerated, however, because of the absence from his census of some important libraries) can be gauged from the fact that no locations at all were traced for 87 items, and for the vast majority only a relatively small number of copies were found: for 105 items one copy was located (and for 28 of these items the sole location was The Hague); for 82 items two copies were found and for 65 items three copies. In other words, no more than 3 copies were traced for 70% of all the located titles (i.e. 252 out of 370). These figures fully support ter Meulen's contention that much of the older peace literature had become 'very rare' and that it was necessary, partly through his bibliography, 'to preserve what exists, to rescue that which is in danger of being lost, and to publicise that which is available' (cf. pp. 5-6 supra). For only 18 items were ten or more copies located. The most frequently available titles were the *Opera Omnia* of Erasmus (21 locations for the edition started in 1703, and 11 for the 1540 edition), of Leibniz (19 locations for the 1768 edition), and of Vives (17 locations for the 1555 edition, even without reference to Spanish libraries). Two editions of Sully's *Mémoires* (1638 and 1662) taken together were reported 27 times, and four editions of Robert Barclay's *An Apology for the true Christian Divinity* 60 times.

Not surprisingly, the language that predominates in works of this early period is Latin (161 items, or almost 30% of the total), followed by French (98), German (72), English (59) and Dutch (48). The remaining 19 works are in a variety of languages, including Italian (9) and Spanish (2). In view of our observation above, no significance should be attached to the latter figures. The predominance of Europe's *lingua franca* progressively declines (in both absolute and relative terms): Latin is the language of nearly 70% of all the works listed for the period 1480-1600, but of less than 30% of the 17th century works, and of less than 10% of the literature for the period 1700-1776. It is interesting to note that for the earliest period (up to 1600), there is only one work in English (the 1533 translation of Erasmus's *Bellum*) whereas there are over a dozen works each in French and German. The next work in English listed is over a century later, namely Richard Ward's *The Anatomy of Warre* (1642)[51]. However, the emergence of Quakerism in the second half of the 17th century resulted in a spectacular increase of works in English which equal the number of titles in French or German (i.e. about 20 for each of these three languages). Lastly, we note that for over half the years (i.e. 67) in the period 1480-1600 no works are recorded; for the 17th century and for the period 1700-1776 entries are absent for 18 and 20 years, respectively.

1776-1898

In his circular of 11 April 1933 ter Meulen had identified the period for the bibliography which he compiled (then the only one thought of) as lying between two historic dates: the American Declaration of Independence (1776) and the First Hague Peace Conference (1899). The chronology itself, however, starts with 1778 and ends in 1898. The small discrepancies at each end of the period are more apparent than real: no literature published in 1776 or 1777 was known to ter Meulen when he published his list, and similar gaps occur for the years 1781, 1783, 1784 and 1789. Such 'blank' years rapidly disappear, as might be expected, as the years progress. For the 19th century only two years, 1805 and 1810, have no publications listed. On the other hand, the same phenomenon, but now working in the opposite direction, may account for the decision to shorten the period by a year: the literature was expanding so rapidly -- partly, no doubt, as a result of the Tsar's manifesto of August 1898 which resulted in the Hague Peace Conference the following year -- that it proved expedient to ignore the last year of the century. Ter Meulen could still argue that it was the Hague Conference, not its actual meeting but its calling, which concluded the period chosen. (As will be seen below, the bibliography was in effect pursued, if not published, up to 1913.)

Particularly for the period 1776-1898 the chronological arrangement of the bibliography enables the reader at a glance to follow the growth of the peace literature (and, presumably, of the peace movement). Whereas one page (two columns) suffices for all the literature originating in the first two decades (1776-1795), two and a half pages (over 5 columns) are needed for the literature published in the last year alone of the period (1898). A full column (comprising about 30 entries) for a single year appears for the first time, and exceptionally, in 1832. Only from the middle of the 19th century does this become the norm. Two columns are for the first time necessary in 1867, and even three the following year. However, this progression is not without its ups and downs and in the period 1876-1888 this increase is not maintained, the average length being only 1-2 columns. This changes dramatically in 1889, the *annus mirabilus* of the peace movement, with the inauguration of the annual World Peace Congresses and those of the Interparliamentary Union. The end of this year also saw the publication of Bertha von Suttner's novel *Die Waffen Nieder! (Lay Down Arms!)*, which stimulated the creation of new peace societies throughout Europe in the following years. (The first edition of 1889 is, surprisingly, not listed by ter Meulen, who first enters the novel the following year)[52] . This increase in peace movement activity and in its institutionalisation is fully reflected in ter Meulen's bibliography: for the last ten years of the century the average length per year becomes an unprecedented five columns.

Given the Anglo-American origins of the 19th century peace

movement, it is not surprising that the literature in English predominates and accounts for some 41% of all entries in the 1934 bibliography. After the early revolutionary years, when French and German publications are most prominent, English reigns virtually supreme until about 1865, when a ten year period of French domination commences, reflecting the creation of new peace societies in France and Switzerland. English dominates the literature again in the last quarter of the century, but less so in the 1890s. French-language items account for about 32% of the total, and German, the third language, for about 13%. Two languages are thus responsible for three-fourths of all entries, and three languages for 86%. Of far less importance in quantitative terms are the next three languages represented: Italian (5%), the Scandinavian group (4%) and Dutch (3%, or about 100 items). Of the remaining 50 items the breakdown according to language is as follows: Russian (15), Spanish (15), Latin (10), Portuguese (4), East European languages (5), Esperanto (1). The extremely low figures for some major countries and tongues suggest that ter Meulen's list has many gaps concerning their peace literature.

Of the approximately 3,500 items in the 1934 bibliography, less than a third are accompanied by the 'P.P.' sign, indicating that the item is in the library of the Peace Palace. It was the aim of ter Meulen to have items missing in The Hague sent to him so that an accurate description could be made of them (and eventually also to acquire such items so that the historical peace collection in the Peace Palace would become the most important one world-wide). Of the 3,500 items some 760 are journal titles listed at the beginning for each year. Only the titles of the journals are included, not individual articles. (A small number of articles on peace *is* included but they are in journals, or even newspapers, which are of a general nature and which do not belong to the peace movement, and which otherwise might easily have been ignored.) These 760 titles refer to, at most, some 100 different periodical publications since ter Meulen repeated the title for each year the publication appeared. In this way, three titles account for about 240 entries (or just under a third of the total). They are the British *Herald of Peace*, the American *Advocate of Peace* (and its predecessors), and *Address(es) and Annual Report(s) of...Peace Society(ies)*. These three titles are included in each year without interruption from 1819 onwards.

A perusal of the journal section for each year shows broadly the same kind of evolution as that observed for the publications in the form of books and pamphlets. Until the 1860s the average number of titles listed per year is 4-5 only, but in the 1870s ten different titles per year are frequently recorded, and this figure increases to 20 or more in the early 1890s and to 30 and over in the last years of the century. Until 1850, the journals listed are in either English or French; German peace journals only really appear in the early 1890s, following the success of Bertha von Suttner's novel. The previous decade saw the emergence of several journals in Scandinavia and Italy.

A word must be said about the first periodical publication entered for each year, from 1816 on, namely *Address(es)* etc. This is in the nature of a generic name or description which ter Meulen apparently included on a 'pro memoria' basis only. We assume that it is meant to refer to the *Annual Reports* of the Peace Society (London, since 1817) and of the American Peace society (since 1828), as well as of those of other peace societies which existed for much shorter periods. If this is indeed the case, several entries which refer to such reports should have been subsumed under this generic heading, rather than separately as is the case now. Examples are the *Annual Report of the Society for the Promotion of...Peace* (London), for which the 1st, 4th, 7th, 8th and 9th reports are listed for the years 1817, 1820, 1823, 1824 and 1825, respectively; the *Third Annual Report of the...Tavistock auxiliary peace society* for 1820 (listed under 1821); and the *Seventh Annual Report of the Rhode-Island...peace society* (listed under 1824; the reference to 1829 is erroneous). It seems that the reports by these three organisations are entered separately because copies of them happened to be present in The Hague (the generic *Address(es)*, on the other hand, is never preceded by the 'P.P' sign). It is no doubt because we are dealing with provisional lists, without any annotations or explanations of the procedure followed, that the system for referring to the annual reports of peace societies is confusing and unsatisfactory.

It is for the same reason that in this working document several entries lack the required information, and others contain question marks. Only on a rare occasion is the same item entered twice (e.g., Lucas 1872 and 1873; since this obviously concerns the same publication, the title of the article is rendered incorrectly for one of the entries). The bibliography contains at least two manuscript items, both present in the library of the Peace Palace (Joubleau, 1842 and den Beer Poortugael, 1875). We know that ter Meulen (encouraged by Curti), rather ambitiously entertained the idea of also incorporating manuscripts in his bibliography. It is obvious that no serious attempt has been made to do so at this stage and the instances noted were readily to hand. Lastly, it may be thought that several items in the bibliography have little to do with peace, including the first one, 'Remarkable speech by a Croatian clergyman' (1778), or such general entries as 'The State' (Wagner, 1815), 'Concerning the future of Germany' (Welcker, 1816), 'Saint Simon and Saint-Simonianism' (Veit, 1834). However, without the benefit of ter Meulen's annotations we can only assume that there are good reasons for their inclusion. Such items, we hasten to add, constitute a minute proportion of the total.

World War II, Grotius

As argued above, ter Meulen's provisional bibliographies are still easily the most comprehensive and useful ones available in the field. Even so, since ter Meulen was librarian of the Peace Palace until 1952 (and lived another ten years in retirement), the question arises as to why the project which he had initiated with so much enthusiasm and pursued with similar energy in the late 1920s and 1930s, remained unfinished in the quarter century before the author's passing. It should be remembered, first of all, that in the years immediately following the publication of the second bibliography in 1936, work on it as well as on the previous one continued to take place[53]. In his annual reports for 1937 and 1938 concerning the work in the Library ter Meulen indicated, e.g., that the library had borrowed respectively 96 and 455 works from libraries abroad for the purpose of completing the two bibliographies[54]. When he came to write his report for 1939 in April 1940, days before the occupation, the effects of the impending war were already in evidence: some library staff had been mobilised, and the total number of books borrowed from abroad had dramatically dropped to thirteen only. The library, however, had received from the curator of the Jane Addams Collection at Swarthmore College, Pennsylvania (Ellen Starr Brinton), 'a very large number' of older peace periodicals, to be used also for completing the bibliographies[55].

The preparation and publication, in 1929 and 1937, of the two supplements to the large printed catalogue of the library of the Peace Palace more or less coincided with research for the peace bibliographies; similar work in anticipation of a further supplement engaged ter Meulen's attention in the subsequent period, including the war years, with the result that work on the completion of the definitive bibliography of the historical peace movement was suspended or slowed down. In his *Report on the Library during the World War 1939-1945* ter Meulen wrote: 'Hoping that time and money may be available for the publication, before long, of a new volume, containing the additions [to the Library] since 1936, we have bestowed all possible care on the preparation for its printing'[56] . Another special project undertaken during the war years was a chronologically arranged catalogue of all books in the library which were published before 1651, with indexes to the names of the countries of publication and to those of the printers. As regards the significance of the date chosen, ter Meulen noted: 'The year 1650 was chosen in connection with the life of Grotius, a man who not only is to be considered, along with Erasmus, as the spiritual father of the Peace Palace, but whose works, moreover, are most completely represented in our Library. This latter fact gave occasion to paying much attention during the past five years to the preparation of an extensive annotated *bibliography of Grotius works*, which we hope will appear in print within a few years'.

It seems that this project quickly put in the shadow the peace bibliographies. J.B. van Hall, one of ter Meulen's successors as director of the library of the Peace Palace, called the Grotius bibliography ter Meulen's 'life work'[57]. During the war years and afterwards, ter Meulen thus returned to a subject on which he had already published bibliographical studies as long ago as 1925[58]. These publications commemorated the tercentenary of the appearance of Grotius's book, the cornerstone of modern international law. The 1950 bibliography of Grotius owed its origin likewise to a commemoration: In his report for 1942 ter Meulen reminded his employers that 1945 was the 300th anniversary of the death of Grotius, and he informed them that he had started preparations to mark the event with the publication of a comprehensive bibliography[59]. The research required turned out to be so vast, however, that already the next year ter Meulen was compelled to note that 'this very extensive task will certainly not be ready in 1945'. Several recent graduates (as well as P.J.J. Diermanse, who had joined ter Meulen in 1939 as a volunteer worker) assisted ter Meulen and, as on a previous occasion, he paid some of these volunteers out of his own pocket[60]. In 1944 and 1945 both the Peace Palace and ter Meulen's house were damaged, the latter severely, by V-weapons which had exploded prematurely. It is not surprising that he wrote in his report for 1945 that the Dutch government had found the circumstances unfavourable for commemorating Grotius's tercentenary in that year and that this had led him to abandon the plan for organising an exhibition to mark the occasion[61]. However, in 1950, albeit later than ter Meulen had originally intended, the Grotius bibliography was successfully completed and published in an impressive volume[62].

It is safe to assume that work on this, together with the disruptive effects of the war and its aftermath, made continued work on the peace bibliographies less of a priority. In his first letter to Brinton after the end of the war in Europe, written in July 1945, he wrote: 'During the years of war Miss Juynboll and I have interrupted the work for the peace-bibliography and we undertook a great bibliography on Hugo Grotius that first must be finished. We are, of course, still much interested in the peace bibliography ... My great job will be however to fill out as soon as possible the gaps in our library of the five years of war, when we were nearly completely isolated, and to give to our institute, the seat of the new international court, a new push in the collection of books on law, history and international relations'. It is difficult to establish to what extent in his retirement years ter Meulen, or his associates, returned to the peace bibliography. The original cards for each entry of the lists have been preserved (and additional ones added). Moreover, there are cards with information for the periods from the Middle Ages to 1500 and from 1899 to the First World War. These cards, as well as others, are stored in 14 drawers, labelled *Histoire du Pacifisme*[63]. Many individual cards contain, in addition to the basic bibliographical data, annotations and comments, e.g. on the significance of the work concerned, or on the identity of its author (with sources). Frequently, the reverse side of the cards has been used for recording this kind of useful information. This is no doubt what ter Meulen had in mind when he referred to 'annotations' which the definitive publication would contain. Looked at from this point of view, the provisional bibliographies were indeed aptly titled since they represented the mere skeleton structure of what was envisaged (and steadily taking shape). It is safe to claim that, had ter Meulen's plans been realised, a work no less voluminous and definitive than the Grotius bibliography would have resulted. It is important to remember (see ter Meulen's reply of 16 November 1934 to Lange, above) that the provisional bibliographies, which are reprinted in this volume, not only are without such annotations but also without the additional titles which ter Meulen had received as a result of the distribution of these bibliographies (initially in part, then in their entirety). This additional literature, as well as corrections to his entries, and places of their location, is incorporated only in the card catalogue preserved in the Peace Palace. (It is very likely, we note in passing, that most of the omissions from the provisional bibliographies which are cited below, by way of illustration, are found in this unpublished data bank.) The bibliographies reprinted here are thus entirely the work of ter Meulen and his immediate assistants, and the significance of the 'Committee for the Bibliography of the Peace Movement in History' of the International Committee of Historical Sciences is largely confined to the help its most active members gave ter Meulen who was very much the heart and soul of the enterprise. One can only admire the enormous effort which ter Meulen, ably assisted over the years by several colleagues and devoted volunteers, invested in this noble project and regret that it never reached full fruition. Is it too much to hope that soon, with the help of modern data-processing techniques not available then, his work can be completed?

Bibliographical Tools & Developments

A further development which has occurred since ter Meulen printed his bibliographies and will also greatly benefit their completion has been the appearance of several major bibliographical works of a general nature[64] . Both the multi-volume *National Union Catalogue, Pre-1956 Imprints* (NUC), published in 1968-1981 in 754 volumes[65] , and the *General Catalogue of Printed Books* of the British Library, published in 1960-1966 in 263 volumes, are obvious starting places in which to check, for instance, for obscure publications of known pacifist authors (the NUC conveniently provides locations as well). Since the secular peace movement was very much a 19th century Anglo-American initiative, the recently started *Nineteenth Century Short Title Catalogue* (NSTC) -- which will, in fact, cover the period 1801-1918, and is based on the holdings of six leading libraries in the U.K. (plus those of Trinity College Dublin and, for later volumes, also of Harvard University and the Library of Congress) -- will be most helpful. For instance, in the most recently published volume[66] we find forty publications entered for Elihu Burritt, an appropriate figure in this context since, more than anyone else, he epitomised Anglo-American collaboration in the mid-19th century peace movement. Although not all of these items are suitable for inclusion in ter Meulen's bibliography (Burritt also wrote books, e.g., based on his walks across the length and breadth of Britain), it is nevertheless likely that several items can now be effortlessly and accurately added to the dozen publications recorded for Burritt by ter Meulen (for the same period, up to 1870).

Another example illustrating the NSTC's usefulness is taken from the first volume, published in 1984. Availing ourselves this time of the subject index we find that the first publication listed under the heading 'International Relations' (there is no separate heading for peace) is Thomas E. Abbott's *Peace: A Lyric Poem* (published in Hull in 1814 and to be found in the British Library only)[67]. This item is absent from ter Meulen's bibliography. It is puzzling to observe that ter Meulen apparently did not use the original STC, namely A.W. Pollard and G.R. Redgrave's *A Short-Title Catalogue of books printed in England,*

Scotland, and Ireland and of English books printed abroad, 1475-1640, published in 1926. The STC records in alphabetical order of author over 26,000 items. For instance, no. 10,466 is Erasmus's *The Complaint of Peace*, published in 1559 in London by Jhon Cawoode in T. Paynell's translation. The STC records only two copies: one in the British Museum (as it was then called), and one in the possession of Sir R.L. Harmsworth[68]. Ter Meulen fails altogether, however, to list this edition[69] and records as the first English translation the one which appeared almost two and a half centuries later, in 1795. It is surprising that this anomaly, namely the apparent absence of a vernacular edition of so popular a tract in such an important tongue, did not occur to him and spur him on to find the 'missing' edition. This is especially so in view of the fact that he conveniently listed, under each *editio princeps*, the various editions and translations (as well as entering these again separately under their respective year of publication)[70]. His entry for the first publication of *Querela Pacis* (1516) shows, for the 16th century alone, two different editions in each of the following languages: Spanish, German, and Dutch. Contemporary translations in English were therefore conspicuously absent[71].

A second edition of the STC has recently been published[72]. It records not only a third copy of *The Complaint of Peace*, in the library of the University of Illinois, Urbana (acquired by it in 1957), but also a change of ownership and location: the Harmsworth copy is now in the Folger Shakespeare Library in Washington (which purchased it in 1938). The second edition of the STC also provides much new information concerning the location of copies of the first English translation of Erasmus's *Bellum* (1533): whereas ter Meulen mentions in the interleaved bibliography only the copy in the British Museum, and the original STC lists another copy in the Huntington Library in San Marino, California, the revised STC has succeeded in locating another five copies (in Oxford, Cambridge, Yale, Urbana, and Folger)[73].

Pollard and Redgrave's work was supplemented for the period 1641-1700 by Donald Wing's now famous *Short-Title Catalogue*, published in three volumes in 1948-1951[74]. Wing enables us, for instance, to supplement ter Meulen's information on the second work in English mentioned in his bibliography, Richard Ward's *The Anatomy of Warre* (1642, cf. p. 18 above). His interleaved bibliography located only one copy of this edition, in the Nobel Institute in Oslo. Wing (who is only concerned with a census of copies in libraries in the United Kingdom and United States) does not list this copy, but records one in the British Museum[75]. A third copy, unknown to Wing, is in the Folger

Shakespeare Library; its published catalogue is another very useful tool for completing the early part of ter Meulen's bibliography[76]. Ter Meulen was unable to provide a single location for the second edition of Ward's tract, published in 1643 as *The Character of Warre*. Wing identified copies of it in the British Museum, the Bodleian, and Trinity College Dublin[77].

A work published a few years before the STC, namely the *Catalogue of the Edward Fry Library of International Law* (which library is housed in the London School of Economics and Political Science), was apparently also ignored by ter Meulen when he compiled his lists. It contains, for instance, an edition of William Ladd's well-known *Essay on a Congress of Nations* published in London in 1840[78]. For the same year ter Meulen only mentions the Boston edition. This omission is all the more surprising since ter Meulen visited London in January 1933, i.e. at least a year before the publication of his first bibliography[79]. As with all his travels, this visit was, at least in part, for professional purposes, and we are left to wonder whether he failed to visit the Edward Fry Library, one of the few specialised libraries at the time in this, ter Meulen's, field. It is likely, however, that he had gathered useful information from his London visit (which is likely to have included the library mentioned) but that it occurred after the printing of the provisional lists for the period 1778-1853. (We know that these were ready when he wrote to the Nobel Committee in May 1933, cf. p. 7 above.) He would have recorded this new information in his central bibliographical data-bank for eventual incorporation into the envisaged definitive bibliography.

Another valuable reference work related to a specialised library in London is the *Catalogue of the Goldsmiths' Library of Economic Literature*, the Library being part of the University of London library. The catalogue was published in four volumes in 1970-1983, and comprises over 37,000 titles published up to 1850[80]. The arrangement is chronological (from 1503 onwards) and, from 1601, also according to subject. (The chronological arrangement, particularly, makes comparison with ter Meulen's bibliography easy and rewarding: For instance, volume 3, p. 158, lists for the year 1816 nine 'miscellaneous' items, four of which are on peace. Three of these are not listed by ter Meulen.) We find, e.g., that the library possesses a copy of the elusive first English translation of Immanuel Kant's *Project of Perpetual Peace*, published in London in 1796. The only other known copies of this edition are in the library of the United Nations in Geneva, of the Johns Hopkins University in Baltimore, and of the Library Company of Philadelphia[81].

This is yet another important translation not recorded by ter Meulen: the first separate publication of Kant's essay in English translation listed by him is that of J. Morell, published in London in 1884. (This edition seems even rarer than the 1796 one: only one copy is listed in the NUC, in the American University library in Washington D.C. It is also the earliest English translation of Kant's essay in the British Library.) The comment made earlier in connection with Erasmus's *The Complaint of Peace* (cf. p. 26 above) also applies here and the absence from ter Meulen's bibliography of the first edition, in English translation, of two famous writings by equally prominent authors, suggests that many rather ephemeral writings, especially in less important languages, are very likely also absent.

Lastly, since ter Meulen's bibliography also includes titles of periodicals, mention must be made of the *British Union Catalogue of Periodicals* (BUCOP), which describes itself as 'a record of the periodicals of the world, from the 17th century to the present day, in British libraries'. The first of this multi-volume publication appeared in 1955 and additional volumes have appeared at least as late as 1975[82]. The *Catalogue* records not only titles but also specifies the completeness of the serial publications and their locations. These details are, for instance, fully recorded for Britain's oldest and most important peace journal, *The Herald of Peace*.

Many other important reference works exist, in a variety of languages and some available only on microfiche or through other means of data storage. In addition, there is the literature on peace itself which has come into existence since ter Meulen's bibliographies were compiled. In the last three decades the history of peace has become a recognised aspect of the history of social and political ideas and movements, and a thriving profession of peace historians has resulted in a sizeable literature[83] . The bibliographies to be found in the works concerned are a prime source for supplementing ter Meulen's. A good example is Peter Brock's monumental *Pacifism in the United States: From the Colonial Era to the First World War* (Princeton: Princeton University Press, 1968) which mentions, in its 30-page bibliography, several items which are missing from ter Meulen's bibliography.

Taken together, the various works referred to above will be of inestimable value in completing the task begun by ter Meulen. The fact that he was not able to draw on some of these modern research tools (whilst ignoring others which *were* available at the time) or on data processing equipment[84], makes his achievement all the more impressive, particularly as he was at the same time involved in the various other projects mentioned. They included the writing of the third and final volume of his great work on the history of the idea of international organisation which was published in 1940 (the two previous volumes were published in 1917 and 1929). To a considerable extent the preparation of this encyclopedic work, which covers the period 1300-1889, provided the initial material for the bibliography of the history of pacifism (cf. p. 11 above)[85] . Although an offshoot of this larger work, it grew into a daunting task once the idea of a separate, annotated, and exhaustive bibliography had taken hold of him. Just how daunting, and how near he came to realising his goal, is suggested by a perusal of the unpublished material in the surviving card catalogues. So far the French saying 'Nothing is as permanent as the provisional' can with justification be applied to ter Meulen's provisional bibliography. But because even in their unfinished form they deserve not merely to survive but to become better known and to be given a new lease of life (all the more so in an age when 'peace history' has established itself as a timely and necessary discipline), their renewed publication following the 75th anniversary of the Peace Palace, is both a tribute to the far-sightedness of its former librarian, and a service to all those who, like him, are interested in the study and pursuit of peace.

Notes

1) The correspondence between Jacob ter Meulen and Christian L. Lange which has been made use of in the first sections of this introduction is incompletely preserved in the Lange archives in the library of the University of Oslo (MS fol. 2521: 88). The correspondence is in French and the translations are mine. Quotations from letters involving ter Meulen or Lange and other correspondents are from the same file, unless otherwise indicated. I am very grateful to Irwin Abrams for bringing these papers to my attention. For concise biographies of Lange and ter Meulen see the entries in Warren F. Kuehl, ed., *Biographical Dictionary of Internationalists* (Westport, Conn.: Greenwood Press, 1983), pp. 417-419 & pp. 712-713, and Harold Josephson, ed., *Biographical Dictionary of Modern Peace Leaders* (Westport, Conn.: Greenwood Press, 1985), pp. 629-631.

2) *Revue de Droit International*, vol. 3 (1929), pp. 589-592, vol. 4 (1929), pp. 706-712, vol. 5 (1930), pp. 397- 404. Jacob ter Meulen, *L'Histoire du Pacifisme* (Extrait de la Revue de Droit International) (Paris: Les Editions Internationales, 1930), 11 pp.

3) On both scores his hopes were justified: it is interesting to note that the *Biographical Dictionary of Modern Peace Leaders* (cf. note 1) is dedicated 'to Merle Curti and the pioneer historians in peace research'. See also Curti's very interesting 'Reflections on the genesis and growth of peace history' in *Peace and Change* (vol. 11, no. 1, Spring 1985), pp. 1-18.

4) For the personal remembrances of the first president of the ICHS see: Halvdan Koht, *The origin and beginnings of the International Committee of Historical Sciences* (Lausanne, 1962).

5) 'Proposition relative à une bibliographie concernant le pacifisme dans l'histoire présentée par M. Ter Meulen', in *Bulletin of the International Committee of Historical Sciences* (vol. IV, part III, no. 16, pp. 419- 422).

6) *Bulletin*, Sept. 1932, o.c., pp. 360-361, 370.

7) Friis had raised this matter with Halvdan Koht who was the president of the ICHS as well as a member of the Norwegian Nobel Committee. (It was in the latter capacity that Koht had spoken in glowing terms of the life and work of Lange on the occasion of the award of the Nobel Peace Prize to him in 1921. Cf. Frederick W. Haberman, ed., *Nobel Lectures - Peace, 1901-1925*.

Amsterdam: Elsevier for the Nobel Foundation, 1972, p.323.)

8) At any rate, in the Lange file of letters concerning ter Meulen there is a gap of three years.

9) Friis had earlier requested Lange's advice, following receipt of ter Meulen's original proposal.

10) Lange had been its first director, from 1904 to 1909, and remained associated with it until the end of his life. Even before the Institute was established (in 1904), Lange had been secretary to the Norwegian Nobel Committee (since 1901).

11) Prophetically, as far as the present author is concerned. See also below, pp. 16-17.

12) The full report of the meeting in The Hague is in *Bulletin*, December 1933 (vol. V, part IV, no. 21, esp. pp. 821 & 841). See also *Bulletin*, Sept. 1932, o.c., pp. 547 & 560.

13) A note to this effect appeared in the *Bulletin* for November 1932 (vol. IV, part IV, no. 17, p. 758): 'Création de la Commission extérieure pour la bibliographie du pacifisme dans l'histoire'. The same issue contained a proposal nominating Rafael Altamira for the 1933 Nobel Peace Prize. He was the Spanish representative of the ICHS, and a judge at the Permanent Court of International Justice.

14) This circular was printed in English and French; the French text, dated 11 April 1933, was also published in the *Bulletin* for May 1933 (vol. V, part II, no. 19, p. 500), together with a specimen list of 7 pages comprising the years 1778-1823.

15) See the annual reports for 1934 and 1935 of the Nobel Committee to the Norwegian Parliament, published respectively as documents no. 6 and 10 in the record of parliamentary debates for 1935 and 1936: *Stortingsforhandlinger*, Part V, Oslo, 1936, pp. 2 & 5 (Document no. 6) & pp. 2 & 4 (Document no. 10). I am grateful to Anne C. Kjelling of the Library of the Norwegian Nobel Institute for bringing these documents to my attention. See also Oscar J. Falnes, *Norway and the Nobel Peace Prize* (New York: Columbia Univ. Press, 1938), pp. 187 & 298-299.

16) Cf. ter Meulen's letter of 6 June 1933 to Curti. He also expressed understanding for the latter's inability, for the time being, to work on the lists (Personal communication from Merle Curti, 28 October 1987).

17) The report, dated 1 August 1933, was printed in the *Bulletin* for March 1935 (vol. VII, part I, no. 26, pp. 114-115): 'Commission pour la Bibliographie du Pacifisme dans l'Histoire: Rapport sur l'activité de la Commission présenté par le secrétaire M. J. ter Meulen'. See also p. 73. Copies of this report, as well as of the third and fourth reports, are present in the Lange papers.

18) The report, dated 20 March 1934, was printed in the *Bulletin* for June 1935 (vol. VII, part II, no. 27, p. 162): 'Commission pour la Bibliographie du Pacifisme dans l'Histoire: Rapport sur l'activité de la Commission'. See also p. 134.

19) A short notice about the appearance of the full list appeared in the *Bulletin* for March 1934 (vol. VI, part I, no. 22, pp. 105 & 112).

20) Lange had recently retired and was now again living in Norway. Ter Meulen was desperate enough to suggest that they could meet even in England or Germany, or elsewhere. However, the latter seemed not to include Norway. Ter Meulen himself apparently shared the view which he had put to Lange in a letter some years previously (12 May 1932), that 'in the eyes of several people, the beautiful capital of Norway is situated pretty far from the centre of Europe'. Of course, modern air travel has revolutionised our geographical notions.

21) That T.P. Sevensma (who was director of the library of the League of Nations) was also preparing a bibliography of the historical peace movement is confirmed in two letters which he sent to ter Meulen towards the end of 1934 (copies of which are preserved in the archives of the library of the League of Nations. I wish to thank Werner Simon of the United Nations Library in Geneva for providing me with copies of Sevensma's letters). On 2 November 1934 he wrote: 'I am still frequently buying all manner of historically interesting brochures (e.g. a journal entitled *Friedens-blatt* of 1869-1870) so that I have not yet decided to print a list'. On 13 December 1934 he wrote, enclosing 'a preliminary list of various old books preserved in my office and of that which has already been catalogued as "peace movement" ... we continue to collect in this area, so that the list is not yet complete'. Other matters discussed in both amicable letters suggest that they frequently helped each other in their professional work. Two years earlier, Sevensma had expressed his great appreciation for the work undertaken by ter Meulen when he reviewed new supplements to the printed catalogues of the library of the Peace Palace. It was to

its 'expert' director that students of international relations owed catalogues which were 'the best and the most complete bibliographies available' ('Der Katalog der Bibliothek des Friedenspalastes', in *Die Friedens-Warte*, vol. 32, November 1932, p. 351). It is doubtless the case that ter Meulen's initiative brought about an increased awareness of, and interest in, the historic peace literature on the part of fellow-librarians such as Sevensma and scholars such as Wehberg. The latter, who edited *Die Friedens-Warte*, devoted a short article to the rare journal, mentioned above, acquired by Sevensma. Cf. 'Eine deutsche Friedenszeitschrift aus den Jahren 1869/70' in *Die Friedens-Warte* (vol. 34, no. 6, 1934, p. 269). Ter Meulen was not aware of this title when his list was printed. Given Wehberg's article, it is surprising that also Karl Ferdinand Reichel fails to list *Friedensblatt* in his *Die pazifistische Presse: Eine Übersicht über die in deutscher Sprache im In‑und Ausland bis 1935 veröffentlichten pazifistischen Zeitschriften und Zeitungen* (Würzburg: Konrad Triltsch Verlag, 1938). This is a unique and valuable compilation, despite its author's anti-semitic and anti-pacifist sentiments.

22) In the margin of this paragraph Lange suggested another starting date, preceding Erasmus by only a few years, namely the beginning of printing.

23) Ter Meulen appended to his letter a sheet with five examples. Against one of them Lange wrote: 'Not pacifism', and against another, a journal which, in ter Meulen's annotation, 'makes propaganda for the delivery of peoples from despotism, [and which] has a revolutionary rather than pacifist character', exclamation marks, implying similar disapproval.

24) Lange's comment in the margin referred to the need to have the language corrected by a native speaker.

25) 'Admirable!' Lange wrote in the margin.

26) Ter Meulen names these 35 individuals and institutions (representing 14 countries) and identifies among them the 17 who have provided him with 'hundreds' of pieces of information each. Among them are several libraries in the U.S.A. and in Germany and France, the library of the Norwegian Nobel Institute and of the League of Nations, the International Peace Bureau in Geneva, Merle Curti. Ter Meulen also identified the four respondents who had been remunerated for their help.

27) It is interesting to note, in view of the discussion between ter Meulen and Lange on the appropriate date for starting the earlier period (cf. note 22), that Lange underlined the first three words of this sentence, and put an exclamation mark next to it. In conception and execution the bibliographies are, indeed, entirely ter Meulen's work and not that of the committee of which he acted as the secretary.

28) The latter source is noteworthy. The State Library in Berlin allowed ter Meulen to borrow this manuscript for a generous period. The second, and smallest, part of it had been published in 1891 and is (unlike the manuscript itself) entered in ter Meulen's bibliography, as are two smaller publications by this author for the years 1887 and 1888. Hetzel wrote in the preface of the book published in 1891: 'In case my work fails to find sufficient support [with the result that the greater part of it would have to remain unpublished], it will upon my death be deposited in the Royal Library in Berlin as a valuable source'. Cf. *Die Humanisirung des Krieges in den letzten hundert Jahren, 1789-1889* (Frankfurt A.D. Oder, 1891, n.p.). The disappointed writer would be gratified to know that his labours were not in vain. Veit Valentin speaks of 'a monumental work ... a source of the first order ... which has also been of great value to us, as it has already been to many others'. He expressed the hope that Hetzel's manuscript (which he used) would soon be printed. Cf. *Geschichte des Völkerbundgedankens in Deutschland: Ein geistesgeschichtlicher Versuch* (Berlin: Hans Robert Engelmann, 1920, pp. 84-85). Whereas ter Meulen made use of the entire manuscript, at about the same time another German scholar referred to the published part as a source book which is 'much used but not always acknowledged'. Cf. Heinrich Rogge, *Nationale Friedenspolitik* (Berlin: Junker & Dünnhaupt Verlag, 1934, p. 5). Fortunately, Hetzel's valuable manuscript survived also the ravages of the Second World War and is now in the Staatsbibliothek Preussischer Kulturbesitz in (W.) Berlin.

29) The traditional neglect of the history of peace ideas had resulted in the virtual oblivion of the names of many important individuals and the movements they created; the documentary evidence relating to both was in real danger of destruction. Almost sixty years after the publication of his first book, *The American Peace Crusade 1815-1860* (1929), Merle Curti commented that 'above all it rescued the leaders of a worthy cause from virtual oblivion'. And of Devere Allen's *The Fight for Peace*, published two years later,

he says that it 'included brief summaries of interesting sources he
[Allen] had in several instances saved from destruction'. Cf. Curti,
'Reflections' in *Peace and Change*, o.c., pp. 5-6. Clearly, ter
Meulen was not exaggerating the problem, and the urgency of the
task which he had set himself was recognised by fellow historians
and chroniclers of the peace idea. The problem became all the
more acute in the 1930s as the political   situation in   Europe
deteriorated. Ellen Starr Brinton, the first curator of the Swarthmore College Peace Collection (from 1935 until her retirement in
1951), frequently expressed her deep anxiety to ter Meulen about
the survival of peace collections in Europe, several of which she
had personal knowledge of. In her letter of 2 June 1938 she
suggested that 'we should pool our strength as well as our financial
resources and endeavor to save from destruction some of these
splendid old collections'. She detailed seven of these in a one-page
'Notes on certain Peace Collections in Europe' which she
appended to her letter of 24 March. 'See if you can devise a means
of reaching the influential persons in charge', she implored ter
Meulen, adding: 'I have done everything I could think of and now
I feel completely baffled'. Later that year (3 December) she
informed him of the tragic stories she was getting from peace
leaders in different countries -- 'one, the owner of a large library,
has written me that it took four nights to destroy the books and
papers before the home was abandoned'. The very interesting
correspondence between ter Meulen and Brinton, covering the
period 1935-1945, is contained in the archival records of the
Swarthmore College Peace Collection itself (rather than in the
Ellen Starr Brinton Papers there). I am very grateful to the present
curator, Wendy E. Chmielewski, for having made the full
correspondence available to me. Perhaps unknown to ter Meulen,
such destruction as described by Brinton was about to take place
on his own doorstep. In May 1940, fearful of the German invader,
Henri van der Mandere (a leading figure in the Dutch peace
movement) destroyed the archives of two organisations which had
played an important role during the First World War, namely the
Dutch Anti-War Council and the Central Organisation for a
Durable Peace. (Cf. the note by P.J.J. Diermanse in the Peace
Movement Collection of the Peace Palace, Z 580-C18.)

30) J. ter Meulen, J. Huizinga, G. Berlage, 'Bibliographie der
Friedensbewegung für die Periode 1480-1776' in *Die Friedens-
Warte* (vol. 36, 1936, no. 2, pp. 82-89 & no. 3/4, pp. 149-161).

The first-mentioned issue comprises the period 1480-1637, the second the period 1638-1776, as well as the index. It is somewhat surprising to find that apparently no mention was made in *Die Friedens-Warte* for 1934 of the appearance that year of the bibliography for the period 1776-1898. This is especially so since its editor, Hans Wehberg, was a member of ter Meulen's committee, and had announced its creation by the ICHS in the November 1932 issue of his journal (in a most interesting article concerning the development of the peace movement before the World War: 'Die Friedensbewegung vor dem Ausbruch des Weltkrieges', vol. 32, pp. 321-328, esp. p. 321).

31) Ter Meulen expressed his regret to learn that Lange had again suffered from a moral depression, adding: 'But I find it very understandable that we internationalists from time to time lose all hope in the future'. He offered to send him a copy of Huizinga's recent book, *In the shadow of to-morrow* (sub-titled: A diagnosis of the spiritual distemper of our time). Lange died in December 1938.

32) Ter Meulen's third and fourth reports do not appear to have been published in the *Bulletin*. In the years 1936-1937 it printed only two small notices on ter Meulen's work: one announcing the extension of the bibliography to an earlier period, and another indicating that this second bibliography had been published in the *Friedens-Warte*. Cf. *Bulletin* for March 1936 (vol. VIII, part I, no. 30, p. 191) and for September 1937 (vol. IX, part III, no. 36, p. 400).

33) A very few copies of the 1934 bibliography were bound in a hard cover, with a printed title on it; they are to be found in the libraries of the Peace Palace, the Norwegian Nobel Institute, and the United Nations in Geneva.

34) Ernst Friedrich opened his disturbing anti-war book, *War against War!* (Berlin: Verlag 'Freie Jugend'/Internationales Haus, 1924) with a defiant invitation to 'the rulers and governments of those countries who fear the truth and who forbid the book', to register their names in the rubric provided. Little can he have realised that only a few years afterwards his book, together with other pacifist literature, would be publicly burnt. Here we encounter one of the traditional causes for the relative rarity of peace literature: the systematic banning and burning to which it has been subjected. In the same year that ter Meulen's first bibliography appeared, Hans

Wehberg wrote an article detailing the extinction of pacifist journals in Nazi-Germany. Cf. 'Das Sterben der pazifistischen Zeitschriften in Deutschland', in *Die Friedens-Warte* (Vol. 34, no. 2, April-May 1934, pp. 80-81). This journal itself only survived because by this time it was published from Geneva where Wehberg, its editor, had been living since 1928. For a brief history of this excellent publication see Friedrich-Karl Scheer's article on it in Helmut Donat & Karl Holl, eds., *Die Friedensbewegung: Organisierter Pazifismus in Deutschland, Oesterreich und in der Schweiz* (Düsseldorf: ECON Taschenbuch Verlag/Hermes Handle-xikon, 1983, pp. 149-152). Reichel provides details of the censorship and prohibition of *Die Friedens-Warte* and other German peace journals; the very first one which he discusses, *Der Völkerfriede*, published in 1851 in Kant's Königsberg, was prohibited by the police after a year. See *Die pazifistische Presse*, o.c., p.3.

35) See also the details given in note 33 above.

36) Both bibliographies proved very useful to Ellen Starr Brinton who had just started putting in order the great quantity of peace literature housed at Swarthmore College, including Jane Addams' library. Brinton first learned of ter Meulen's bibliographies through Merle Curti, who loaned them to her. 'This bibliography of yours is a priceless aid to me', she wrote ter Meulen on 7 July 1936, and 'Your bibliographies are most valuable' (9 February 1937). In her letter of 27 October 1940 (there would not be another one until May 1945) she wondered whether he was able to complete 'the bibliography which so many of us would treasure'. Brinton was able to provide him with many new items not yet recorded in the bibliographies.

37) It is mentioned in *A London Bibliography of the Social Sciences* (London: British Library of Political and Economic Science/LSE, vol. VIII, 1954, p. 872).

38) Theodore Besterman, *A World Bibliography of Bibliographies* (Lausanne: Societas Bibliographica, 4th ed., vol. III, 1965, columns 4458-4460). The reference in the heading ('Peace - see also War') is rather misleading: the three columns devoted to 'Peace' compare unexpectedly favourably with the two columns devoted to 'War' (the latter are in vol. IV, 1966, columns 6482-6483); however, the fuller entry for this subject is to be found under the heading 'Military arts and sciences' and runs to almost 40 columns (cf. vol.

III, columns 3912-3950).

39) Besterman's precise estimates are 2,222 and 2,500 entries, respectively.

40) Since Besterman's work was published, several important bibliographies on aspects of peace have appeared, for instance Martin Anderson's *Conscription: A Select and Annotated Bibliography* (Stanford, CA: The Hoover Institution Press, 1976), which has 'some 1,385 entries, over ten times the number of the next largest annotated bibliography known' (p. XIV). (Most of these recent bibliographies are mentioned in the work referred to in the next note). In her decennial supplement to Besterman, *A World Bibliography of Bibliographies 1964-1974* (Totowa, N.J.: Rowman & Littlefield, 1977), Alice F. Toomey lists 7 entries for 'peace', none of them being as comprehensive as the bibliographies contained in Besterman's own compilation (cf. vol. 2, pp. 820-821).

41) Berenice A. Carroll, Clinton F. Fink & Jane E. Mohraz, *Peace and War: A Guide to Bibliographies* (Santa Barbara, CA: ABC-Clio, 1983, pp. 229-231).

42) Blanche Wiesen Cook, ed., *Bibliography on Peace Research in History* (Santa Barbara, CA: ABC-Clio, 1969, p. 9, no. 98). The publisher appears, interestingly but erroneously, as Nijhoff.

43) Alex H. Swinne, *Bibliographia Irenica 1500-1970: Internationale Bibliographie zur Friedenswissenschaft: kirchliche und politische Einigungs- und Friedensbestrebungen, Oekumene und Völkerverständigung* (Hildesheim: Gerstenberg/Studia Irenica No. 10, 1977, 319 pp.).

44) The reader constantly encounters juxtapositions such as the following (taken from p. 32, no. 211 & no. 212): 'Dimensions of defense opinions. The American public. In: *Papers, Peace Research Society, 1966'* and *'Eclaircissement* de la question pourquoy le Synode National tenu a Charenton l'an 1631 a admis a sa communion les Lutheriens potost [sic] que ceux de l'Eglise Romaine. Charenton, 1658'.

45) Gerardo Zampaglione, *The Idea of Peace in Antiquity* (Notre Dame, Ind.: Univ. of Notre Dame Press, 1973, p. 15).

46) Christian L. Lange & August Schou, *Histoire de l'Internationalisme* (Oslo: H. Aschehoug/Publications de l'Institut Nobel

Norvégien, vol. 2, 1954, pp. VIII & 111). This volume had been started by Lange but was completed by Schou.

47) Théodore Ruyssen, *Les Sources Doctrinales de l'Internationalisme* (Paris: Presses Universitaires de France, vol. 2, 1958, pp. 592 & 602). Ruyssen wrongly gives the date as 1938. One of the very few other studies to refer to ter Meulen's bibliographies is Kurt von Raumer's *Ewiger Friede: Friedensrufe und Friedenspläne seit der Renaissance* (Freiburg: Karl Alber, 1953, p. 498 & pp. 507-508).

48) It is surprising to find, however, that several of the earliest editions of Erasmus's *The Complaint of Peace* (in Latin as well as in German and Spanish translations), which are recorded in the *Catalogue Général des Livres Imprimés de la Bibliothèque Nationale* (Paris: Imprimerie Nationale, 1911, vol. 47) are, as regards their presence in the Bibliothèque Nationale, not noted in ter Meulen's interleaved copy. For two translations (German, 1521 and Spanish, 1529), ter Meulen records only one known copy; for two Latin editions (1525 and 1530) only two copies each. However, according to its catalogue, the Bibliothèque Nationale possesses copies of all four editions. These omissions suggest that ter Meulen failed to consult this catalogue which lists very systematically the Bibliothèque's extensive collection of works by Erasmus. Their number runs to 958, comprising nearly 70 pages of double columns. (Cf. columns 751-882, esp. columns 859-860, no. 747-754). For evidence of ter Meulen's failure to use other important reference works see note 50 and infra. Given his preeminence as a cataloguer and bibliographer this is surprising.

49) Brigitte Hannemann, ed., Erasmus von Rotterdam. *"Süss scheint der Krieg den Unerfahrenen"*. (Munich: Chr. Kaiser, 1987, p. 31).

50) Copies of the 1607 edition have been located, however, in the city library in Breslau and the university library in Giessen. Cf. Ferdinand Vander Haeghen et al., *Bibliotheca Erasmiana. Bibliographie des oeuvres d'Erasme*: Adagia (Ghent: C. Vyt, 1897, p. 479). This volume provides not only a very comprehensive catalogue of all editions of *Bellum* but also of their locations which are frequently more numerous than the information provided in the interleaved copy (Cf. pp. 445-527). It seems that both ter Meulen and Hannemann did not consult this standard work on Erasmus. It is of course possible that Vander Haeghen's census must be revised in the light of the destruction caused by the two world wars.

51) The first 200 works listed, comprising the period up to 1643, consist of 120 titles in Latin, 30 in German, 25 in French, but only 2 in English!

52) Both novel and author are similarly absent from the chapter 'Das Jahr 1889' in the final volume of his large work *Der Gedanke der Internationalen Organisation in seiner Entwicklung*, vol. 2, part 2, 1867-1889 (The Hague: Martinus Nijhoff, 1940, pp. 246-259).

53) Cf. p. 12 above, and p. 17 concerning the interleaved copy.

54) *Verslag betreffende de Bibliotheek van het Vredespaleis over het kalenderjaar 1937* (The Hague: Library of the Peace Palace, 1938, p. 13); Verslag ... 1938 (1939, p. 15). From 1924 to 1950, ter Meulen wrote an annual report on the library for his employers, the Trustees of the Board of the Dutch Carnegie Foundation. Typescript copies of these very interesting and informative reports have been preserved in the library of the Peace Palace.

55) *Verslag ... 1939* (1940, pp. 5, 14). The exchange of duplicate material between ter Meulen and Brinton is fully documented in their correspondence.

56) Dr. Jacob ter Meulen, *Report on the Library during the World War 1939-1945* (The Hague: Library of the Peace Palace, 1945, pp. 4-5, in English). In 1954 the first (of six) supplements for the period 1937-1952 was published. However, these supplementary volumes were no longer properly printed, and it seems significant that by this time ter Meulen had retired; see also note 58.

57) Kuehl, *Biographical Dictionary*, o.c., p. 713. Arthur Eyffinger's comments on the Grotius bibliography can be applied to ter Meulen's other works too: ' ... is definite and will remain forever authoritative in the field, thanks to the author's painstaking research, the work's completeness and its virtual faultlessness'. See the interesting sketch of ter Meulen in his book *The Peace Palace: Residence for Justice. Domicile of Learning* (The Hague: Carnegie Foundation, 1988, pp. 180-84) as well as in the foreword to the present volume. Ellen Starr Brinton thus got much more than she had bargained for: In 1938 she had queried: 'The name of Hugo Grotius is nowhere mentioned in your bibliographies. We are wondering why' (10 February). Ter Meulen replied: 'We consider Hugo Grotius more a jurist than a pacifist in the strict sense of the word, although he was deeply interested in the subject and had made great efforts towards the unity of the churches' (22

February).

58) *Liste Bibliographique de 76 éditions et traductions de 'De Iure Belli ac Pacis' de Hugo Grotius* (Leyden: Bibliotheca Visseriana V, 1925); *Concise Bibliography of Hugo Grotius* (Leyden: A.W. Sijthoff, 1925). Another commemorative publication appeared in 1926, *Eenige brieven betreffende de eerste uitgave van Hugo de Groot's De Iure Belli ac Pacis* [Some letters concerning the first edition of -] (Amsterdam: Lettergieterij "Amsterdam"). Edited by Dr. A. Lysen, the conservator of the Peace Palace Library, this bibliophile edition contained a revealing introduction by ter Meulen in which he eloquently wrote that books should be esthetically pleasing and that in their production the need for harmony of form and content should be observed.

59) *Verslag ... 1942* (1943, pp. 9-10).

60) *Verslag ... 1943* (1944, p. 15).

61) *Verslag ... 1944* (1945, p. 3); Verslag ... 1945 (1946, pp. 3-4).

62) Jacob ter Meulen & P.J.J. Diermanse, *Bibliographie des écrits imprimés de Hugo Grotius* (The Hague: Martinus Nijhoff, 1950, 708 pp.).

63) Signature Z 580a: 'Bibliographie sur fiches concernant l'histoire du pacifisme'. Half of these drawers (those numbered B3-B9) contain, in chronological order, names of authors and titles of books (etc.) from the Middle Ages to the First World War, as follows: B3 (1050-1599), B4 (1600-1775), B5 (1776-1839), B6 (1840-1867), B7 (1868-1883), B8 (1884-1895), B9 (1896-1913). It will be noted that only parts of B3 and B9 have been published in the provisional bibliographies which, presumably, it was intended to extend in the definitive bibliography both backwards to 1050 and forwards to 1913 - thus detailing the history of pacifist literature over a millennium. A good case can be made, however, for confining the historical peace movement to the period represented by the published bibliographies and which are reprinted here, namely 1480-1898. The first date coincides with the beginning of printing and, practically, with Erasmus's writings. It is difficult to think of a more appropriate trail-blazer of the modern peace movement than Erasmus. With the First Hague Peace Conference, pacifist ways of thought entered the conferences of statesmen and increasingly were no longer confined to the traditional (oppositional and minority) peace movement. The experiences of the First

World War and the advent of the nuclear era have further reinforced this tendency. Drawers C10-C12 contain, in alphabetical order, the names of authors and of titles of books (etc.). The remaining drawers, A1-A2, contain a subject index and is entitled 'History of pacifism, arbitration, portraits, etc.'; D13 contains references to periodicals, undated works and duplicates (present in the Peace Palace?); lastly, E14 ('Divers') lists, in chronological order, titles for the period 1480-1898. The whole collection is most impressive.

64) For an overview of one very important kind of bibliographical tool, see Robert Collison, *Published Library Catalogues* (London: Mansell, 1973), which describes some 600 such catalogues in the English-speaking world alone.

65) The NUC has been described as 'the most extensive general bibliographical compilation of all times. It contains more than 12 million entries in 754 huge folio volumes ... and is the best record we shall ever have of the first 500 years of printing'. Cf. Bernard H. Breslauer & Roland Folter, *Bibliography: Its History and Development.* Catalogue of an exhibition ... to mark the completion of The National Union Catalog: Pre-1956 Imprints (New York: The Grolier Club, 1984, p. 213). The fascinating history of the NUC is related in John Y. Cole, ed., *In Celebration: The National Union Catalog, Pre-1956 Imprints* (Washington: Library of Congress, 1981).

66) *Nineteenth Century Short Title Catalogue* (Newcastle-upon-Tyne: Avero Publ., 1987), Series II, Phase I, 1816-1870, vol. 7, B-C, pp. 228-229.

67) o.c., Series I, Phase I, 1801-1815, vol. 1, A-C, pp. 3 & 520.

68) (London: The Bibliographical Society, 1926, p. 228).

69) The interleaved copy contains no additional titles (and thus also not this edition) since it only indicates locations, other than those in the Peace Palace, for the titles which are already listed in the provisional bibliography. (See note 51 above and the discussion preceding it.)

70) However, ter Meulen adopted this procedure only for the 1936 bibliography. This is, although understandable, a pity since it would have been convenient also to have seen listed, for instance, under the entry for its *editio princeps* of 1795, all editions and translations of Kant's *Essay on Perpetual Peace*. This is now not

the case and in order to trace all editions of a particular title in the 1934 bibliography the author index must be consulted. The practice followed in the 1936 bibliography contained another useful feature: all editions of a particular work were listed, even if these were published after 1776. This enables the reader to establish without much difficulty that many items published in the period 1776-1898 (and mentioned in the 1936 bibliography) were missed out in the earlier bibliography covering this period. This applies, for instance, to a dozen editions (including one in Welsh) of Erasmus's *Bellum* which were all published between 1817 and 1856 and listed in the entry for the *editio princeps* in the 1936 bibliography (but which are all absent from the 1934 one). Since all these editions were also present in the standard bibliography of the works of Erasmus published in 1893, we find further confirmation (see note 50 above) that it also was not used by ter Meulen for the compilation of the 1934 bibliography. Cf. Ferdinand Vander Haeghen, *Bibliotheca Erasmiana: Répertoire des Oeuvres D'Erasme* (Ghent: 1893; 2nd reprint, Nieuwkoop: B. de Graaf, 1972 - pp. 22-23 for *Bellum*).

71) The same applies to contemporary French translations, except that in this case ter Meulen can hardly be blamed for their absence from his bibliography: only one exists, and this was presumed lost until recently, when two copies (printed in Lyon in about 1531) were located in the Houghton Library at Harvard University and in the Royal Library in Brussels. Cf. James E. Walsh, 'The *Querela Pacis* of Erasmus: The "Lost" French Translation', in *Harvard Library Bulletin* (vol. 17, no. 4, 1969, pp. 374-384). The translation was condemned by the Faculty of Theology of the University of Paris in 1525, and the translator, Louis de Berquin, burned at the stake four years later. A facsimile was published in 1978: Emile V. Telle, ed., Le Chevalier de Berquin, *La Complainte de la Paix* (Paris-Geneva: Droz). The *Catalog of Printed Books of the Folger Shakespeare Library, Washington, D.C.* (Boston: G.K. Hall, 1970, vol. 9, p. 144) seems to suggest that an original copy of Berquin's translation is also to be found in that library; this is not the case since it is only a microfilm of the Harvard copy. (I am grateful to Nati H. Krivatsy of The Folger Shakespeare Library for this clarification). The next French translation occurred almost four centuries later, in 1924, but ter Meulen erroneously gives this date as 1925 in his entry under the *editio princeps*. Here, Berquin's translation is hidden in the last entry where ter Meulen notes

another five editions which are all without date and place of publication and 'one of which is in French'. Ter Meulen does not give the title unlike Vander Haeghen in the work mentioned in the previous note (p. 167).

72) This second edition of the STC was begun by W.A. Jackson and F.S. Ferguson, and completed by Katharine F. Pantzer (London: The Bibliographical Society, Vol. 1, A-H, 1986; vol. 2, I-Z, 1976). Details of the acquisition of *The Complaint of Peace* (which follow) I owe to Nancy Romero of the library of the University of Illinois at Urbana-Champaign, and to Elizabeth A. Walsh of The Folger Shakespeare Library.

73) For *The Complaint of Peace*, see vol. 1, p. 467, no. 10,466; for *Bellum*, vol. 1, p. 466, no. 10,449.

74) Donald Wing, comp., *Short-Title Catalogue of books printed in England, Scotland, Ireland, Wales, and British America, and of English books printed in other countries, 1641-1700* (New York: Printed for the Index Society by Columbia Univ. Press, 1945, 1948, 1951). This catalogue lists nearly 90,000 titles. The three volumes of the second, revised, edition were published in 1972, 1982, and 1988 (New York: Index Committee of the Modern Language Association of America). This edition contains approximately 120,000 titles.

75) Wing, vol. 3 (1951), p. 451, no. 800.

76) Cf. note 71; for Ward (1642) see vol. 27, p. 564.

77) Wing, vol. 3 (1951), p. 451, no. 801. I have been unable to consult the revised (1988) edition of this volume.

78) B.M. Headicar, ed., *Edward Fry Library of International Law: Catalogue* (etc.) (London: St. Clements Press, 1923, p. 38).

79) *Verslag ... 1933* (1934, p. 16).

80) Margaret Canney & David Knott, comp., *Catalogue of the Goldsmiths' Library of Economic Literature* (Cambridge: Cambridge Univ. Press for the Univ. of London Library, vol. 1, Printed books to 1800, 1970; vol. 2, Printed books 1801-1850, 1975). Vol. 3 concerns additions to the printed books to 1850 as well as periodicals and manuscripts; vol. 4 is an index. (The last 2 volumes were published in 1982 and 1983, respectively, by the Athlone Press.)

81) For Kant's essay see the Goldsmiths' Library Catalogue, o.c., vol. 1, p. 787; the various editions and translations of Kant's essay occupy almost three pages in the NUC (vol. 289, pp. 319-321).

82) (London: Butterworths Scientific Publ.)

83) See note 3 above and also Charles F. Howlett & Glen Zeitzer, *The American Peace Movement: History and Historiography* (Washington: American Historical Association, 1985).

84) The most recent development in this field, which is of the greatest importance, is the conversion of the British Library printed *General Catalogue of Printed Books to 1975* into machine-readable form, to produce the CD-ROM edition. This project, which started in 1987 and is expected to be completed in 1991, will allow searching by, e.g., date of publication, keyword, and shelfmark, thus enabling the user to a level of subject access (e.g. for 'peace', 'pacifism') never before available. Cf. Saztec Europe Ltd. & Chadwyck-Healey, *The most famous library catalogue in the world - The most important development in its history* (Cambridge, England: Chadwyck-Healey, 1988, 6 pp.).

85) Whereas the 1917 volume has an extensive bibliography, the two later volumes refer to the literature used only in notes, and there is no bibliography appended. This was an unusual procedure for ter Meulen and an anomaly which he explained as follows (in the foreword of the 1940 volume): 'The Library of the Peace Palace is sufficiently well known. Its extensive printed catalogues are widely available ... He who would like to study a certain topic in greater depth is, moreover, well advised to contact the Library of the Peace Palace where ... very extensive bibliographical data in the field of the history of the peace movement (especially since the end of the Middle Ages) are being collected and where also the greatest part of this literature is available' (p. XIV). Earlier in the foreword, ter Meulen had thanked the various assistants for the peace bibliography (p. XIII). Apparently he was not inclined to compile yet another bibliography, especially since his two comprehensive, albeit provisional, bibliographies were available, and their definitive version was envisaged. If so, this was an error of judgement, and one can agree with Hans Wehberg's view that the absence of a bibliography for the last volumes is a serious deficiency. (Cf. 'Die Entwicklung des Gedankens der internationalen Organisation: Zum Vollendung des grossen Werkes von Jacob

ter Meulen', in *Die Friedens-Warte*, vol. 41, no. 5/6, 1941, pp. 217-236, at p. 222.)

INDEX

BIBLIOGRAPHY OF THE PEACE MOVEMENT BEFORE 1899, 1480–1776

BIBLIOGRAPHIE DU MOUVEMENT DE LA PAIX[1]
BIBLIOGRAPHY OF THE PEACE MOVEMENT[1]

1480-1776[2]

P.P. = Bibliothèque du Palais de la Paix, La Haye.
= Library of the Palace of Peace, The Hague.

1480
P.P. Sensuyt le testamèt de la guerre qui regne a p̃sent sur la terre. [Par **Jehan Molinet**. (A la fin:) On les vend à Lignan, près du grant pont de boys, à lenseigne des Deux Jousteux]. S. d. 8º. 4 ff. n. ch., car. goth., fig. au titre.
Voir aussi 1531 et 1537.

1483
.... **Dialogus**, cuius collocutores sunt milites duo, unus Francus alter Anglus, contendentes de querelis Franciæ et Angliæ. [Dans :] **Johannis Gersonis** opera omnia. Coloniæ (Johannes Koelhoff) 1483-1484. Vol. IV, fol. CLXXIIII-CLXXXII.
Voir pour les éditions suivantes : 1488 Strassbourg ; 1489 Bâle ; 1494 Strassbourg ; 1606 Paris ; 1706 Anvers ; 1728 La Haye.

1488
.... **Dialogus**, cuius collocutores sunt milites duo, unus Francus alter Anglus, contendentes de querelis Franciæ et Angliæ. [Dans :] **Johannis Gersonis** opera omnia. Argentorati (Martin Flach) 1488-1502. Vol. II, fol. 52, littera X sqq. 1re éd. 1483.

1489
.... **Dialogus**, cuius collocutores sunt milites duo, unus Francus alter Anglus, contendentes de querelis Franciæ et Angliæ. [Dans :] **Johannis Gersonis** opera omnia. Basiliæ (Nicolaus Kessler) 1489. Vol. II, fol. 52, littera X sqq. 1re éd. 1483.

1494
.... **Dialogus**, cuius collocutores sunt milites duo, unus Francus alter Anglus, contendentes de querelis Franciæ et Angliæ. [Dans :] **Johannis Gersonis** opera omnia. Argentorati 1494. Vol. II, fol. 52, littera X sqq. 1re éd. 1483.

1504
.... **Erasmus, Desiderius**, Ad illustrissimū principē Philippū, archiducem Austriæ... de triūphali profectione Hispaniensi... panegyricus. Antwerpiæ [Th. Martinus] 1504. 4º.
Voir pour les éditions suivantes : 1504 Paris ; 1516 Bâle, 2x ; 1516 Louvain ; 1518 Bâle ; 1518 Venise ; 1519 Bâle ; 1519 Florence ; 1520

Bâle ; 1540 Bâle ; 1611 Hannover ; 1613   ; 1703 Leyde.
.... **Erasmus, Des.**, Ad illustrissimū principē Philippū... panegyricus. Parisiis 1504. 4º.
Voir ci-dessus.

1514??
.... **Erasmus, Des.**, Roterodamus clarissimo D. ac reverendo in Christo patri D. Antonio a Bergis abbati Sancti Bertini S. D. [Lettre du 14 mars 1514, dans **Allen**, Opus epistolarum. Oxford 1906 —. Vol. I, p. 551].
La publication de la lettre en 1514 en latin n'est pas certaine. Voir pour les éditions suivantes : 1514 s. l., en allemand ; 1540 Bâle ; 1703 Leyde.

1514
.... **Herre Erasmus** Roterodamus Epistel zu herr Antony von Berg, Apt zu Sant Bertin, von den manigfältigen schäden des Krieges und was übels, nachteyls und unwesens usz den Kriegen erwechst. [Trad. par **George Spalatinus**.] S. l. ni d. [1514?] Six feuilles in-4º.
Voir ci-dessus.

1515
.... **Erasmus, Des.**, Epistola ad Leonem X... [Dans :] **Ian. Damianus** Sen., Ad Leonem X de expeditione in Turcas elegeia. Bas. (I. Froben) m. aug. 1515. 4º.
Voir pour les éditions suivantes : 1516 Leipsic ; 1517   ; 1540 Bâle ; 1703 Leyde ; s. d., s. l.
.... **Erasmus, Des.**, Institutio principis christiani saluberrimis referta præceptis. Lovanii (Th. Martinus Alost.) 1515. 4º.
Voir pour les éditions suivantes : 1515 Venise ; 1516 Bâle, 3x ; 1516 Louvain. 3x ; 1517 Bâle ; 1517 Paris ; 1518 Bâle ; 1518 Venise ; 1519 Paris ; 1519 Florence ; 1519 Bâle ; 1520 Bâle ; 1521 Augsbourg, en allemand ; 1521 Zürich, en allemand ; 1523 Cologne ; 1524 Cologne ; 1525 Cologne ; 1529 Cologne ; 1534 Roskylde, en danois ; 1534, en danois ; 1540 Bâle ; 1543 Paris, 2x ; 1546 Paris, en français ; 1549 Paris, 3x, dont 2 en français ; 1550   , en français ; 1554 Paris, en français ; 1574 Paris ; 1591 Lemgo ; 1628 Leyde ; 1628 Amsterdam ; 1641 Leyde, 2x ; 1665 Amsterdam, 2x en français ; 1666 s. l., en français ; 1667 s. l., en fran-

---

[1] Les auteurs espèrent recevoir toutes les informations nécessaires relatives aux erreurs et lacunes qui se trouvent dans cette liste, ainsi qu'aux endroits (bibliothèque, institution, etc.) où se trouve le matériel déjà mentionné ou non encore mentionné dans la liste.

The editors hope to obtain all information necessary concerning errors and omissions in this list, as well as concerning the places (library, institute, etc.) where the material mentioned, or not yet mentioned, in the list is to be found.

[2] Des exemplaires de la liste provisoire imprimée pour la période 1776-1898 peuvent être demandés à la Bibliothèque du Palais de la Paix, La Haye, Pays-Bas.

Copies of the printed provisional list for the period 1776-1898 may be obtained from the Library of the Peace Palace, The Hague, Netherlands.

çais ; 1703 Leyde ; 1721 Stockholm, en suédois ;
1921 Londres, en anglais ; s. d. Rotterdam, en
hollandais ; s. l., s. d., en allemand.

.... **Erasmus, Des.,** Institutio principis.... Venetiis
(Aldus) 1515. 8º.
Voir ci-dessus.

.... **Erasmus, Des.,** Proverbiorum chiliades. Basil.
(J. Frobenius) 1515. 8º.
Cette troisième édition des Adages contient
sous le Nº 3101 la première publication de
« Dulce bellum inexpertis ».

.... **Leo X papa,** breve ad Des. Erasmum Rot. Ejus-
dem ad Henricum Angliæ regem alterum breve
pro Erasmo. Basil. (Froben.) 1515. 4º.

1516

.... **Erasmus, Des.,** Ad illustris·ímū principē Philippū... panegyricus. [A la suite de :] **Erasmus,
Des.,** Institutio principis.... Basil. (I. Frobenius) mense aprili 1516. 4º.
1ʳᵉ éd. 1504.

.... **Erasmus, Des.,** Epistola ad Leonem X... [Dans :]
Erasmus, Des., Epistolæ. Lypsiæ (Val. Schumann) 1516. 4º.
1ʳᵉ éd. 1515.

.... **Erasmus, Des.,** Institutio principis.... Basil.
(Io. Frobenius) m. martio 1516. 4º.
1ʳᵉ éd. 1515.

.... **Erasmus, Des.,** Institutio principis.... Basil.
(Io. Frobenius) mense aprili 1516. 4º.
1ʳᵉ éd. 1515.

.... **Erasmus, Des.,** Institutio principis.... cum aliis
nonnullis pertinentibus, quorum catalogum in
proxima reperies pagella..... Basiliæ (Jo.
Frobenius) mense maio 1516. 4º.
C2.v.-q6. v., (113 p.) : Institutio principis....
1ʳᵉ éd. 1515.
A1-N2. (99 p.) : Panegyricus gratulatorius....
1ʳᵉ éd. 1504.

.... **Erasmus, Des.,** Institutio principis.... Louanii
(Th. Martinus Alost. pour Gilles de Gourmont
à Paris) 7 Aug. 1516. 4º.
1ʳᵉ éd. 1515.

.... **[Erasmus, Des.]** Institutio principis christiani
saluberrimis referta præceptis per Erasmum
Roterodamum cum aliis nonnullis eodem pertinentibus quorum catalogum in proxima
reperies pagella. Lovanii (Apud Th. Martinum
Alustensem) mense Augusti 1516. 4º.
C 1r-O 4v : Institutio principis christiani ....
1ʳᵉ éd. 1515.
P 1r-a 1v : Ad Philippum panegyricus.... 1ʳᵉ
éd. 1504.

.... **Erasmus, Des.,** Querela pacis undique gentium
ejectæ profligatæque. Basileæ 1516.
Voir pour les éditions suivantes : 1517 Bâle ;
1518 Venise ; 1518 Bâle, 2x ; 1518 Louvain, 2x ;
1518 Cracovie ; 1518 Leipsic ; 1519 Florence ;
1519 s. l.; 1520 Séville, en espagnol ; 1521
Augsbourg, en allemand ; 1521 Mayence ; 1521
Zürich, en allemand ; 1522 Strassbourg ; 1522
Bâle ; 1523 Deventer ; 1523 Strassbourg, 2x ;
1525 Paris ; 1529 Bâle ; 1529 Lyon ; 1529 Alcala
de Henares, en espagnol ; 1530 Paris ; 1534
Cracovie ; 1540 Bâle ; 1567 s. l. ,en hollandais ;
1583 Anvers, en hollandais ; 1590 Cologne ;
1611 Amberg ; 1612 Leuwarden, en hollandais ;
1616 Rotterdam, en hollandais ; 1622 Francfort, en allemand ; 1627 s. l.; 1628 Leyde ; 1634
Bâle, en allemand ; 1641 Leyde ; 1672 Harder-

wyck ; 1703 Leyde ; 1795 Londres, en anglais ;
1802 Londres, en anglais ; 1813 Boston, en
anglais ; 1917 Londres, en anglais ; 1925 Paris,
en franç'ais ; 1934 Berne, en allemand ; s. d.
Cologne ; s. d. Louvain, 2x ; s. d., s. l., 5x,
dont 1 en français.

.... **Listrius, Gerard.,** Elogiæ et Epodi in detesta-
tionem belli. — Encomiasticum Pacis. — [A la
suite de :] Carmen Sapphicum.... Daventriæ
(Alb. Palfraet) Nov. 1516.

1517

.... **Erasmus, Des.,** Bellum (Dulce Bellum Inexpertis).
Basileæ (apud J. Frobenium) mense Aprilii
1517. 4º.
Voir pour la première publication : 1515,
Erasmus, Proverbiorum Chiliades.
Voir pour les éditions suivantes : 1517 Louvain ;
1519 Bâle, en allemand ; 1520 Strassbourg ;
1520 Cologne ; 1520 Zwolle ; 1521 Leipsic, 5x ;
1521 Mayence ; 1523 Strassbourg ; 1523 Paris ;
1524 Anvers ; 1525 Paris ; 1527 Paris ; 1530
Paris ; 1533 Londres, en anglais ; 1540 Bâle ;
1590 Cologne ; 1607 s. l., en allemand ; 1611
Amberg ; 1622 s. l., en hollandais ; 1622 Rostock ; 1629 Zwolle, en hollandais ; 1633 Amsterdam, en hollandais ; 1635 Amsterdam ; 1644
Campen, en hollandais ; 1659 s. l., en allemand ;
1664 Utrecht, en hollandais ; 1670 Amsterdam,
en hollandais ; 1672 Brunswig ; 1674 Irenopolis ;
1703 Leyde ; 1709 Amsterdam, en hollandais ; 1724 Halle ; 1794 Londres, en anglais ;
1795 Boston, en anglais ; 1813 Boston, en anglais ; 1813 New-York, en anglais ; 1817 Londres,
en anglais ; 1818 Londres, en anglais ; 1819
Londres, en français ; 1820 Londres, en anglais ;
1822 Londres, en français ; 1824 Londres, en
français ; 1828 Londres, en français ; 1829
Londres, en français ; 1830 Londres, en anglais ;
1832 Londres, en anglais ; 1840 Londres, en
anglais ; 1850 Furnes, en français ; 1851 Londres
en allemand ; 1853 Londres, en anglais ; 1855
Londres, en kymrique ; 1856 Londres, en français ; 1887 Nîmes, en français ; 1891 s. l., en
français ; 1907 Boston, en anglais ; 1909
Londres, en anglais ; s. d. Londres, en anglais ;
s. d. Paris ; s. d. Cologne ; s. d. Amsterdam ;
s. d., s. l.

.... **Erasmus, Des.,** Bellum. Louanii (Theod. Martinus
Alost.) mense octobri 1517. 4º.
1ʳᵉ éd. 1517.

.... **Erasmus, Des.,** Epistola ad Leonem X.....
, 1517.
1ʳᵉ éd. 1515.

.... **Erasmus, Des.,** Institutio principis.... [Parisiis]
(in ædib. Ascensianis) cal. mart. 1517. 8º.
1ʳᵉ éd. 1515.

.... **Erasmus, Des.,** Institutio principis.... Basileæ
(Jo. Frobenius) 1517.
1ʳᵉ éd. 1515.

.... **Erasmus, Des.,** Querela pacis.... Basil. (Io. Frobenius) mense decembri 1517. 4º.
1ʳᵉ éd. 1516.

1518

.... **Erasmus, Des.,** Institutio principis.... cū aliis
nōnullis eodē pertinētibus, quorū catalogū in
proxima reperies pagella ....Basiliæ (Jo. Frobenius) mense julio 1518. 4º.
Pag. 9-128 : Institutio boni et Christiani
principis.... 1]ᵉ éd. 1515.

Pag. 142-242 : Panegyricus gratulatorius....
1re éd. 1504.

.... [Erasmus, Des.,] Quæ toto volumine continentur.
Venetiis (Aldus et A. Socer) mense sept.
1518. 8º.
Fol. 4-26 : Pacis querela.... 1re éd. 1516.
Fol. 38-102 : Institutio principis.... 1re éd.
1515.
Fol. 103-157 : Panegyricus ad Philippum....
1re éd. 1504.

.... Erasmus, Des., Querela pacis.... Basileæ (A. Cratander) 1518.
1re éd. 1516.

.... Erasmus, Des., Querela pacis.... Lovanii (Theod.
Martinus Alost.) [1518]. 4º.
1re éd. 1516.

.... Erasmus, Des., Declamationes aliquot. Lovanii
(Theod. Martinus Alost.) tercio Idus Mart. An.
MDXVIII.
a1-h4. : Querimonia pacis undiq̇. profligatæ...
1re éd. 1516.

.... Erasmus, Des., Querela pacis. Cracoviæ (Scharff)
1518. 4º.
1re éd. 1516.

.... Erasmus, Des., [In hoc libello continentur Querela
pacis.... [In fine : Basiliæ apud Joannem
Frobenium mense novembri. Anno M.D.XVIII].
1re éd. 1516.

P.P. Erasmus, Des., Querela pacis.... ; Eiusdēq ;
ī genere consolatorio. de morte Declamatio.
[Lipsiæ (Schumañ) 1518]. 4º. [38 p.].
1re éd. 1516.

P.P. Isocratis Atheniensis oratoris ac philosophi gravissima oratio, de bello fugiendo et pace ser-
vanda, ad populum Atheniensem. Petro Mosel-
lano Protegense [= Pierre Schade de Bruttig]
interprete. [Lipsiæ ?] 1518. 6º. [37 p.]
Voir pour les éditions suivantes : 1529 Paris, en
grec ; 1579 Lyon, en français ; s. l. s. d.

1519
P.P. [Clichtoveus, Jodocus,] De regis officio opusculũ :
quid optimum quemque regem deceat, ex sacris
literis et probatoris authorũ sentscijs
historijsque depromens. Parisiis (Henricus
Stephanus) 1519. 4º.
Le nom de l'auteur est indiqué à p. 3.

.... Erasmus, Des., Dulce bellum inexperto. Eyn
gemeyn Sprũchwort.... durch U. Varnbüler
geteutscht. Basel (Andr. Cratander) sechster
Tag Nov. 1519. 4º.
Voir éd. latine 1517.

.... Erasmus, Des., Institutio principis.... [A la suite
de :] Fr. Patricius, Compendiosa s. rerum memorandarum descriptio. Paris. (P. le Brodeur),
1519. 8º.
1re éd. 1515.

.... [Erasmus, Des.], Quæ toto volumine continentur.
Florentiæ (per hæredes Philippi Juntæ) mense
febr. 1519. 8º.
Fol. 3-23 : Pacis querela.... 1re éd. 1516.
Fol. 33-95 : Institutio principis.... 1re éd. 1515.
Fol. 96-148 : Panegyricus ad Philippum....
1re éd. 1504.

.... [Erasmus, Des.], Institutio principis.... cũ aliis
nõnullis eõdē ptinētibus, quorũ catalogũ in
ṗxima reperies pagella.... Basiliæ (Jo. Frobenius) mense iunio 1519. 4º.
Pag. 9-146 : Institutio principis.... 1re éd.
1515.

Pag. 163-281 : Panegyricus gratulatorius....
1re éd. 1504.

P.P. Erasmus, Des., Querela pacis.... S. l. [1519].
4º. 44 p.
1re éd. 1516.

1520
.... Erasmus, Des., Bellum. Argentorati (Joh. Prijs)
1520. 8º.
1re éd. 1517.

.... Erasmus, Des., Dulce bellum inexpertis. Coloniæ
1520. 4º.
1re éd. 1517.

.... Erasmus, Des., Bellum [Zwolle (Simon Korver)
c. 1520] 4º.
1re éd. 1517.

.... Erasmus, Des., Institutio principis.... Basileæ
1520. 4º.
1re éd. 1515.

.... Erasmus, Des., Panegyricus.... [Dans :] Pane-
gyrici veteres.... ed. Beatus Rhenanus.
Basil. (Frobenius) 1520. 4º.
1re éd. 1504.

.... [Erasmus, Des.], Querella de la paz desechada
y huyda de todos las gentes y estados. Compues-
ta por Erasmo, doctor muy famoso. [Dans :]
Tractado de la miseria de los cortesanos que
escrivio el papa Pio ante que fuesse sũmo pon-
tifice a un cauallo su amigo. Y otro tractado
de como se quexa la paz. Compuesto por
Erasmo varon doctissimo. I sacados de latin
en romance por.... don Diego Lopez. Sevilla
(Jacobo Cromberger) [1520]. Fol. c-ij.
Voir éd. latine 1516.

1521
.... Erasmus, Des., Elegans adagium.... Dulce
bellum inexpertis. Moguntiæ (Joh. Schoeffer)
1521. 4º.
1re éd. 1517.

.... Erasmus, Des., Elegans adagium.... Dulce
bellum inexpertis. Lipsiæ (Melch. Lotherus)
1521. 8º.
1re éd. 1517.

.... Erasmus, Des., Elegans adagium.... Dulce
bellum inexpertis. Lipsiæ (Val. Schumann)
1521. 8º. [64] p.
1re éd. 1517.

.... Erasmus, Des., Ein nutzliche underwisung eines
christl. fürsten wol zu regieren (durch Leo Jud
geteuscht). Zürich (Christ. Froschauer) 1521. 4º.
Voir éd. latine 1515.

.... Erasmus, Des., Die Unterweysung aines frummen
und christl. Fürsten.... durch G. Spalatinũ
geteuscht. Augspurg (S. Grimm und M. Wir-
sung) 1521. 4º.
Voir éd. latine 1515.

.... Erasmus, Des., Das cristlich büchlein.... die
clage des Frids.... durch Georg. Spalatinum
verteütscht. [Augspurg, (S. Grym und M. Wir-
sung.) Anno dni M.D.XXI] 4º. 70 p.
Voir éd. latine 1516.

.... Erasmus, Des., Ein Klag des Frydens.... durch
Leo Jud verteutscht. Zürich (Christ. Froschauer)
1521. 4º.
Voir éd. latine 1516.

.... Erasmus, Des., Querela pacis.... Moguntiæ
(Joh. Schoeffer) 1521. 8º.
1re éd. 1516.

.... **Petra Chelcziczkeho** sit wiery.... [In fine : Sko-
nawagi se knihy, genž sloww siet wiery,
skrze snaznu peczi Chwala Dubanka ten
cztwrtck przed vtiessenu Pamatku wssech
swatych Leta od narozenie syna božieho
Tisycieho pietisteho dwadczateho prwnieho
na Klassterze Wylemowskem].
(Le réseau de la foi de Pierre Chelcicky....
[In fine : Ici finissent les livres qui s'appellent
le réseau de la foi par les bons soins de Chwal
Dubanek, le jeudi avant Toussaint en l'an de
grâce 1521 dans le cloître Wilemow]).

1522

.... **Erasmus, Des.,** Querela pacis.... Basileæ (Thom.
VVolf.) 1522. 4º.
1re éd. 1516.

.... **Erasmus, Des.,** Querela pacis.... Argentinæ (Io.
Knoblouchus) mense martio 1522. 8º.
1re éd. 1516.

1523

P.P. **Clichtoveus, Judocus,** De bello et pace opusculum,
Christianos principes ad sedandos bellorum
tumultus et pacem componendam exhortans.
Parisiis (Simon Colinaeus) 1523. 8º. 53 p.
Le nom de l'auteur est indiqué à p. 1.

P.P. **Erasmus, Des.,** Bellum.... Argentorati (Io.
Cnoblochus) mense novembri 1523. 8º. 23
[, 23] p.
1re éd. 1517.

.... **Erasmus, Des.,** Bellum.... Parisiis (P. Gro-
morsus et J. Parvus) 1523. 8º.
1re éd. 1517.

.... **Erasmus, Des.,** Institutio principis.... Coloniæ,
mense aug. 1523. 8º.
1re éd. 1515.

.... **Erasmus, Des.,** Querela pacis.... Deventer (Alb.
Pafraet) mense Mart. 1523.
1re éd. 1516.

.... **Erasmus, Des.,** Querela pacis.... Argentinæ
(Io. Knoblochus) mense julio 1523. 8º.
1re éd. 1516.

P.P. **Erasmus, Des.,** Querela pacis.... Argentorati
(Io. Cnoblochus) mense novembri 1523. 8º.
1re éd. 1516.

1524

.... **Erasmus, Des.,** Bellum.... [Antverpiæ] (Mich.
Hillenius) 1524. 8º.
1er éd. 1517.

.... **Erasmus, Des.,** Institutio principis.... Coloniæ
1524. 8º.
1re éd. 1515.

P.P. **Sauromanus, G.,** proc. caes. ad principes Christianos de religione ac communi concordia. [In
fine : Romæ. An. Chris. sal. MDXXIIII.
Clemente. VII. Pont. opt. max. fluctuantis
reipu. Christianæ gubernacula æquabiliter
moderante]. 4º. [81 feuilles non chiffrées].

1525

.... **Erasmus, Des.,** Bellum.... Parisiis (Sim. Colinæus) 1525. 8º.
1re éd. 1517.

.... **Erasmus, Des.,** Institutio principis.... Coloniæ
(Euch. Cervicornus) 1525, mense januario. 8º.
1re éd. 1515.

.... **Erasmus, Des.,** Querimonia pacis.... Parisiis
(Sim. Colinæus) 1525. 8º.
1re éd. 1516

1526

P.P. **[Joannes Maria = Julius III]**
Johannis Mariæ, Archiepiscopi Sipontini ad
principes Christianos Oratio de pace. [In fine :
Impressum Romæ per Ludovicum Vicentinum
Anno a Partu Viriginis MDXXVI.] 8º. 14 f.

.... **Vives Valentinus, Johannes Ludovicus,** De Euro-
pæ dissidiis, et Republica ad Adrianum VI
Pon.... De Europæ dissidiis et bello Turcico..
ad Thomam cardinalem Angliæ.... Brugis
(Hubertus de Croock) 1526, mense Decemb. 8º.
Fol. 1.r.-10.r. : De Europæ dissidiis et repu-
blica.
Fol. 23.r.-44.r. : De Europæ dissidiis et bello
Turcico dialogus.
Pour l'édition suivante voir 1555 Bâle.

1527

.... **Erasmus, Des.,** Bellum.... Parisiis 1527. 8º.
1re éd. 1517.

1529

.... **Erasmus, Des.,** Institutio principis.... Coloniæ
(E. Cervicornus) 1529. Imp. G. Hittorpii,
mense maio. 8º.
1re éd. 1515.

P.P. **Erasmus, Des.,** Querela pacis.... Lugd[uni]
(S. Gryphius) 1529. 8º. [45] p.
1re éd. 1516.

.... **Erasmus, Des.,** Libellus.... de pueris.... insti-
tuendis, cum aliis compluribus, quorum catalogum indicabit versa pagella. Basiliæ (Hier.
Frobenius, Jo. Hervagius, Nic. Episcopius)
mense septembri 1529.
Pag. 218-270 : Querela pacis.... 1re éd. 1516.

.... **Erasmus, Des.,** Tractado de las ꝗrellas de la paz...
traduz. per **D. Lopez.** Alcala de Henares (Mig.
de Eguia) 1529. 8º.
Voir éd. latine 1516.

.... **Isocrates,** Oratio de pace. [En grec.]
[Parisiis (Christ. Wechel)] 1529. 8º.
Voir éd. latine 1518.

.... **Vives, Johannes Ludovicus,** De concordia et
discordia.... libri quattuor. De Pacificatione,
Lib. unus... Antwerpiæ (Mich. Hillenius) 1529.
8º.
Fol. 2.r.-216 r. : De concordia et discordia.
Fol. 217.r.-260 r. : De pacificatione.
Voir pour les éditions suivantes : 1532 Lyon ;
1555 Bâle ; 1578   , en allemand.

1530

.... **Erasmus, Des.,** Bellum.... Parisiis (Simon Colinæus) 1530.
1re éd. 1517.

.... **Erasmus, Des.,** Querimonia pacis.... Parisiis
(S. Colinæus) 1530. 8º.
1re éd. 1516.

.... **Erasmus, Des.,** Utillissima consultatio de bello
Turcis inferendo. Basiliæ (Frobenius) 1530. 8º.
Voir pour les éditions suivantes : 1530 Cologne ;
1530 Paris ; 1530 Vienne ; [1530?] Anvers ;
1540 Bâle ; 1547 Bâle ; 1547 Cologne ; 1643
Leyde ; 1703 Leyde ; s. l. s. d., en allemand.

.... **Erasmus, Dec.,** Utilissima consultatio de bello
Turcis inferendo. Coloniæ (   )
1530. 8º.
1re éd. 1530.

.... **Erasmus, Des.,** Utilissima consultatio de bello
Turcis inferendo. Parisiis (Chr. Wechel) 1530. 8º.
1re éd. 1530.

1530-1549 57

... **Erasmus, Des.,** Utilissima consultatio de bello
Turcis inferendo. Viennæ 1530. 8°.
1re éd. 1530.
.... **Erasmus, Des.,** Utilissima consultatio de bello
Turcis inferendo. Antwerpiæ (Michel Hillenius)
[1530?]. 8°.
1re éd. 1530.

1531
.... **Molinet, Jehan,** Sensuyt le testament de la guerre,
qui règne à présent sur la terre. [Dans :] Molinet,
Faitz et dictz.... Paris (J. Longis et la veufve
feu J. St. Denys) 1531. Fol. Fol. 124-132.
Voir aussi 1480.

1532
.... **Vives, Joh. Lud.,** De concordia et discordia in
humano genere. — De pacificatione. — Quam
misera esset vita Christianorum sub Turca.
Lugduni (Melch. et Gasp. Treschêl) 1532. 8°.
1re éd. 1529.

1533
.... **Erasmus, Des.,** Bellum. translated into englyshe.
Londini (Tho. Berthelet) 1533 [A la fin : 1534].
8°.
Voir éd. latine 1517.

1534
.... **Erasmus, Des.,** Een christelig oc nyttelig bog
om kongers, fursters riigts landte oc stoeders
regiminge digthet.... och kaldett een christen
furstis underwiisning och laere. Roschildie
1534.
Voir éd. latine 1515.
.... **Erasmus, Des.,** Institutio principis...., danico
idiomate a Paulo Eliae. 1534. 8°.
Voir éd. latine 1515.
.... **Polidamus, Valentinus,** Querela communis populi
de pace ad christianos principes contra ethni-
cos, et Erasmi Rot. quercla de pace. Cracoviæ
(Math. Scharffenberck) 1534. 8°.... 1re éd.
1516.

1537
.... **[Grevenbroich, Guillaume de],** Oratio suasoria
ad Carolum Cæs. Imp. Aug. et Franciscum
Galliarum Regem, de pace et concordia inter
ipsos constituenda. Gulielmo Insulano Menapio
Grevibrocensi Autore. Basiliæ (Robert Winter)
1537. 8°. 44 p.
.... **Molinet, Jehan,** Sensuyt le testament de la guerre
qui règne à présent sur la terre. [Dans :] Molinet,
Faicts et dicts.... Paris (J. Petit) 1537. 8°.
Fol. 218.
Voir aussi 1480.

1539
.... **Wernstreyt, Friderich,** [= Sebastian Franck]
Das Kriegs-büchlin des Frides. Ein Krieg des
Frides wider alle Lermen, Auffruer und Un-
siñigkait zu kriegen, mit gründlicher Anzai-
gung etc., das der Krieg nicht allein in das
Reich Christi nit gehöre, sonder auch nicht
sey dan ein teuflisch Ding. S. l. 1539. 8°.
CVII ff.
Voir pour les éditions suivantes : 1550 Franc-
fort ; 1618 Gouda, en hollandais.

1540
.... **Erasmus, Des.,** Opera omnia quæcumque ipse
autor pro suis agnovit, novem tomus distincta,
vita autoris describente. Basileæ (per Frobenium et N. Episcopum) 1540. 9 vol. in fol.
Vol. II, p. 845 : Bellum.... 1re éd. 1517.

Vol. III, p. 63 : Epist. ad Ant. à Berg.... 1re éd.
1514 ?
Vol. III, p. 63 : Epist. ad Leonem X.... 1re éd.
1515.
Vol. IV, p. 390 : Panegyricus ad Philippum....
1re éd.1504.
Vol. IV, p. 433 : Institutio.... 1re éd. 1515.
Vol. IV, p. 486 : Querela pacis.... 1re éd. 1516.
Vol. V, p. 292 : Consultatio utilissima....
1re éd. 1530.

1543
.... **Aureus Codiculus** de institutione principis christiani ex libro Erasmi novissime excerptus
[auct. Aeg. d'Aurigny. A la suite de :] Franc.
Patricius, Compendiosa rerum memorandarum
descriptio.... Parisiis (Car. Langelier) 1543.
16°.
Voir éd. latine 1515.
.... **Aureus codiculus** de institutione principis christiani ex libro Erasmi novissimè excerptus
[auct. Aeg. d'Aurigny. A la suite de :] Franc.
Patricius, Compendiosa rerum memorandarum
descriptio.... Parisiis (Poncet le Preux) 1543.
16°.
Voir éd. latine 1515.

1544
P.P. **De nova Christiani orbis pace oratio.** [Romæ
Habita in æde Virginis supra Mineruam à
Philippo Archinto. Quarto idus Octobris
M.D.XLIIII.] Romæ (Bladus) 1544. 4°. 11 p.

1546
.... **Erasmus, Des.,** Petit livre précieux comme l'or,
dit l'enseignement du prince chrestien [trad.
de l'Aureus codiculus de Gilles d'Aurigny].
Paris (Ch. Langelier) 1546. 8°.
Voir éd. latine 1515.

1547
.... **Erasmus, Des.,** Utilissima consultatio de bello
Turcis inferendo. Basil. (in off. Frobeniana)
1547. 8°.
1re éd. 1530.
.... **Erasmus, Des.,** Utilissima consultatio de bello
Turcis inferendo. Coloniæ (   ) 1547. 8°.
1re éd. 1530.
.... **Luther, M.,** Erklerung von der Frage die Noth-
wehr belangend. Wittenberg (H. Lufft) 1547.4°.
46 p.
.... **Menius, J.,** Von der Notwehr unterricht. Wittem-
berg 1547. 4°.

1549
.... **Brief recueil du livre d'Erasme** de l'enseignement
du prince chrestien. [A la suite de :] Fr. Patri-
cius, Le livre de la police humaine, extrait par
G. d'Aurigny, trad. par J. Leblond. Paris
(Ch. L'Angelier) 1549. 16°.
Voir éd. latine 1515.
.... **Brief recueil du livre d'Erasme** de l'enseignement
du prince chrestien. [A la suite de :] Fr. Patri-
cius, Le livre de la police humaine ,extrait par
G. d'Aurigny, trad. par J. Leblond. Paris
(Oudin) 1549. 16°.
Voir éd. latine 1515.
.... **Codiculus** de institutione principis ex libro
Erasmi excerptus. [A la suite de :] Fr. Patricius,
Compendiosa rerum memorandarum descriptio.
Parisiis (Audoënus Petit) 1549. 12°.
1re éd. 1515.

.... **Sadoleti, Jacobi,** cardinalis oratio de pace ad imperatorem Carolum Quintum Cesarem Augustum. [Dans :] **Sebastianus de Monte Sacrato,** Oratio de studiis liberalium artium.... Epigrammata diversorum auctorum quam elegantissima. Lucæ (apud V. Busgradum) 1549.

1550

.... **Brief recueil** du livre d'**Erasme** de l'enseignement du prince chrestien [A la suite de :] **Fr. Patricius,** Le livre de la police humaine, extrait par **G. d'Aurigny,** trad. par **J. Leblond.** 1550. 8º. Voir éd. latine 1515.

... **Franck, Sebastian,** Krieg Büchlin des Friedes. Ein Krieg des frides wider alle lärmen, aufrůhr und onsinnigkeit zů krygen.... Hiebey auch von dem grewlichen Laster der Trunckenheyt. Gedruckt zu Francfordt am Mein, durch Cyriacum Jacobum zum Bock. Anno M.D.L. 8º. 307 p.
Kriegb. p. 1-232..... 1re éd. 1539.
Laster. p. 233-307.

.... **Niclaes, Hendrick,** Vorkündighe von dem Vrede up Erden, un von dem genedigen tijdt, idt Goldenjär ofte anghenäm fär des Heren. [± 1550].

1554

.... **Brief recueil** du livre d'**Erasme** de l'enseignement du prince chrestien. [A la suite de :] **Fr. Patricius,** Le livre de la police humaine, extrait par **G. d'Aurigny,** trad. par **J. Leblond.** Paris (Guill. Thiboust) 1554. 16º. Voir éd. latine 1515.

1555

.... **Vives, Johannes Ludovicus,** Opera omnia. Basiliæ (Nic. Episcopius) 1555. 2 vol. Fol.
Vol. II, p. 257-283 : Concio de sudore nostro et Christi. [In fine : Brugis Mense Novemb. M.D.XXIX].
Vol. II, p. 760-861 : De concordia et discordia.... 1re éd. 1529.
Vol. II, p. 863-881 : De pacificatione.... 1re éd. 1529.
Vol. II, p. 934-939 : De Europæ statu ac tumultibus. Joh. Lud. Vives Adriano VI P.M.S. Lovanii. 12.X.1522.
Vol. II, p. 939-941 : Henrico VIII regi Angliæ inclyto S. de Francisco Galliæ rege a Cæsare capto. Oxford 12.III.1525.
Vol. II, p. 941-947 : Henrico VIII regi Angliæ inclyto S. de pace inter Cæs. et Franciscum Galliarum regem : deque optimo regni statu. Brugis 8.X.1525.
Vol. II, p. 947-959 : De Europæ dissidiis et bello Turcico dialogus.... 1re éd. 1526.

1558

P.P. **Discorso** intorno alle cose della guerra [di **Antonio Girardi**], con una oratione della pace. Venetia 1558. 4º.

1559

.... **Aubert, Guillaume,** Oraison de la paix et les moyens de l'entretenir et qu'il n'y a aucune raison suffisante pour faire prendre les armes aux Princes Chrestiens les uns contre les autres. Paris (Vincent Sertenas) 1559. 4º. 22 ff. Voir aussi 1560.

.... **Possevino, Antonio,** Libro nel qual s'insegna a conoscer le cose pertinenti all' honore, et a ridurre ogni querela alla pace. Con due tavole. Ferrara (Gabriel Giolito) 1559. 8º. 72 p.

1560

.... **Aubert, Guillaume,** Oratio [traduction en latin de l'Oraison de 1559 par **Martin Hesseling.** Paris] 1560. 4º. 52 p.
Voir aussi 1559.

1567

.... **Erasmus, Des.,** Een christelyke noodtwendige clage des vreedts. S. l. 1567. 4º.
Voir éd. latine 1516.

1568

.... **Traicté** du bien et utilité de la paix et des maux provenans de la guerre. Paris (Micard) 1568.

1574

.... **De institutione** principis christiani ex lib. Des. Erasmi brevis collectio. [A la suite de :] **Fr. Patricius,** compendiosa epitome commentariorum. Parisiis (Hier. de Marnef et G. Cauellat) 1574. 16º.
1re éd. 1515.

1576

.... **La Boëtie, Etienne,** De la Servitude volontaire ou Le contr'un. [Dans :] Mémoires de l'estat de la France sous Charles IX [par **Simon Goulart**]. 1576.

P.P. **Discours,** sur les moyens de bien gouverner et maintenir en bonne paix un Royaume ou autre Principauté. [par **Innocent Gentillet**]. S. l. 1576. 8º. [XIII,] 656 p.

1578

.... **Vives, Joh. Lud.,** Von der Einigkeit und Zwytracht in dem menschlichen Geslecht.   1578. Ed. orig. 1529.

1579

P.P. **Isocrate,** Sincère exhortation à la paix.... Trad. par **M. Philippes Robert**.... Lyon (J. Stratius) M.D.LXXIX. 8º. [XIV,] 60 p.
Voir éd. latine 1518.

1583

.... **Albergati, Fabio,** Del modo di ridurre alla pace le inimicizie private. Roma 1583.
Voir pour les éditions suivantes : 1587   ; 1621 Milan.

.... **Erasmus, Des.,** Een christelycke noodtwendige clage des vreedts. T' Hantwerpen (Arn. s' Coninx) 1583. 8º.
Voir éd. latine 1516.

1585

P.P. **Apologie** de la paix. Representant tant les profficts et commodités qu'à la paix nous produict, que les malheurs, confusions, et desordres qui naissent durant la guerre. Paris 1585. 8º.

1587

.... **Albergati, Fabio,** Del modo di ridurre alla pace le inimicizie private. 1587.
1re éd. 1583.

1588

.... **Erhardt, Christ.,** Gründliche Historia der Münster. Wiedertäufer. München (A. Berg) 1588. 4º.
Dans ce livre on trouve sur p. 20 l'épître de **Jacob Hutter** à Johann Kuna von Kunstadt, seigneur de Lukow, dans laquelle est exposée la doctrine orthodoxe des anabaptistes concernant la non-résistance.

1590

.... **Erasmus, Des.**, Libelli tres utiles ac salutares....
piis hominibus et pacis amatoribus. Coloniæ
Agrippinæ (Joh. Gymnicus) 1590. 8°.
Pag. 1-124 : De sarcienda Ecclesiæ concordia,
deque sedandis opiniorum dissidiis.
A1.r.-E3.v., (70 p.): Querela pacis.... 1ʳᵉ éd.
1516.
A1.r.-E3.v., (69 p.): Πολεμος sive Belli Detestatio.... 1ʳᵉ éd. 1517.

P.P. **De l'obéissance** deue au prince. Pour faire cesser
les armes et restablir la Paix en ce Royaume.
Au Roy. Caen (Iaques le Bas) 1590. 4°. 39 p.

1591

.... **Erasmus, Des.**, De institutione principis christiani.... Lemgoviæ (hæred. Conr. Grotheni)
1591.
1ʳᵉ éd. 1515.

1595

.... **Panigarola, Francesco**, Specchio di guerra. Bergamo 1595. 8°. 227 ff.

1597

.... **Musculus, Michael**, Kriegsbüchlein. Leipzig 1597.

.... **Verantwoordinge** eender Requeste door eenige
van den Predicanten in den Steden van Wal-
cheren berispt zynde : Daarin getrackteert
worde, oft Oorlogh.... gheoorlooft zy. Door
I. P. S. l. (Gillis Mesdagh) 1597. Met een Cort
Antwoort.

1601

P.P. **Stuckius, Joh. Guillielmus**, Irene Gallica, Hoc
est, De pace et concordia in Gallis sancita....
[Tiguri] 1601. 8°. 191 p.

1604

.... **Ostorodt, Christoph**, Unterrichtung von den vor-
nehmsten Hauptpunkten der christlichen Reli-
gion, in welcher begriffen ist fast die ganze
Confession oder Bekenntnisz der Gemeinen im
Königreich Polen. Rakow 1604.
Voir les éditions suivantes : 1612 Rakow ; 1623
Rakow.

1605

.... **L'Hostal, Pierre**, Le soldat françois. 1605. 191 p.
Le pacifique ou l'anti-soldat françois [par
Du Souhait ?] 1604. 168 p. S. l. 1604. 1605.
2 t. en 1 vol. 16°.

1606

.... **Dialogus**.... de querelis Franciæ et Angliæ.
[Dans :] **Johannis Gersonis** opera omnia. Parisiis 1606. Vol. II, p. 854-860.
1ʳᵉ éd. 1483.

.... **Rathschlag** zum Frieden. Magdeburg 1606.

1607

P.P. **Een cleyn Poetelick Tractaet** betreffende des
Vreeds en Oorloghs vruchten.... By een
verghadert door **G[idion] M[orris] N. P.** Vlis-
singhe (van der Nolck) 1607. 4°. 18 p.

... **Erasmus, Des.**, Das alte, zierliche.... Sprich-
wort Dulce bellum inexpertis.... Ueber-
setzt durch **Fridericum Cornelium von Friedens-
berg.** S. l. 1607. 4°. 24 ff.
Voir éd. latine 1517.

1608

.... **Brederodii, [Petri,]** Representatio generalis inter
orbis christiani Reges Principes et status, pon-
tificum et sedis Romanæ sollicitudine pro-
curatæ. 1603.

1611

.... **Erasmus, Des.**, Panegyricus.... ad Philippum...
Han. 1611.
1ʳᵉ éd. 1504.

.... **Irene Germanica,**.... Qua hoc libello conti-
neantur, seq. pagina ostendet. Ambergæ (Typis
Johannis Schönfeldii) 1611. 12°.
Pag. 1-76 : **Des. Erasmi** Rot. Querela pacis.
....1ʳᵉ éd. 1516.
Pag. 77-156 : Eiusdem **Erasmi** Declamatio....
Dulce Bellum inexpertis.... 1ʳᵉ éd. 1517.
Pag. 193-221 : **Michaelis Virdungi** oratio de
Concordia et Discordia earundemque fructibus.

.... **Virdungi, Michaelis,** voir ci-dessus : Irene Germanica.

1612

.... **Erasmus, Des.**, Querela pacis, dat is Vreden-
clacht. Leeuwarden (Abr. van den Rade)
1612. 4°.
Voir éd. latine 1516.

.... **Ostorodt, Christoff,** von Goslar. Unterrichtung
Von den vornemsten Hauptpuncten der Christlichen Religion... Rackaw (Sebastian Ster-
natzki) 1612. 8°. 14 p., 17 ff. non chiffrées,
442 p., 1 f. errata, non chiffrée.
1ʳᵉ éd. 1604.

1613

.... **Erasmus, Des.**, Panegyricus ad Philippum....
[Dans :] Orationes gratulatoriæ. 1613. 8°.
1ʳᵉ éd. 1504.

1614

.... **Smalcius, Valentinus,** Refutatio thesium Wolfg.
Franzii de præcipuis religionis christianæ capi-
tibus. Racov. 1614.

1616

.... **Erasmus, Des.**, Een christelijcke noodtvvendige
clage des vreedts.Rotterdam (Matth.Bastiaensz)
1616. 4°.
Voir éd. latine 1516.

1618

.... **Franck, Seb.,** Krijgh-boeck des vredes. Eenen
Krijgh des vredes tegen alle allarmen, oproer
ende onsinnigheydt tot krijghen.... nu in
Nederduytsch overgheset door **David Willemsz
Camerlinck.** Ter Goude (by Jasper Tournay,
voor Andries Burier) 1618. 4°.
1ʳᵉ éd. 1539.

1621

P.P. **Albergati, Fabio,** Trattato del modo di ridurre à
Pace l'inimicitie priuate. Terz. impr. Milano
(Bidelli) 1621. 8°. [VI,] 423 p.
1ʳᵉ éd. 1583.

.... **Breen, Daniel de,** Examen tractatus a magistro
Simone Episcopio conscripto an liceat Chris-
tiano magistratum gerere. [1621.]

1622

.... **De la Justice** et de la Paix, de l'Injustice et de la
Guerre, les Misères et fin luctueuse des guerres
civiles et étrangères ; et qu'il n'y a rien au
monde si désirable que la Paix. Paris (Louys
Boulanger) 1622. [Auteur : **Charles Chappuzeau ?**].

P.P. **Erasmus, Des.**, De On-ervaren Krijghsman, ofte
Verhandelinge van het oude spreeck-woort,
Dulce bellum inexpertis.... uyt het Latijn....
door **H. R.** Noch het spreeckwoort : Sileni
Alcebiadis [sic], Of Schijn bedrieght. Vertaelt

door **I. R.** Alles voor ontrent hondert en ses
jaren, in sijn Adagien of Spreeckwoorden
ghestelt ende uytghegheven. S. l. 1622. 4°.
53 p.
Voir éd. latine 1517.

.... **Erasmus, Des.,** Bellum.... Rostochi 1622.
1re éd. 1517.

P.P. **Erasmus Des.,** Teutscher Friedens-Bott d. i....
Weheklag des.... Jungfräulein Friede welches
der blutdürst. Mars mit Schwert, Mord,
Raub.... verjagt hat.... Franckfurt 1622.
4°. 26 p.
Voir éd. latine 1516.

1623
.... **Chappuzeau, Charles,** De la société de la vie
humaine, des alliances et ambassades des
princes et devoirs des ambassadeurs.... Paris
(P. Recollet) 1623.

.... **Le nouveau Cynée** ou Discours d'Estat repré-
sentent les occasions et moyens d'establir une
paix generalle, et la liberté du commerce par
tout le monde. Aux Monarques et Princes
souverains de ce temps. Em[eric] Cr[ucé]
Par[isius]. Paris (Jacques Villery) 1623. 8°.
[IX,] 226 p.
Voir ci-dessous.

... **Le nouveau Cynée** ou Discours des occasions et
moyens d'establir une paix generale et la
liberté du commerce par tout le monde.
Em[eric] Cr[ucé] P[arisius]. Paris (Jacques
Villery) 1623. 8°. [IX,] 226 p.
Voir aussi sous 1624.

.... **Ostorodt, C.,** Unterrichtung von der Christlichen Religion. Rakov. 1623.
1re éd. 1604.

.... **Schürstabius, Johannes Philippus,** Bellum et
pax. Wegen einander Haltung und Vergleichung
desz Kriegs und Friedens, was deren Operation
und Würckung seye. Nürmberg 1623. 16°.
[XVI,] 80 p.

1624
.... **Crucé, Em.,** Le Cinée d'Estat sur les occurrences
de ce temps. Aux Monarques et Potentats de
ce Monde. Paris (Jacques Villery) 1624. 8°.
[IX,] 226 p.
Voir les éditions de 1623, appartenant au
même tirage que celle-ci.

... **Rijs, Hans de, en Lubbert Gerritsz,** Korte belij-
denisse des geloofs, der voornaamste stukken
der Christlijke leere, opgestelt door — en —.
't Amstelredam. De Rijp (Claes Jacobse) 1624.

1627
.... **Erasmus, Des.,** Querela pacis [Dans:] **Chemnitz,**
Senatus Deorum. S. l. 1627. 8°.
1re éd. 1516.

.... **[Menno Simons],** Een gantz duidelijck ende klaer
bewijs.... dat Jesus Christus is de rechte
belovede David.... S. l. 1627. 12°. 32 p.

1628
.... **Erasmus, Des.,** Institutio principis.... Amsterdam 1628. 12°.
1re éd. 1515.

.... **Erasmus, Des.,** Institutio principis.... cui Adiun-
ximus Querela Pacis.... Lugd. Batavor.
(Apud Andream Cloucquiū) 1628. 32°.
Pag. 14-211 : Institutio principis.... 1re éd.
1515.
Pag. 212-287 : Querela pacis.... 1re éd. 1516.

1629
P.P. **Erasmus, Des.,** Belli detestatio. Ofte Oorlogs
vervloeckinge. Swol (Z. Heyns) 1629. 4°.
Voir éd. latine 1517.

1630
.... **Irenaromachia.** Das ist Eine Newe Tragico-
comoedia. Von Fried und Krieg. Auctore
Johann Rist sub nomine **Ernst Stapelius.**
Hamburgi 1630.
Voir pour les éditions suivantes 1636 s. l.;
1639 Breslau.

1631
P.P. **Twisck, Pieter Jansz,** Oorloghs-Vertooninghe :
Ofte Teghen die Krijch en voor de Vrede....
Hoorn (Zacharias Cornelissz.) 1631. 16°. 166 p.

1632
.... **Schaffshausen, Nicolaus,** Discursus academicus
de pace constituenda, firmanda et conservanda. Wittenberg (Helwig) 1632.
Ed. suiv. 1640 Hambourg.

1633
.... **Callot, Jacques,** Les miseres et les malhevrs de la
guerre. Représentez par —, noble lorrain, et
mis en lumiere par **Israel,** son ami. Paris 1633,
18 gravures. 8°.
Comparer l'éd. de 1636.

P.P. **Erasmus, Des.,** De Onversochte Krijghsman, Of
Verklaringe van 't oude Latijnsche spreeck-
woord, Dulce bellum inexpertis.... Alles int
Latijn beschreven door — van Rotterdam.
Maer nu ten dienst der Liefhebberen vertaelt.
Amstelredam (Dirck Pietersz.) 1633. 4°. 75 p.
Voir éd. latine 1517.

1634
.... **Erasmus, Des.,** Klags des an allen Orten und
enden vertribenen und ausgejagten Friedens...
Uebers. von **Samuel Grynaeus.** Basel (J. J.
Geneth) 1634.
Voir éd. latine 1516.

1635
.... **Erasmus, Des.,** Libellus aureus de bello.... ad
adagium : Dulce bellum inexpertis [Dans :] **Joh.
A. Werdenhagen,** Synopsis.... de republica.
Amst. (J. Janssonius) 1635. Pag. 832. 12°.
1re éd. 1517.

P.P. **Tilemann, Johann Andreas,** Disputatio de Pace.
[Halle (Faber) 1635?] 4°.

1636
.... **Callot, Jacques,** Misères de la guerre faict par
— et mis en lumière par **Israel Henriet.**
Paris 1636. 7 gravures. Pet. 12°.
Comparer l'éd. de 1633.

.... **Irenaromachia.** Eine Tragi-comoedia von Fried
und Krieg. [Auctore **Johann Rist,** sub nomine
Ernst Stapelius.] S. l. 1636.
1re éd. 1630.

.... **Unvorgreiffliches Bedencken :** Welcher Gestalt
ein Land, so durch Krieg, oder in andere Weg
verderbt, und öd gemacht, vermittelst Göttli-
cher Gnaden, widerumb auffzubringen. S. l.
1636.

1637
.... **[Comenius, J. A.],** Cesta pokoge.... Leszno 1637.
(La voie à la paix.... Lissa 1637).

1638

.... **Golaw, Salomon von,** [= Friedrich von Logau],
Zwey hundert teutscher Reimensprüche. Bres-
lau 1638.
Voir l'éd. suivante 1654.

P.P. [**Sully, Maximilian de Béthune, duc de,**], Mémoires
des sages et royalles œconomies d'estat, domestiques, politiques et militaires de Henry le
Grand.... Et des servitudes.... de Maximilian de Béthune.... Amstelredam s. a. [Le
livre a été imprimé au Château de Sully vers
1638]. 2 tom. en 1 vol. Fol.
Voir les éditions suivantes : 1638 Amsterdam ;
1649 Rouen ; 1652 s. l. ; 1662 Paris, 2x ; 1663
Paris ; 1663 Rouen ; 1663-1664 Paris ; 1664
Paris, 3x ; 1683 Paris ; 1723 Amsterdam, 2x ;
1725 Amsterdam ; 1768 Dresde ; 1775 Amsterdam ; 1778 Paris ; 1783-1786 Zürich, en allemand ; 1788 Paris ; 1810 Altona, en allemand ;
1820-1821 Paris ; 1822 Paris ; 1822 Londres,
en anglais ; 1837 Paris ; 1850 Paris ; 1889 Paris ;
1921 Londres, en anglais.
Ed. M.L.D.L.D.L. : 1745 Londres, 2x ; 1747
Londres, 2x ; 1752 Londres ; 1752 Genève ;
1756 Londres, en anglais ; 1757 Londres, en
anglais ; 1761 Londres, en anglais ; 1763 Londres ; 1767 Londres ; 1768 Londres ; 1778
Londres, 2x ; 1778 Londres, en anglais ; 1781
Londres, en anglais ; 1788 Liège ; 1805 s. l., en
anglais ; 1810 Londres, en anglais ; 1812
Londres, en anglais ; 1814 Paris ; 1819 Edinburgh, en anglais ; 1827 Paris ; 1856 Londres,
en anglais ; 1892 Londres, en anglais ; s. d.
Berlin.

P.P. [**Sully, Maximilian de Béthune, duc de,**], Mémoires
des sages et royalles œconomies d'estat, domestiques, politiques et militaires de Henry le
Grand.... Et des servitudes.... de Maximilian de Béthune. Tome[s I et] II. Amstelredam
[c.à.d. au château de Sully 1638?] 2 tom. en
1 vol. Fol.
1re éd. 1638.

1639

P.P. **Friedensrede** in gegenwart vieler Fürsten....
fürgebracht und abgeleget durch einen funftze-
hen jährigen edelen Knaben [= Paris von dem
Werder.] [Par **Dietrich von dem Werder.**]

[Cöthen?] 1639. 4º. 46 p.
Voir l'éd. suivante 1640.

.... **Stapelius, Ernst,** Eine newe Tragi-comœdia von
Fried und Krieg. Breslau 1639. 8º.
1re éd. 1630.
L'auteur est **Johan Rist.**

1640

.... **Breen, Daniel de,** De qualitate regni Domini
nostri Jesu Christi : quodque illud totum in
spirituali dominio constat. 1640.
Voir les éd. hollandaises 1641 et 1657.

.... **Schaffshausen, Nicolaus,** Tractatus de pace constituenda, firmanda et conservanda. Ed. reit.
et auct. Hamburgi 1640. 16º. 408 p.
1re éd. 1632.

.... **Werder, Dietrich von dem,** Friedens-Rede. Hamburg (T. Gundermann) 1640. 8º. 20 p.
1re éd. 1639.

1641

.... **Breen, Daniel van,** Van de hoedanigheyd des
rijks Christi, de tweede druk. Amsterdam 1641.
8º.
Voir éd. latine 1640.

.... **Erasmus, Des.,** Institutio principis.... Lugd.
Bat. (Jo. Maire) 1641. 12º.
1re éd. 1515.

.... **Erasmus, Des.,** Principis Christiani institutio
per aphorismos digesta. Lugd. Bat. 1641. 8º
1re éd. 1515.

.... **Erasmus, Des.,** Querela pacis.... Lugduni Batav.
(Jo. Maire) 1641. 12º.
1re éd. 1516.

1642

.... **W[ard], R[ichard],** The anatomy of warre, or,
warre with the wofull fruits, and effects thereof,
laid out to the life.... London s. d. [1642]. 4º.
Voir l'éd. 1643.

1643

P.P. **Bonbra, Franciscus David,** Ars belli et pacis, sive
de bello feliciter gerendo, et pace firmiter
stabilienda. Straubingæ 1643. 2 tom. en
1 vol. Fol.

Rappel :

Les auteurs espèrent recevoir toutes les informations nécessaires relatives aux erreurs et lacunes qui se
trouvent dans cette liste ainsi qu'aux endroits (bibliothèque, institution, etc.) où se trouve le matériel déjà
mentionné ou non encore mentionné dans la liste.

The editors hope to obtain all information necessary concerning errors and omissions in this list, as well
as concerning the places (library, institute, etc.) where the material mentioned, or not yet mentioned, in the list
is to be found.

Des exemplaires de la liste provisoire imprimée pour la période 1776-1898 peuvent être demandés à la Bibliothèque du Palais de la Paix, La Haye, Pays-Bas.

Copies of the printed provisional list for the period 1776-1898 may be obtained from the Library of the
Peace Palace, The Hague, Netherlands.

.... **Erasmus, Des.,** Utilissima consultatio de bello
Turcis inferendo. Lugd. Bat. (Jo. Maire) 1643.
8°.
1re éd. 1530.

.... **Ley, John,** The fury of warre, and folly of sinne,
(as an incentive to it) declared and applyed.
London (Chr. Meredith) 1643. 8°. 74 p.

.... **W[ard,] R[ichard],** The character of warre, or
warre with the wofull fruits and effects thereof,
laid out to the life.... London 1643. 8°.
Voir l'éd. 1642.

1644

.... **Erasmus, Des.,** Colloquia familiaria.... Hierach-
ter zijn bijgevoegt de verklaringen van ver-
scheyden spreeck-woorden.... Campen (Arent
Benier) 1644. 4°.
Pag. 3-32, De onversochte Kryghman of verklaringe van 't oude Latijnsche spreeckwoort
Dulce bellum inexpertis.... 1re éd. 1517.

.... **Idea** pacis generalis inter orbis christiani principes. Antwerpiæ 1644. 8°.

1646

.... **Loycx, Petrus,** Sæculum aureum, sive de Pace
libri duo.... Antverpiæ, 1646. Fol.

P.P. **Neander, C. Nic.,** Pax profuga, seu querela pacis
exulantis eiusdemque revocatio et triumphus.
Coloniæ Agrippinæ 1646. 4°. [22 p.]

P.P. **Starovolscius, Simon,** Ad principes Christianos
De Pace inter se componenda Belloque Turcis
inferendo. Protrepticon. S. l. [1646.] 4°.

1647

.... **Balde, Iacobus,** Poesis Osca sive drama Geor-
gicum in quo Belli mala, Pacis bona....
Repræsentantur.... [Monachii (Wagner) 1647].
Voir éd. suiv. 1660 Cologne.

.... **Bracht, T. van,** Angstigh Swanen-Gesangh of
Troostelooze Vrede. Dordrecht (Jacob Braat)
1647.

.... **[Rist, Johann,]** Das Friedewünschende Teutschland. In einem Schauspiele öffentlich vor-
gestellt und beschrieben durch einen Mitge-
nossen der Fruchtbringenden Gesellschaft.
Amsterdam (Elzevir) 1647. 12°.
Voir les éditions suivantes : 1647 Hambourg ;
1648 Amsterdam ; 1649 Hambourg ; 1649
Cologne ; 1653 Nürnberg ; 1806 s. l. ; s. l. s. d.

.... **[Rist, Joh.],** Das Friedewünschende Teutschland.
Hamburg (Wärners Wittwe) 1647. 12°.
1re éd. 1647.

1648

.... **[Rist, Johann,]** Das Friedewünschende Teutschland.... [Amsterdam?] 1648. 16°.
1re éd. 1647.

1649

.... **[Rist, Johann,]** Der Herr Sawsewind oder desz
edlen Joh. Risten Friedewünschendes und
nunmehr Friedebeseeligtes Teutschland....
Cölln (Andr. Binghen) 1649.
1re éd. 1647.

.... **[Rist, Johann,]** Das Friedewünschende Teutschland.... Hamburg (H. Wärners Wittwe) 1649.
12°.
1re éd. 1647.

.... **Sully, Maximilian de Béthune, duc de,** Mémoires
des sages et royales œconomies d'Estat....
Rouen 1649. 2 vols. Fol.
1re éd. 1638.

1650

P.P. **Lang(en), Johann, e.a.,** Zehen Christliche Danck-
und Friedenspredigten.... Ulm (Kühn) 1650.
12°. [II,] 629 p.

.... **Schookius, Mart.,** Tractatus de pace, speciatim
de pace perpetua que Fœderatis Belgis singulari Dei muneri contigit.... Amst. (J. Jan-
sonius) [1650].
Voir l'éd. suivante 1651 Groningue.

P.P. **Tempel** des Friedens und gegenüber gesetztes
Castel des Unfriedens. [S. l. 1650?]. Plano. 1 p.

1651

.... **Schookius, Martinus,** Tractatus de pace, speciatim de pace perpetua, quæ Fœderatis Belgis
singulari Dei muneri contigit. Groningæ. 1651.
4°.
1re éd. 1650.

1652

.... **Caussinus, Nic.,** Angelus pacis.... [Parisiis 1652].
Voir l'éd. suivante 1667.

P.P. **Erich, Christophorus,** Disputatio de Jure Pacis.
Jenæ (Nis) 1652. 4°. 14 p.

P.P. **[Sully, Maximilian de Béthune, duc de,]** Mémoires
des sages et royales œconomies d'estat domestiques, politiques et militaires de Henry le
Grand.... S. l. 1652. 4 vols. 16°.
1re éd. 1638.

1653

.... **[Rist, Johann,]** Das Friedewünschende Teutschland.... Nürnberg (Wolffgang d. J. und Joh.
Andr. Endtern?) 1653.
1re éd. 1647.

.... **Rist, Johann,** Das Friedejauchzende Teutschland,
welches vermittelst eines neuen Schauspieles....
denen, mit guter Ruhe und Frieden nunmehr
wolbeseligten Teutschen, Teutsch und treu-
meinentlich vorstellet Johann Rist. Nürnberg
(Wolffgang d. J. u. Joh. And. Endtern) 1653.
8°. 40 + 262 p.

1654

.... **[Logau, Friedrich von,]** Salomons von Golaw
deutscher Sinngedichte drei Tausend. 1654.
1re éd. 1638.

1656

.... **Lith, Nicolaus à,** Laus pacis. Amstelodami (Paulus
Matthias) 1656. Pet. 4°. 4 ff. non chiffrées.

1657

.... **Breen, Daniel van,** Van de hoedanigheyd des rijks
Christi de derde druck..... 1657. 8°.
Voir éd. latine 1640.

1658

.... **[Zwicker, Daniel,]** Irenicum irenicorum : Sive
reconciliatoris Christianorum hodiernorum nor-
ma triplex, sana ratio, scriptura sacra et tra-
ditiones, exempla doctrinæ de Christo ob
oculos posita. [Amsterdam 1658.]
Voir l'éd. hollandaise 1678.

1659

.... **Erasmus, Des.,** .... Dulce Bellum Inexpertis....
Verdeutscht durch **Caspar Meuslern**.... S. l.
1659. 12°.
Voir éd. latine 1517.

.... **[Plockhoy,] Peter Cornelius,** van Zurick-Zee,
The way to the peace and settlement of these
nations.... London 1659.

1660

.... **Balde, Jacobus,** Poesis Osca s. drama Georgicum in quo belli mala, pacis bona representantur. [Dans :] **Balde,** Poemata. Coloniæ 1660. 12°. 1re éd. 1647.

.... **Fox, George,** J.e.a., A declaration from the harmless and innocent people of God called Quakers, against all sedition, plotters and fighters in the world.... Presented to the King upon the 21st day of the 11th month 1660.

.... **Hessen-Rheinfels, Ernst von,** Der so wahrhafte als ganz aufrichtige und discretgesinnte Katholischer.... über den heutigen Zustand des Religions-Wesens in der Welt.... Köln 1660. Voir l'éd. abrégée 1673.

1661

.... **Penington** the Younger, **Isaac,** Somewhat spoken to a weighty Question, concerning the Magistrates Protection of the Innocent, wherein is held forth the blessing and peace, which Nations ought to wait for, and embrace in the later days.... London (Thomas Simmons) 1661. 4°. 2 ff.

Voir pour les éditions suivantes 1681 London ; 1746 London ; 1756 Salop ; 1761 London ; 1784 London ; 1861-1863 Sherwood N. Y.

.... **Smith, William,** The banner of love under which the royal army is preserved and safely conducted. Being a clear and perfect way out of all wars and contentions, with a short testimony unto the way of peace.... London (Robert Wilson) 1661. 4°. 3 ff.

1662

.... **Bayly, William,** A briefe Declaration to all the World from the innocent People of God, called Quakers, of our Principles and Beleif concerning Plottings and Fightings with Carnal Weapons, against any People, Men or Nations.... S. l. (Printed for W. M.) 1662. 4°. 1 f.

P.P. **Sully, Maximilian de Béthune, duc de,** Mémoires ou œconomies royales d'estat, domestiques, politiques et militaires de Henry le Grand. Tome[s] troisiesme [et] quatriesme. Paris (Courbé) 1662. 2 tomes en 1 vol. Fol. 1re éd. 1638.

.... **Sully, Maximilian de Béthune, duc de,** Mémoires ou œconomies royales d'estat.... Nouv. éd. Paris (Courbé). Vol. I et II. 1662 et 1664. 1re éd. 1638.

1663

.... **[Spremberg, Jac. Sturm von],** Augspurgische Friedens-Freud und Krieges-Leid, poetisch besungen. Nürnberg 1663.

.... **Sully, Maximilian de Béthune, duc de,** Mémoires ou œconomies royales d'estat.... Imprimés à Rouen, et se vendent à Paris (Vol. 1-4 chez L. Billaine ; vol. 5-8 chez A. Courbé), 1663. 4 parties en 8 vol. 12°. 1re éd. 1638.

.... **Sully, Maximilian de Béthune, duc de,** Mémoires ou œconomies royales d'estat.... Paris (Jolly) 1663. 2 tomes. Fol. 1re éd. 1638.

.... **Sully, Maximilian de Béthune, duc de,** Mémoires ou œconomies royales d'estat.... Paris (Billaine) 1663-1664. 5 vols. 12°. 1re éd. 1638.

1664

.... **Erasmus, Des.,** Dulce bellum inexpertis, dat is den krijg is den onversochten soet. [A la suite de :] **Erasmus,** Colloquia.... vertaelt. Utrecht (Gijsb. van Zijl) 1664. 8°. Voir éd. latine 1517.

.... **[Kempe, Anders,]** Perspicillum bellicum. Det ähr krigz-perspectiv : uthi hwilket man kenna kan, hwad krig är, hwadan det kommer, och om een christen wäl met gåt samwet kan krig föra, emot sina fiender, för troon och religionen.... Amsterdam 1664. 8°. 118 p.

... **Sully, Maximilian de Béthune, duc de,** Mémoires ou œconomies royales d'estat.... Paris (Joily) 1664. 3 tomes. Fol. 1re éd. 1638.

.... **Sully, Maximilian de Béthune, duc de,** Mémoires ou œconomies royales d'estat.... Paris 1664. 4 tomes en 2 vols. Fol. 1re éd. 1638.

P.P. **Sully, Maximilian de Béthune, duc de,** Mémoires ou œconomies royales d'estat.... Paris (Billaine) 1664. 4 tomes en 2 vols. 6° et 4°. 1re éd. 1638.

1665

... **Erasmus, Des.,** Codicille d'or, ou petit recueil tiré de l'Institution du prince chrestien. Trad. par **Cl. Joly.** S. l. [Amst., Elzevier,] 1665. 12°. 189 p. et 1 p. non cotée. Voir pour les éditions suivantes : 1665 Amsterdam ; 1666 s. l. ; 1667 s. l. Ed. orig. 1515.

.... **Erasmus, Des.,** Codicille d'or, ou petit recueil tiré de l'Institution du prince chrestien. Trad. par **Cl. Joly.** S. l. [Amst. (Elzevier)] 1665. 12°. 187 p. et 2 ff. non cotées. 1re éd. 1665. Voir l'éd. orig. 1515.

.... **Joly, Claude,** Le traité des restitutions des grands. Amsterdam (Elzevier) 1665.

1666

... **[Comenius, J. A.,]** De rerum humanarum emendatione consultatio catholica, ad genus humanum, ante alios vero ad Eruditos, Religiosos, Potentes, Europæ. Amsterdam 1666. Voir l'éd. suivante 1702 Halle.

.... **Erasmus, Des.,** Codicille d'or, ou petit recueil tiré de l'Institution du prince chrestien. Trad. par **Cl. Joly.** S. l. 1666. 12°. 1re éd. 1665. Voir l'éd. orig. 1515.

1667

.... **[Comenius, J. A.,]** Angelus pacis ad Legatos pacis Anglos et Belgas Bredam missus. Indeque ad omnes Christianos per Europam, et mox ad omnes populos per orbem totum mittendus. Ut se sistant, belligerare desistant, pacisque principi, Christo, pacem gentibus jam loquuturo, locum faciant. S. l. Anno 1667, Mense Maio.

.... **Erasmus, Des.,** Codicille d'or, ou petit recueil tiré de l'Institution du prince chrestien. Trad. par **Cl. Joly.** S. l. 1667. 1re éd. 1665. Voir l'éd. orig. 1515.

P.P. **Pomey, Franc,** Candidatus Rhetoricæ, seu Apthonii Progymnasmata.... Accessit Angelus Pacis ad Principes Christianos **Nic. Caussini.** Monachii (Wagner) 1667. 12°. [X]456, 58 p. Pag. 1-456, ... Pag. 3- 58 : Angelus Pacis.... 1re (?) éd. 1652.

1668

.... **Comenius, J. A.,** Unum necessarium, scire quid sibi sit necessarium, in vita et morte, et post mortem. Amsterodami (Christoph. Cunradus) 1668.
Voir pour les éditions suivantes : 1682 Francfort s. Oder; 1690 Lüneburg, en allemand; 1724 Leipsic; 1725 Leipsic, en allemand; 1735 Leipsic, en allemand; 1755 Leipsic, en allemand.

.... **Socini, Faust.,** Senensis, Opera omnia. Amsterdam (F. Kuyper) 1668. 2 vols. Fol.

1669

.... **[Grimmelshausen, Hans Jakob Christoffel,]** Neu eingerichteter und viel verbesserter Simplicissimus. Mömpelgard 1669.
Il y a de nombreuses éditions du Simplicissimus : souvent le titre a subi des variations ou bien on a ajouté des chapitres nouveaux. De plus Grimmelshausen a eu beaucoup d'imitateurs. Afin de ne pas encombrer la liste, le livre a été mentionné une fois seulement.

P.P. **Milichius, Gottlieb,** Dissertatio politica de Pace Aeterna. Lipsiæ (Michaelis) [1669]. 4°. [19 pag.]

1670

.... **Erasmus, Des.,** .... Belli detestatio ofte Oorloghs vervloeckinge. Amsterdam (Ch. Cunradus voor A. Micker) 1670. 12°.
Voir éd. latine 1517.

1671

.... **Bentley, Thos.,** An examination of the Doctrine of Non-Resistance, as held by the people called Quakers. 1671.

1672

.... **Burrough, Edward,** The memorable works of a son of thunder and consolation.... [London] 1672. Fol.

.... **Erasmus, Des.,** Bellum. Brunsvicæ 1672. 8°. 1re éd. 1517.

.... **Erasmus, Des.,** Querela pacis. Hardervici (Petr. van den Berge) 1672. 12°.
1re éd. 1516.

1673

.... **[Hessen-Rheinfels, Ernst von,]** Extract desz Veri, sinceri et discreti Catholici, oder eines gewissen Buchs.... vom Author selbsten.... Zusammengesetzt. S. l. 1673. 8°.
Voir l'éd. complète 1660.

1674

.... **Erasmus, Des.,** Gravissima epistola ad Christianissimum Galliarum Regem Franciscum I.... Cum eiusdem Erasmi elegantissima dissertatione de Bello annotationibus historicis illustrata.... Irenopoli 1674. 12°.
Pag. 41-138 : Dissertatio de bello.... 1re éd. 1517.
Pag. 139-234: Annotationes historicæ in Dissert. Erasmi de Bello.

1675

P.P. **Lügenfeind, Wahrnoldo Melancholico,** [= Daniel Lossius ?], Dulcipaciphili und Horribellifacii Seltsame Kriegs- und Friedens-Grillen.... S. l. [1675]. 4°. [VI] 86 p.

1676

.... **Barclay, Robert,** Theologiæ verè Christianæ Apologia. Amstelodami (Jacob Claus) 1676. 4°.
Voir pour les éditions suivantes : 1678 Aberdeen, en anglais; 1678 Londres, en anglais; 1684 s. l., en allemand; 1701 Londres, en anglais; 1702 Londres, en français; 1703 Londres, en anglais; 1710 Londres, en espagnol; 1728 s. l., en anglais; 1729 Londres; 1736 Londres, en anglais; 1737 Dublin, en anglais; 1738 Londres, en danois; 1740 s. l., en allemand; 1757 Amsterdam, en hollandais; 1765 Londres, en anglais; 1765 Birmingham, en anglais; 1774 s. l., en anglais; 1775 Philadelphia, en anglais; 1776 Germantown, en allemand; 1780 Londres, en anglais; 1780 Dublin, en anglais; 1780 Philadelphia, en anglais; 1789 Philadelphia. en anglais; ·1797 Londres, en français; 1800 Dublin, en anglais; 1805 Philadelphia, en anglais; 1815 Londres, en anglais, abrégée; 1817 Sunderland, en anglais, abrégée; 1822 Londres, en anglais, abrégée; 1825 Londres, en anglais; 1827 New York, en anglais; 1837 Lindfield, en anglais, sélection; 1841 Londres, en anglais; 1848 Stavanger, en danois; 1849 Londres, en anglais; 1850 Manchester, en anglais; 1855 Philadelphia, en anglais.

.... **Der alte und neue** treyhertzig und tieffgesinnte frantzmänische **politicus** welcher die Mittel des friedens.... an die hand giebet.... S. l. 1676. 144 p.

P.P. **Gessi, Berlingiero,** Lo scettro pacifico. Venetia (Baglioni) 1676. 12°. 166 [, XIV] pag.

.... **W[olzogen], J. L.,** De werelose Christen, verbeeldende de Nature en Hoedanigheyt van het Rycke Christi.... Trad. du Latin par P. L[angedult]. S. l. 1676.

1677

.... **Barclay, Robert,** Universal love considered and established upon its right foundation.... S. l. 1677. 4°.
Voir l'éd. suivante : 1799 Londres.

P.P. **Fürstnerius, Caesarinus,** [= G. G. Leibniz], De jure suprematus ac legationis principum Germaniæ. S. l. [Amsterdam ?] 1677. 8° [XIV,] 245 p.
Voir les éditions suivantes : 1678 Londres; 1768 Genève.

1678

.... **Barclay, Robert,** An Apology for the True Christian Divinity.... [Aberdeen ?] 1678. 4°.
Il y a encore deux éditions anglaises de la même année, publiées probablement à Londres. Voir éd. latine 1676.

.... **Barclay, Robert,** Epistle of Love and Friendly Advice to the Ambassadors of Europe met at Nimeguen (in Dutch). Rotterdam (J. P. Sroenwort) 1678.
Voir les éditions suivantes : 1679 Londres; 1684 s. l. en hollandais; 1717 Londres.

.... **[Barclay, R.,]** Een brief van liefde.... aan de ambassadeurs van.... Europa.... tot Nimwegen vergadert..., waar in.... de.... remedie tot.... vrede aangewesen word. In 't Engelsch geschreven door R. Barclay. S. l. 1678. Voir l'éd. orig. ci-dessus.

P.P. **Fürstnerius, Caesarinus,** [= **G. G. Leibniz**], Tractatus de jure suprematus ac legationis principum Germaniæ. Editio 2ᵃ. Londini 1678. 8⁰. [XXII,] 357 p. 1ʳᵉ éd. 1677.

.... **[Kuijper, F.]**, De Recht weerlooze Christen. Of verdediging van het gevoelen der eerste Christenen, en gemartelde Doops-gezinden; weegens het Overheyds-ampt, Oorlog en geweldige teegenstand.... Rotterdam (P. Terwout) 1678. 4⁰. XXX, 132 p.

P.P. **[Nalson, John,]** The project of Peace, or Unity of Faith and Government, the only Expedient to Procure Peace.... London 1678. 8⁰. 394 p.

... **Verburg, Jan Dionijssen,** De Recht weerlooze Christen. Rotterdam (P. Terwout) 1678.

.... **Zwicker, D.,** Gecensureerde.... vredeschrift der vredeschriften.... [Préface et traduction de **Adr. Swartepaard.**] S. l. 1678. Voir l'éd. orig. 1658.

1679

.... **Barclay, Robert,** Epistle of Love and Friendly Advice to the Ambassadors of Europe met at Nimeguen. London (B. Clark) 1679. 8⁰. 1ʳᵉ éd. 1678.

1680

.... **Lurting, Thomas,** Letter. [Dans :] George Fox, To the Great Turk and his King at Argiers. London (Ben. Clark) 1680. 4⁰. Ed. origin. de The Fighting Sailor. Voir pour les éditions suivantes : 1710 Londres; 1711 Londres; 1720 Londres; 1766 Londres; 1801 Londres; 1811 Leeds; 1813 Londres; 1821 s. l.; 1824 Londres; 1842 Londres; 1855 Londres; 1863 Christiania, en norvégien; Londres, s. d.

1681

.... **Penington, Isaac,** The works.... London (B. Clark) 1681. Fol. In two parts. Part I, p. 143, To the Army. Part. I, p. 320 : Somewhat spoken to a weighty question.... 1ʳᵉ éd. 1661.

1682

.... **Comenius, J. A.,** Unum necessarium.... Francfort s. Oder 1682. 1ʳᵉ éd. 1668.

1683

.... **Sully, Maximilian de Béthune, duc de,** Mémoires ou œconomies royales d'estat.... Paris 1683. 4 tomes en 2 vols. 1ʳᵉ éd. 1638 .

1684

.... **Barclay, Robert,** Eine Apologie oder Verthei-digungs, Schrift der Recht Christlichen Gotts-Gelahrtheit. S. l. 1684. 4⁰. Voir éd. latine 1676.

.... **Barclay, Robert,** Epistle of Love (in Dutch). [Dans :] De oude waarheyd ontdekt. p. 85. 1684. 4⁰. 1ʳᵉ éd. 1678.

1687

.... **Eeghem, Adriaan van,** Catechismus ofte Onderwijzinge in de Kristelijke Godsdienst. Middelburg (M. v. Hoekke) 1687.

1688

.... **Toornburg, Klaas,** Schriftuurlijcke Verhandelingh voor de wraek en weerloose lijdsaemheijt en volmaecte liefde. Alckmaar (G. J. Haseven) 1688.

.... **Toornburg, K.,** Verhandeling tegen het eedzweeren en voor de weerloosheyt. Alcmaar 1688. 8⁰.

1689

.... **Sivers, Henricus,** De studio belli ac pacis. Kiel 1689. 8⁰. 64 p.

1690

.... **Comenius, J. A.,** Unum necessarium.... Lüneburg 1690. (Traduction allemande). 1ʳᵉ éd. 1668.

1691

.... **Goudet, Huit** entretiens, ou Irène et Ariste fournissent des idées pour terminer la présente guerre par une paix générale. Genève 1691.

1693

.... **[Penn, William,]** An essay towards the present and future peace of Europe by the establishment of an European Dyet, Parliament or Estates. S. l. 1693. 12⁰. Voir pour les éditions suivantes : 1693 Londres; 1696 Londres; 1702 Londres; 1726 Londres; 1897 Boston.

.... **Penn, William,** An essay towards the present and future peace of Europe by the establishment of an European Dyet, Parliament or Estates. London (Randal Taylor) 1693. Pet. 8⁰. 1ʳᵉ éd. voir ci-dessus.

1696

.... **Penn, William,** An essay towards the present and future peace of Europe by the establishment of an European Dyet, Parliament or Estates. London (E. Whitlock) 1696. 12⁰. 42 p. 1ʳᵉ éd. 1693.

1697

P.P. **Lescailje, Kataryne,** Daphnis Harderszang op de Vrede. Amsteldam (Lescailje) 1697. 4⁰. 8 p.

P.P. **Lomannus, W.,** Vredezang aan de Vrye Nederlanders. 's-Gravenhage (Van Limburg) 1697. 4⁰. 8 p.

P.P. **Obrecht, Ulricus,** Biga dissertationum academicarum.... Prior de ratione belli, vulgo raison de guerre, posterior de sponsoribus pacis.... S. l. 1697. 4⁰. 76 p.

P.P. **Rotgans, L.,** Vredetriomf. Utrecht (Halma) 1697. 4⁰. 8 p.

1698

P.P. **Perizonius, Jac.,** Orationes duæ de pace.... Lugd. in Bat. (Haring) 1698. 4⁰. [IV,] 62 p.

.... **Valckenaer, Is.,** Oratio de pace. Leod. [= Leovardiæ ?] 1698.

1701

.... **Barclay, Robert,** An apology for the True Christian Divinity.... The 4th ed. London (T. Sowle) 1701. 8⁰. Voir éd. latine 1676.

1702

.... **Barclay, Robert,** Apologie de la véritable Théologie Chrétienne.... Londres (T. Sowle) 1702. Voir éd. latine 1676.

.... **Comenius, J. A.,** De Rerum Humanarum emendatione Consultatio catholica ad genus Humanum ante alios vero ad eruditos, religiosos, potentes Europæ. Halæ 1702.
1re éd. 1666.

.... **Penn, William,** An essay towards the present and future peace of Europe.... London (A. Baldwin) 1702. 12º. IV, 42 p.
1re éd. 1693.

1703
P.P. **Barclay, Robert,** An apology for the true Christian divinity.... The 5th ed. London (Sowle) 1703. 8º. [XII.] 574 [,XXII] p.
Voir éd. latine 1676.

.... **Erasmus, Des.,** Opera omnia [edidit J. Clericus]. Lugd. Bat. (P. van der Aa) 1703-1706. Fol. 10 tom. en 11 vols.
Vol. II, col. 951 : Bellum.... 1re éd. 1517.
Vol. III. 1, col. 122 : Epist. ad Ant. à Bergis.... 1re éd. 1514 ?
Vol. III, 1, col. 149 : Epist. ad Leonem X.... 1re éd. 1515.
Vol. IV, col. 505 : Panegyricus ad Philippum... 1re éd. 1504.
Vol. IV, col. 561 : Institutio principis.... 1re éd. 1515.
Vol. IV, col. 625 : Querela pacis.... 1re éd. 1516.
Vol. V, col. 345 : De bella Turcico.... 1re éd. 1530.
Vol. VIII, col. 545 : Oratio de pace et discordia.

1706
.... **Dialogus**.... de querelis Franciæ et Angliæ. [Dans :] Johannes Gerson, Opera omnia. Ed. Dupin. Antwerpen 1706. Vol. IV, col. 844-859. 1re éd. 1483.

1709
.... **Erasmus, Des.,** Belli detestatio.... in rijm gebracht door **Korn. v. Vleuten.** Amsterdam (Pieter Visser) 1709. 8º.
Voir éd. latine 1517.

P.P. **[N. N.,]** Helden-roem op de vertraagde vrede, tusschen de ontzaglicke Bondgenooten en Louïs de XIV. Rotterdam (Pieter de Vries) 1709. 4º. 8 p.

1710
.... **Barclay, Robert,** Apologia de la verdadera Theologia Christiana.... Transl. p. **A. de Alvarado.** Londres (J. Sowle) 1710. 8º.
Voir éd. latine 1676.

.... **Bellers, John,** Some reasons for an European State proposed to the powers of Europe.... London 1710. 4º.

.... **The fighting sailor,** turn'd peaceable Christian, manifested in the convincement and conversion of **Thomas Lurting.** London (J. Sowle) 1710. 8º.
Voir l'éd. orig. 1680.

1711
.... **The fighting sailor,** turn'd peaceable Christian, manifested in the convincement and conversion of **Thomas Lurting.** London (J. Sowle) 1711. 8º.
Voir l'éd. orig. 1680.

1712
.... **[Fleetwood, William,]** A sermon on the fast-day, January the sixteenth 1711/12. Against such as delight in war. London (S. Buckley) 1712. 23 p.

P.P. **[Saint-Pierre, Charles Irénée Castel, abbé de,]** Mémoires pour rendre la paix perpétuelle en Europe. Cologne (Jacques le Pacifique) 1712. Pet. 8º.
Voir pour les différentes rédactions et éditions : 1713 Utrecht ; 1713 Lyon ; 1714 Londres, en anglais ; 1716 Utrecht ; 1717 Utrecht ; 1729 Rotterdam ; 1729, 1733, 1738 Rotterdam-Paris ; 1761 Londres, en anglais.

1713
P.P. **[Saint-Pierre, Charles Irénée Castel, abbé de,]** Projet pour rendre la paix perpétuelle en Europe. Utrecht (A. Schouten) 1713. 2 vols. 8º.
Voir 1712.

.... **[Saint-Pierre, Charles Irénée Castel, abbé de,]** Projet pour rendre la paix perpétuelle en Europe. Lyon 1713.
Voir 1712.

.... **Trapp, Joseph,** Peace. A poem : inscribed to.... Lord Viscount Bolinbroke.... London (J. Barber) 1713. 22 p.

1714
P.P. **Gysen, Jan van,** De vreeden op haar zeegen, en Mars in een rolwagen.... Amsterdam (Van Egmont) 1714. 16º. 15 p.

.... **St. Pierre, The abbot,** A project for settling an ever lasting peace in Europe... London (J. Watts) 1714.
Voir 1712 et 1761. On prétend que « le projet » fut traduit en plusieurs langues Nous ne connaissons que le titre de cette édition anglaise.

1716
P.P. **Saint-Pierre, [Ch. I. Castel,] abbé de,** Projet de traité pour rendre la paix perpétuelle.... Utrecht (Schouten) 1716. 8º. 456 p.
Voir 1712.

1717
.... **Barclay, Robert** An epistle of love and friendly advice to the Ambassadors.... of Europe met at Nimeguen.... London 1717.
1re éd. 1678.

P.P. **Saint-Pierre, [Ch I. Castel,] abbé de,** Projet de traité pour rendre la paix perpétuelle.... Utrecht (Schouten) 1717. 16º. XLIV, 456 p.
Voir 1712.

1718
P.P. **[Poot, H. K.,]** Het nut van den vrede. Aen Zyne Excellentie Willem, Graeve van Kadogan. enz.... Gedicht. Delft 1718. 4º. 16 p.
Voir aussi 1722.

1720
.... **Leibniz, G. W.,** Observations sur le projet d'une paix perpétuelle de M. l'abbé de **Saint-Pierre.** [Dans :] Recueil de diverses pièces sur la philosophie.... Amsterdam 1720. Tome II, p. 173.
Voir pour l'éd. suivante 1768 Genève.

.... **The fighting Sailor** turn'd peaceable Christian, manifested in the convincement and conversion of **Thomas Lurting.** London (J. Sowle) 1720. 8º.
Voir l'éd. orig. 1680.

1721
.... **Erasmus, Des.,** En christelig furstes uptuchtelse uti wissa reglor och Läre-puncter förestäld. Stockholm (Kongl. boktryckeriet) 1721. 8º.
Voir éd. latine 1515.

1722

.... **Poot, H. K.,** Het nut van den vrede. [Dans :] Gedichten. Rotterdam 1722. Pag. 328-29.
Voir aussi 1718 Poot.

1723

.... **Sully, Maximilian de Béthune, duc de,** Mémoires ou œconomies royales d'estat.... Amsterdam (Trevoux) 1723. 12 vols. Pet. in 12º.
1re éd. 1638.

.... **Sully, Maximilian de Béthune, duc de,** Mémoires ou œconomies royales d'estat.... Amsterdam (Trevoux) 1723. 15 vols.
1re éd. 1638.

1724

.... **Comenius, J. A.,** Unum necessarium, scire quid sibi sit necessarium, in vita et morte, et post mortem. Lipsiæ 1724.
1re éd 1668.

.... **Erasmus, Des.,** Enchiridion militis Christiani.... cum auctoris commentatione in proverbium Dulce Bellum inexpertis.... Halæ (Orphano-dochii) 1724. 8º.
Pag. 169-204 : Bellum.... 1re éd. 1517.

1725

.... **Comenius, J. A.,** Unum necessarium, scire quid sibi sit necessarium, in vita et morte, et post mortem. Leipzig 1725. (Traduction allemande).
Voir éd. latine 1668.

.... **Sully, Maximilian de Béthune, duc de,** Mémoires ou œconomies royales d'estat. Amsterdam (aux dép. de la Compagnie) 1725. 12 vols. 12º.
1re éd. 1638.

1726

.... **Penn, William,** A collection of the works of —. Edited by **Joseph Besse.** London (J. Sowle) 1726. 2 vol. Fol.
Vol..... p..... : An essay towards the present and future peace of Europe.... 1re éd. 1693.

1728

.... **Barclay, Robert,** An Apology for the True Chris- tian Divinity.... (Edition published under the Sanction of the Yearly Meeting of Friends in New England). 1728.
Voir éd. latine 1676.

... **Dialogus....** de querelis Franciæ et Angliæ. [Dans :] **Johannis Gersonis** opera omnia. 2a ed. **Du Pin.** Hagæ Comitum 1728. Tom. IV, p. 844-859.
1re éd. 1483.

.... **Projet** de traité pour rendre la paix perpétuelle entre les Souverains Chrétiens, pour maintenir toujours le commerce entre les nations et pour affermir beaucoup davantage les maisons Sou- verains sur le throne.... 1728.
Voir aussi l'éd. 1747.

1729

.... **Barclay, Robert,** Theologiæ vere Christianæ Apologia. Ed. sec. priore emendatior. Londini (J. Sowle) 1729. 8º.
1re éd. 1676.

P.P. **Saint-Pierre, [Charles Irénée Castel,] abbé de,** Abrégé du projet de paix perpétuelle.... Rotterdam (Beman) 1729. 227 p.
Voir 1712.

P.P. **Saint-Pierre, [Charles Irénée Castel,] abbé de,** Abrégé du projet de paix perpétuelle.... Rot- terdam (Beman), Paris (Briasson) 1729. 8º. 227 p.
Voir 1712 et 1738.

1733

P.P. **Le vrai intérêt** des princes, établi sur la paix. Utrecht 1733. 8º. 11 p.

P.P. **Saint-Pierre, [Charles Irénée Castel,] abbé de,** Ouvraje(s) (de) politique(s) (et de morale). Rotterdam (Beman) (, et se trouve à Paris, chéz (Briasson)) 1733-1741. 16 (ou 17) vols. 8º.

.... **Tome I,** contenant l'Abrégé du projet de paix perpétuelle, inventé par le roi Henri le Grand... 1733.
Voir 1712, Mémoires pour rendre la paix, etc.

P.P. **Tome II,** p. 3-83 : Suplément à l'abréjé du projet de paix perpétuele. 1733.

.... **Tome VIII,** p. 156-169 : Observation VI. Importante. Sur le système de l'équilibre en Europe.... et.... avantages.... pour préfé- rer l'établissement de la Diète europaine. 1734.

P.P. **Tome X,** p. 260-264 : Comparaizon entre le système de l'équilibre des deux principales puissances, et le sistème de la diète europaine. 1735.
Pag. 447-451 : Articles fondamentaux de l'éta- blissement de la diète européaine. 1735.
Pag. 452-458 : Observations sur le plan des médiateurs. 1735.

.... **Tome XI,** p. 317-332 : Observations sur les dernières paix. 1737.

P.P. **Tome XV,** p. 1-37 : Règle pour discerner le droit du tort, le juste de l'injuste entre nasion et nasion. 1741.
Pag. 100-112 : Conséquances du progrez néces- saire et indéfinie de la Raizon humaine, malgré les interruptions des guerres. 1741.

.... **Tome XVI,** p. 117-142 : Sur le sistème de la paix perpétuèle en Europe. [Correspondance de l'Abbé de Saint-Pierre avec le Cardinal de Fleury.] 1741.... Voir 1712.
Pag. 459-534 : Réfiexions sur l'Anti-Machiavel de 1740. 1741.

P.P. **Saint-Pierre, [Charles Irénée Castel,] abbé de,** Ouvrajes politiques. Rotterdam (Beman), Paris (Briasson) 1733. 8º.
Tome II, p. 1-73 : Suplément à l'abréjé du projèt de paix perpétuèle. 1733.
Existe-t-il encore d'autres volumes de cette édition des Ouvrajes politiques ?

1734

.... **Saint-Pierre, Ch. I. Castel, abbé de,** Observation VI Importante. Sur le système de l'équilibre en Europe.
Voir 1733 Ouvraje(s) (de) politique(s) etc.

1735

.... **Comenius, J. A.,** Unum necessarium, scire quid sibi sit necessarium, in vita et morte, et post mortem. Leipzig 1735. (Traduction allemande).
Voir éd. latine 1668.

P.P. **Saint-Pierre, Ch. I. Castel, abbé de,** Comparai- zon....
Voir 1733, Ouvraje(s) (de) poiitique(s) etc.

P.P. **Saint-Pierre, Ch. I. Castel, abbé de,** Articles fon- damentaux de l'établissement de la diète europaine.
Voir 1733, Ouvraje(s) (de) politique(s) etc.

P.P. **Saint-Pierre, Ch. I. Castel, abbé de,** Observations sur le plan des médiateurs.
Voir 1733, Ouvraje(s) (de) politique(s) etc.

1736

.... **[Alberoni, Guilio,]** Scheme for reducing the Tur- kish Empire to the obedience of Christian Princes and for a partition of the conquests, together with a scheme of a perpetual dyet for establishing the public tranquility. Translated from the Italian manuscript. London 1736.

P.P. **Ontwerp** van den Kardinaal **Alberoni**, om het Turksche Rijk onder de gehoorzaamheit van de Christen Mogentheden te brengen, en van de wijze, op welke ze dat over wonnen hebbende, onder hun zouden konnen verdeelen ; als mede ontwerp van een altijt durende Rijksdag, om de algemeene rust vast te stellen en voor altoos te verzekeren. Uit het Italiaansch vertaalt na een oirspronkelijk manuscript, etc. Delf 1736. 8⁰.

.... Des Weltberühmten Cardinals **Alberoni** Vorschlag das Türkische Reich unter der Christlichen Potentaten Botmässigkeit zu bringen. Samt der Art und Weise, wie dasselbe nach der Ueberwindung unter Sie zu vertheilen a.a. Aus dem Italienischen nach dem Original, welches in eines vornehmen Ministers Händen ist, übersetzt. Frankfurt u. Leipzig 1736.

P.P. **Barclay, Robert,** An Apology for the True Christian Divinity.... The 6th ed. London (T. Sowle Raylton) 1736. 8⁰.
Voir éd. latine 1676.

1737

.... **Barclay, Robert,** An Apology for the True Christian Divinity.... The 7th ed. Dublin (Mary Fuller) 1737. 8⁰,
Voir éd. latine 1676.

... **Saint-Pierre, Ch. I. Castel, abbé de,** Observations...
Voir 1733, Ouvraje(s) (de) politique(s).

P.P. **Turretini, Jean Alphonse,** Orationes academicæ. Genevæ (Barrillot et fils) 1737. 4⁰. [II,] 355 p. Pag. 323-337 : Oratio undecima, seu, votum pro Pace Europæ.... Voir aussi 1748.

1738

.... **Barclay, Robert,** Forsvar for den Sande Christelige Theologi.... Oversat af **C. Meidel,** London (T. Sowle Raylton) 1738. 8⁰.
Voir éd. latine 1676.

P.P. **Saint-Pierre, [Ch. I. Castel,] abbé de,** Ouvrajes de politique. Tome premier. Contenant l'abrégé du projet de paix perpétuelle.... Segonde édition, revue et augmantée. Rotterdam (Beman), Paris (Briasson) 1738. 4⁰. [XII.] 352 p. Voir 1729. Existe-t-il encore d'autres volumes de cette édition des Ouvrajes de politique ?

1740

.... **Barclay, Robert,** Eine Apologie oder Vertheidigungs-Schrift der Recht Christlichen Gotts-Gelahrtheit. S. 1. 1740. 8⁰.
Voir éd. latine 1676.

.... **Saint-Pierre, [Ch. I. Castel,] abbé de,** Bedenkingen op den Anti-Machiavel. Rotterdam (Beman) 1740. 8⁰.
Voir les éditions suivantes (holl. et fr.) 1741.

1741

.... **Saint-Pierre, abbé de,** Bedenkingen op den Anti-Machiavel, eerst gedrukt in 't jaar 1740. Rotterdam 1741.
1ʳᵉ éd. 1740.

P.P. **Saint-Pierre, [Ch. I. Castel,] abbé de,** Règle pour discerner le droit du tort....
Voir 1733, Ouvraje(s (de) politique(s) etc.

P.P. **Saint-Pierre, [Ch. I. Castel,] abbé de,** Conséquances du progrez nécessaire et indéfini de la Raizon humaine. Malgré les interruptions des guerres.
Voir 1733, Ouvraje(s) (de) politique(s) etc.

... **Saint-Pierre, [Ch. I. Castel,] abbé de,** Sur le sistème de la paix perpétuèle en Europe. [Correspondance de l'abbé de Saint-Pierre avec le cardinal de Fleury].
Voir 1733, Ouvraje(s) (de) politique(s) etc.

P.P. **Saint-Pierre, Charles Irénée Castel, abbé de,** Réflexions sur l'Antimachiavel de 1740. Rotterdam (Beman) 1741. 16⁰. 64 p.
Voir aussi les éditions hollandaises de 1740 et 1741.

.... **Saint-Pierre, [Ch. I. Castel,] abbé de,** Réflexions sur l'Anti-Machiavel de 1740.
Voir 1733, Ouvraje(s) (de) Politique(s) etc.

1742
P.P. **Haren, Willem van,** Lof der Vrede. 's Gravenhage (Beauregard) 1742. 8⁰. [36 p].

1743
.... **Beweis** das die Universalmonarchie vor die Wohlfahrt von Europa und Ueberhaupt des menschlichen Geschlechts die grösste Glückseligkeit würcken würde (in der dem Grundgedanken St. Pierres zugestimmt wurde). Frankfurt 1743.
Voir aussi 1747.

.... **Saint-Pierre, Ch. I. Castel, abbé de,** Motifs pour préférer de beaucoup la voie de l'arbitrage europain.... à la voie des armes, pour terminer les différans entre deux souverains, et pour randre ainsi l'Alliance ou la Ligue europaine...
Rotterdam 1743. 8⁰. 28 p.

P.P. **Tresenreuter, Joh. Udalricus,** [Oratio de pace. Coburgi (Otto) 1743]. 4⁰. [6 p.].

1745
.... **Langendijk, Pieter,** Spoor tot een algemeenen Vrede. Haarlem (P. v. Assendelft) [1745].
Voir aussi 1751.

P.P. **Projet** d'un nouveau système de l'Europe, préférable au système de l'équilibre entre la maison de France et celle d'Autriche. S. 1. 1745. 4⁰. 32 p.
Voir l'éd. anglaise 1746.

P.P. **Sully, Maximilien de Béthune, duc de,** Mémoires. Mis en ordre, avec des remarques, par **M. L. D. L. D. L.** [= Pierre Mathurin de l'Ecluse des Loges.] [Et un supplément à la vie du duc de Sully, depuis sa retraite]. Londres [= Paris] 1745. 8 vols. 8⁰.
Voir l'éd. originale 1638.

P.P. **Sully, Maximilien de Béthune, duc de,** Mémoires. Mis en ordre, avec des remarques par **M. L. D. L. D. L.** Londres [= Paris] 1745. 3 vols. 4⁰. Ed. origin. 1638 ; 1ʳᵉ éd. M. L. D. L. D. L. Voir ci-dessus.

1746
.... **[Finch, Richard,]** The nature and duty of self-defence : addressed to the people called Quakers. London (M. Cooper) 1746. 8⁰.
Voir encore 1755 Second Thoughts....

.... **Langendijk, P.,** Herdersklagt over de Rampen des Oorlogs. Haarlem (P. van Assendelft) 1746.
Voir aussi 1751.

... **[Penington, Isaac,]** The doctrine of the people called Quakers in relation to bearing arms and fighting ; extracted from the works of a learned

and approved writer of that persuasion [with a preface by **Joseph Besse**, under the signature of « **Irenicus** »]. London (T. Sowle Raylton and L. Hinde) 1746. 8⁰.
1ʳᵉ éd. 1661 sous le titre : Somewhat spoken to a weighty question etc.

... **The new System**.... London 1746.
Voir l'éd. origin. française 1745.

.... **Trostschreiben** an alle betruebte Teutschen, die Widerwartigkeiten zu besiegen, entworfen von einem wahren Menschenfreunde. Jena 1746.

1747

.... **A modest plea** in behalf of the people called Quakers in answer to a pamphlet, intituled « The nature and duty of self-defence.... » London (C. Corbett) s. d. 8⁰ [1747 ?].

.... **An enquiry** into the validity of a late discourse intituled « The nature and duty of self-defence ». [Signed **Philanthropus = Joseph Besse**.] London (T. Sowle Raylton and L. Hinde) 1747. 8⁰. Edition suivante : s. l. s. d.

.... **Beweis** das die Universal-Monarchie vor die Wohlfahrt von Europa, und überhaupt des Menschlichen Geschlechts die grösste Glückseligkeit würcken würde. Frankfurt a/M. 1747. 1ʳᵉ éd. 1743.

.... **Loen, J. M. v.**, Entwurf einer Staatskunst worin die natürlichste Mittel entdecket werden, ein Land mächtig, reich und Glücklich zu machen. Frankfurt a/M. 1747.
Voir la 3ᵉ éd. 1751. Le titre et la date de la 2ᵉ éd. sont incertains.

.... **Projet de traité** pour rendre la paix perpétuelle entre les Souverains chrétiens, pour maintenir toujours le commerce entre les nations et affermir beaucoup davantage les maisons Souverains sur le throne.... 2ᵉ éd. S. l. 1747. 8⁰.
Voir l'éd. 1728.

P.P. **Projet** d'une paix perpétuelle et générale entre toutes les puissances de l'Europe. S. l. 1747. 16⁰. 88 p.

P.P. **Sully, Maximilien de Béthune, duc de**, Mémoires. Mis en ordre par **M. L. D. L. D. L.** Londres [= Paris] 1747. 3 vols. 4⁰.
1ʳᵉ éd. 1638 ; 1ʳᵉ éd. M. L. D. L. D. L. 1745.

.... **Sully, Maximilien de Béthune, duc de**, Mémoires. Mis en ordre par **M. L. D. L. D. L.** Londres [= Paris] 1747. 8 vols. 12⁰.
1ʳᵉ éd. 1638. 1ʳᵉ éd. M. L. D. L. D. L. 1745.

1748

P.P. **[Meijer, J.,]** De voor-bodinne der vrede verwellekomt in Nederland.... [Amsterdam (Jacobus Bremer)] 1748. 8⁰. 14 p.

P.P. **Patriotische Vorschläge**, wie zu Vermeidung blutiger Kriege unter freien Völckern dauerhafte Verträge und nach diesen Grund-Sätzen der allgemeine Friede in Europa heilsam zu schliessen. Aachen 1748. 4⁰.

P.P. **[Turretini, J. A.,]** Dilucidationes philosophico-theologico-dogmatico-morales. Lugduni Batavorum (Jaeger) 1748. 4⁰.
Pag. 419-433 : Oratio XI. seu votum pro pace Europæ.
Voir aussi 1737.

1749

P.P. **[Cahusac, L. de,]** Naïs, opéra pour la paix, représenté par l'Académie royale de musique, pour la première fois, le mardi vingt-deux avril 1749. [Musique de **Rameau**]. [Paris] 1749. 4⁰. 60 p.

.... **Langendijk, Pieter**, Op den Triumfdag over den Vreede gesloten binnen Aken. 1748. Haarlem (P. van Assendelft) [1749].
Voir aussi 1751.

.... **Pater, Lucas**, Leeuwendaal hersteld door de Vrede. Zinnespel. S. 1. 1749.

1751

.... **Langendijk, Pieter**, De gedichten van —. Haarlem (J. Bosch). 4 vols. 4⁰. — Les volumes I et II ne portent aucune date ; le vol. III est daté 1751, le vol. IV 1760.
Vol. III, p. 26-35 : Spoor tot een algemeenen Vreede.... Voir aussi 1745.
Vol. III, p. 35-45 : Herdersklacht over de Rampen des Oorlogs.... Voir aussi 1746.
Vol. III, p. 50-59 : Op den Triumfdag over den Vreede gesloten binnen Aken.... Voir aussi 1749.

P.P. **Loen, J. M. von**, Entwurf einer Staats-Kunst, worinn die natürlichste Mittel entdecket werden ein Land mächtig, reich, und glücklich zu machen. 3. Auflage. Frankfurt-Leipzig (Fleischer) 1751. 8⁰. [XIV.] 240 pag.
1ʳᵉ éd. 1747. Le titre et la date de la 2ᵉ édition sont incertains.

1752

P.P. **Loen, J. M. von**, Freie Gedanken zu Verbesserung der menschlichen Gesellschaft. 3tte verb. Aufl. Frankfurt-Leipzig (J. F. Fleischer) 1752. 8⁰.
Chapitre XIV, p. 248-295 : Von der Universal-Monarchie.

P.P. **Sully, Maximilien de Béthune, duc de,** Mémoires... Mis en ordre par **M. L. D. L. D. L.** Nouv. éd. revue et corrigée. Londres 1752. 8 vols. (8⁰ ou 12⁰ ?).
1ʳᵉ éd. 1638 ; 1ʳᵉ éd. M. L. D. L. D. L. 1745.

.... **Sully, Maximilien de Béthune, duc de ,**Mémoires... Mis en ordre par **M. L. D. L. D. L.** Genève 1752. 8 vols. 12⁰.
1ʳᵉ éd. 1638 ; 1ʳᵉ éd. M. L. D. L. D. L. 1745.

P.P. **[Toze, E.,]** Die algemeine christliche Republik in Europa, nach den Entwürfen Heinrich des Vierten.... des Abts von St. Pierre, und anderer vorgestellet.... Göttingen (Vandenhoecks seel. Witwe) 1752. 8⁰.
Même tirage que 1763, Der ewige und allgemeine Friede....

1755

.... **Comenius, J. A.**, Unum necessarium, scire quid sibi sit necessarium, in vita et morte, et post mortem. Leipzig 1755. (Traduction allemande). Voir éd. latine 1668.

P.P. **[Finch, Richard,]** Second thoughts concerning war.... by the author of a late pamphlet intitled : The nature and duty of self-defence Nottingham (M. Cooper) 1755. 8⁰.
Voir pour The nature and duty.... 1746.

1756

.... **An historical account** of the rise and establishment of the people called Quakers.... In which the doctrine of peace and obedience to Government are considered. Extracted.... By a Friend. London (J. Newbery) 1756. 8⁰.

.... **Penington, Isaac**, The doctrine of the people called Quakers, in relation to bearing arms and fighting.... [Edited with a preface by **J**. Besse under the signature of « **Irenicus** ».] Salop (J. Cotton and J. Eddowes) 1756. 8⁰.

Voir pour la 1re éd. 1661, Somewhat spoken to
a weighty question.

.... **Roman politique** sur l'état présent des affaires
de l'Amérique, ou Lettres de M*** à M***, sur
les moyens d'établir une paix solide et durable
dans les colonies.... [Par **Saintard**.] Amster-
dam-Paris (Duchesne) 1756. 12º.
Pag. 293-352 : Système d'une paix universelle
en Europe.
Autres éditions 1757 et 1779.

.... **Sully, Maximilian de Béthune, duc de,** Memoirs...
Transl. by **Charlotte Lennox.** London 1756.
3 vols.
1re éd française 1638.

1757
.... **Barclay, Robert,** Verantwoording van de ware
Christelijke Godgeleertheid.... In 't Neder-
duitsch vertaald door **J. H. Glazemaker.**
Tweede druk. Amsterdam (A. Waldorp) 1757.4º.
Voir éd. latine 1676.

P.P. **Der neutrale Philosoph** bey dermaligen krieger-
ischen Zeiten. O. O. 1757. 4º.

P.P. [**Goudar, Ange,**] La paix de l'Europe ne peut
s'établir qu'à la suite d'une longue trève, ou
projet de pacification générale.... Par **M. le
Chevalier G***** [= **Ange Goudar**]. Amsterdam
(Chastelain) 1757. 12º.
Voir aussi 1761.

.... **Roman politique** sur l'état présent des affaires
de l'Amérique, ou Lettres de M*** à M*** sur les
moyens d'établir une paix solide et durable
dans les colonies.... [Par **Saintard**.] Amsterdam
Paris (Duchesne) 1757. XLVII, 352 p. 8º.
Voir aussi les éd. 1756 et 1779.

P.P. **Sully, Maximilian de Béthune, duke of,** Memoirs..
Transl. by **Charlotte Lennox.** 2nd ed. London
1757. 5 vols. 8º.
1re éd. française 1638.

1758
.... **Lostwaters, Johan,** Reise nach Mikroseuropien.
Glückstadt 1758.

.... **Palthen, Joh. Franz v.,** Versuche zum Vergnügen.
Rostock und Wismar 1758. 8º.
Erste Sammlung, p. 71-84 : Projekt einen immer
währenden Frieden in Europa zu erhalten.

1759
.... **Aceldama** neu Faes y Gwaed.... allan o Ddau
Lythyr a 'scrifennwyd yn gyntaf yn y Jaith
Germanaidd (neu Dutch) gan.... Sorge yn
Shilberg, yn Newmark, ar y 13 a'r 14 o Hydref,
yn y Flwyddyn 1758.... Wedi ei gyhoeddi yn
Saesonaeg gan.... **George Whitfield.** A'i
gyfiaethu i'r Gymroaeg gan.... **Daniel Row-
land**... Caerfyrddin (Evan Powel) 1759.
[= **Aceldama**, ou le Champ du sang.... Tiré
de deux lettres écrites par.... Sorge de
Schildberg dans le Neumark, le 13 et 14 octobre
1758.... Traduit en anglais par.... George
Whitfield et puis traduit en Kymrique par....
Daniel Rowland. Caerfyrddin [= Carmarthen
(Evan Powel) 1759.]

P.P. [**Justi, J. H. G. von,**] Wohlgemeynte Vorschläge
eines die jetzigen unglücklichen Zeiten beseuf-
zenden Menschenfreundes auf was vor Bedin-
gungen die jetzo in Krieg befangenen Mächte
zu einem dauerhaftigen.... Frieden gelangen
könnten.... Friedensnah 1759. 4º. 54 p.

.... **Projet de paix** générale. Traduit de l'allemand
du docteur **Sertorius.** Dresde 1759.

1760
.... **Justi, J. H. G. von,** Untersuchung ob Europa in
eine Staatsverfassung gesetzt werden könne,
wobei ein immerwährender Friede zu hoffen ?
[Dans :] Historische und juristische Schriften.
Frankfurt-Leipzig 1760. Vol. I, p. 171 sqq.

1761
.... [**Goudar, Ange.**] La paix de l'Europe ne peut
s'établir qu'à la suite d'une longue guerre....
par le chevalier G*** [= **Ange Goudar**.] Amsterdam (Van der Kroe) 1761. 12º.
Voir aussi 1757.

.... **Penington, Isaac,** The works.... 2nd ed. Col-
chester (J. and Th. Kendall) 1761. 2 vols. 4º.
Vol. I, p. 227 : To the army.... Voir 1681.
Vol. I, p. 443 ; Somewhat spoken to a weighty
question.... 1re éd. 1661.

.... **Prusse, A. B.,** Vollkommen begründetes Urteil....
vom Kriege, und von den sichersten Mitteln das
Ende desselben.... zu fördern, welche zu....
schleuniger Wiederherstellung eines.... dauer-
haften Friedens abgehandelt werden. Breslau-
Leipzig 1761.

P.P. **Rousseau, J. J.,** Extrait du projet de paix per-
tuelle de Monsieur l'abbé de **Saint-Pierre.** S.
l. 1761. 16º. 114 p.

.... **Rousseau, J. J.,** Extrait du projet de paix perpétuelle de Monsieur l'abbé de **Saint-Pierre.**
Amsterdam (M. M. Rey) 1761. 12º.
Selon **B. Laserstein** (J. J. Rousseau's Schriften
Zum ewigen Frieden, Berlin 1920) il existe
quatre éditions de 1761, dont deux sont impri-
mées à Amsterdam.

.... **Rousseau, J. J.,** A project for perpetual peace.
Transl. from the French. London (M. Cooper)
1761.
Voir aussi l'éd. 1767.

.... **St. Pierre, The Abbot,** A project for settling an
everlasting peace in Europe.... Translated.
London (J. Watts) 1761.
Voir l'éd. 1714, et l'éd. orig. 1712.

P.P. **Sully, Maximilian de Bethune, duke of,** Memoirs.
To which is added the tryal of Ravaillac. The
3rd ed. London (Millar) 1761. 3 vols. 8º.
1re éd. française 1638.

1762
P.P. **Die Verwüstungen** und Schrecken des Krieges,
geschildert in einer Ode an den Herrn Professor
Gellert, von B** Leipzig (Gollner) 1762. 8º.
16 p.

P.P. **Maubert de Gouvest, [Jean-Henri,]** La paix générale ou considérations du **Docteur Man'lover
d'Oxfordt.** Mises en françois par **Maubert de
Gouvest** [= l'auteur]. [Berlin] (De l'imprimerie du futur Congrès) 1762. 16º. 267 p.

1763
P.P. **Ballhorn, L. W.,** Pax in terris profanis etiam et
bellicosissimis olim populis exoptatissimum
omnium munus prolusione succincta declara-
tur.... Hannoveræ (Schlüter) 1763. 4º. 8 p.

P.P. **Europäische Friedens-Gedanken** des grossen
Gottes.... Bey völlig wiederhergestelltem
Frieden.... besungen von **Einem beständigen
Liebhaber der Evangelischen Wahrheiten.**
Franckfurt am Mayn (Diehl) 1763. 4º. 8 p.

.... **Sully, Maximilien de Béthune, duc de,** Mémoires...
Mis en ordre par **M. L. D. L. D. L.** Nouv. éd. rev.
et corr. Londres [= Paris-Lyon] 1763. 8 vols.
12⁰. 1ʳᵉ éd. 1638 ; 1ʳᵉ éd. M. L. D. L. D. L. 1745.
Cette édition renferme le supplément.

.... **Thomas, A. L.,** Lettres sur la paix. Lyon 1763. 8⁰.

P.P. [**Toze, Eobald,**] Der ewige und allgemeine Friede
in dem durch ein beständiges Bündniss in
einem Staatskörper zu vereinigenden Christlichen Europa, nach den Entwürfen Henrichs
des Vierten, des Abts von St. Pierre und anderer
vorgestellet.... Göttingen 1763. 8⁰.
Même tirage que 1752, Die allgemeine Christliche Republik....

.... **Tucker, J.,** The case of going to war for the sake
of.... trade.... being a fragment of a greater
work. London 1763.

1764

.... **Jay, John,** Address on the advantages of peace.
Probably never printed ; voir aussi 1881
dans nos Listes provisoires 1776-1898.

1765

.... **Barclay, Robert,** An apology for the true Christian
Divinity.... The 7th ed. London (W. Richard-
son and S. Clark) 1765. 8⁰.
Voir éd. latine 1676.

.... **Barclay, Robert,** An apology for the true Christian
Divinity.... The 8th ed. Birmingham (J. Bas-
ville) 1765. 4⁰.
Voir éd. latine 1676.

1766

.... **Benezet, Anthony,** Thoughts on the nature of
war in its repugnance to the Christian Life.
Philadelphia 1766.

.... **The Fighting Sailor** turn'd peacable Christian ;
manifested in the convincement and conversion
of **Thomas Lurting.** London 1766. 8⁰.
Voir l'éd. orig. 1680.

1767

P.P. **Gaillard, [G. H.,]** Les avantages de la paix....
Paris (Regnard) 1767. 8⁰. 47 p.
Voir aussi 1806 dans nos Listes provisoires
1776-1898.

P.P. **La Harpe, [J. F.] de,** Des malheurs de la guerre
et des avantages de la paix.... Paris (Regnard)
1767. 8⁰. 40 p.

P.P. [**Lilienfeld, Jakob Heinrich von,**] Neues Staats-
Gebäude. In drey Büchern. Leipzig (Breit-
kopf) 1767. 4⁰.

.... **Rousseau, J. J.,** A project for perpetual peace.
Transl. from the French. 2nd ed. London
(M. Cooper) 1767.
1ʳᵉ éd. 1761.

P.P. **Schill, F. A.,** Pacis commendatio. [Diss. ac.]
Vitebergæ (Gerdes) 1767. 4⁰. 32 p.

P.P. **Sully, Maximilien de Béthune, duc.de,** Mémoires.
Mis en ordre, avec des remarques par **M. L. D.
L. D. L.** Nouv. éd. revue et corrigée. Londres
1767. 8 vols. 8⁰.
1ʳᵉ éd. 1638 ; 1ʳᵉ éd. M. L. D. L. D. L. 1745.

1768

P.P. **Leibniz, Godefridus Guilielmus,** Opera omnia....
collecta.... studio **Ludovici Dutens.** Genevæ
1768. 6 vols. 4⁰.
T. IV, pars III. p. 329-497 : **Cesarinus Fürstnerius.**Tractatus de jure suprematus ac legationum
Principum Germaniæ.... 1ʳᵉ éd. 1677.

T. V, p. 56-60 : Observations sur le projet d'une
paix perpétuelle de M. l'Abbé de **Saint-Pierre**...
1ʳᵉ éd. 1720.
T. V, p. 61-62 : Lettre à M. l'Abbé de **Saint-
Pierre.**

.... **Loen, J. M. von,** Freye Gedanken vom Hof, der
Policy, dem gelehrten, bürgerl. und Bauern-
stand, der Religion und einem beständigen
Frieden in Europa. 3. Aufl. Frankfurt-Leipzig
1768.

P.P. [**Sully, Maximilian de Béthune,**] duc de, Esprit
de Sully ou extrait de tout ce qui se trouve dans
les Mémoires de Béthune, duc de Sully....
concernant son administration des finances
et ses maximes de police, etc. Dresde-Varsovie
(Michel Groell) 1768. 16⁰. 374 p.
Comparer la 1ʳᵉ éd. 1638.

.... **Sully, Maximilien de Béthune, duc de,** Mémoires.
Mis en ordre.... par **M. L. D. L. D. L.** Nouv. éd.
revue, corrigée et augmentée. Londres [Amster-
dam ?] 1768. Supplément. Nouv. éd. consid.
augmentée. Amsterdam 1768. 9 vol. 8⁰.
1ʳᵉ éd. 1638 ; 1ʳᵉ éd. M. L. D. L. D. L. 1745.

1769

P.P. **De la paix** perpétuelle, par **Le Docteur Goodheart**
[= **Voltaire.**] [S. l. 1769.] 8⁰. 74 p.

1774

.... **Barclay, Robert,** An apology for the true Christian
Divinity.... (An edition published under the
sanction of the Yearly Meeting of Friends in
New England.) 1774.
Voir éd. latine 1676.

.... **Cesare, D. Bartolomeo de,** La pace della società
fondata su i doveri della christiana religione.
Napoli 1774. 8⁰. 216 p.

P.P. **Gattinara, Domenico da,** La pace. Poema epico.
Brunsuic (Vedova Bindseil) 1774. 2 parties en
1 vol. 8⁰.

1775

.... **Barclay, Robert,** An apology for the true Christian
Divinity.... (The 9th ed. in English). Phila-
delphia (J. Crukshank) 1775. 8⁰.
Voir éd. latine 1676.

P.P. **Saint-Pierre, Ch. I. Castel, abbé de,** Les rêves d'un
homme de bien, qui peuvent être réalisés ; ou
les vues utiles et pratiquables de M..., choisies
dans ce grand nombre de projets singuliers,
dont le bien public était le principe [par
P. A. Alletz]. Paris 1775. 12⁰.
Pag. 171-198 : Sur la paix. Moyens de faire
régner une Paix perpétuelle en Europe. [Partie
de l'] Extrait [de **Jean-Jacques Rousseau**] du
Projet de Paix perpétuelle de M. l'abbé de
Saint-Pierre.
Voir ci-dessus sous 1761.

.... **Sully, Maximilien de Béthune, duc de,** Mémoires.
Nouv. éd. par M. l'abbé **Baudeau.** Amsterdam
et se trouve chez tous les libraires de Paris et
du Royaume. 1775. 8⁰.
1ʳᵉ éd. 1638.
Cette édition devait avoir douze volumes, mais
l'éditeur n'en a publié que deux.

1776

.... **Barclay, Robert,** Apologie oder Vertheidigungs-
Schrift der wahren Christlichen Gottes-gelahrt-
heit,.... Germantown (Ch. Saur) 1776. 8⁰.
Voir éd. latine 1676.

Dans la liste précédente sont mentionnées sous le titre de l'édition princeps des éditions non-datées autant que nous en avions connaissance. Voir :

In the preceding list undated editions that came to our knowledge are entered under the title of the first edition.　See :

1515, Erasmus, Epistola ad Leonem X.
1515, Erasmus, Institutio.
1516, Erasmus, Querela pacis.
1517, Erasmus, Bellum.
1518, Isocrates.
1530, Erasmus, Consultatio utilissima.
1638, Sully.
1647, Rist.
1680, Lurting.
1747, Enquiry.

En dehors de ces ouvrages non-datés, nous donnons ici encore quelques autres écrits non-datés qui tombent également dans la période 1480-1776 :

Besides these undated works some more undated writings belonging to the same period 1480-1776 may be mentioned here :

A letter to the People called Quakers, on the enormous and ridiculous Inconsistency of their Conduct in refusing to find Substitutes to serve in the militia.... S. l. n. d.

Essai d'un projet pour rendre la paix de l'Europe solide et durable : Par l'établissement d'une diète générale composée des députés de tous les princes et états souverains. S. l. n. d. 8º. 80 p.

Plutarchi Oratio consolatoria ad Apollonium. Demosthenis.... Orationes Olynthiacae III.... Eiusdem de pace Oratio.... Isocratis Sermo de pace.... S. l. n. d. 8º. —

INDEX, 1480-1776

INDEX ALPHABÉTIQUE DES AUTEURS

L'index donne les noms propres ou des mots d'ordre lorsqu'il s'agit d'ouvrages sans indication d'auteur [1].

ALPHABETICAL AUTHOR INDEX

according to the name of the author, or to the first word or substantive for works without author's name [1].

---

[1] s (= suivantes) signifie que l'ouvrage mentionné a été publié en plusieurs éditions. Le titre de l'édition princeps est suivi d'une énumération de ces éditions, qui naturellement sont en outre signalées chaque fois à l'année de leur publication.

s (= suivantes) means that the work mentioned has been published in several editions. The title of the first edition is followed by an enumeration of those editions, which are, of course, entered under their successive years of issue as well.

BIBLIOGRAPHY OF THE PEACE MOVEMENT BEFORE 1899, 1776–1898

1778
.... Merkwaardige redevoering van een Kroatischen geestelijke. Amsterdam 1778.

1779
.... Embser, Joh. Val., Die Abgötterei unseres philos. Jahrhunderts. 1er Abgott. Ewiger Friede. Mannheim 1779.
.... Embser, Joh. Val., L'idolatrie de ce siècle philos. 1re idole : la paix perpétuelle. Mannheim 1779.
.... Kahrel, H. F., Oelzweig des Friedens. Marburg 1779.

1780
.... Olpe, Chr. F., Bellorum crudelitas Christ. religionis lenitate mitigata. Dresdae (1780).
.... Schlettwein, Joh. A., Der Krieg in seinen wahren .... Folgen (dans :) Archiv für den Menschen und Bürger I, pag. 367. Leipzig 1780.

1782
.... Causes politiques secrètes .... Suivies d'un projet de haut-pouvoir conservateur .... Par un Ministre d'état .... Ouvrage traduit de l'Anglais. Londres 1782.
.... Derschau, Chr. Fr. von, Ueber die Verminderung der Kriege. Dessau 1782.
.... Etrennes de l'empereur de la Chine aux souverains de l'Europe pour l'année 1782. Constantinople 1782.
.... G(argaz), P. A., Conciliateur de toutes les nations d'Europe. Passy 1782.

1785
.... Le triomphe du Nouveau-Monde par l'Ami du corps social (Jos. And. Brun). 2 vols. Paris 1785.

1786
P.P. De l'état naturel des peuples (par Gavoty). 3 vols. Paris 1786.

1787
.... Idee von der Möglichkeit eines allg. und ew. Friedens (dans :) Niederelbisches hist.-pol.-litt. Magazin I. 2, p. 935 s. (Hamburg) 1787.

1788
.... Nouvel essai sur le projet de la paix perpétuelle (par A. Polier de Saint Germain). En Suisse (Lausanne) 1788.
.... Schinly, J. G. (= Schindler), Was ist den grössern Fürsten zu rathen. Wien, etc. 1788.

1790
P.P. Pétion de Villeneuve, Discours sur le droit de faire la paix. Paris 1790.

.... Réflexions philos. sur le projet de l'abbé de Saint-Pierre par M. L. (A. M. Lemaître). 1790.
.... Tchoulkoff, M. D., Proekt traktata mejdou evropeïskimi gossoudariami. (En Russie ± 1790).

1791
P.P. Cloots, An., L'orateur du genre-humain. Paris 1791.
.... Schlettwein, J. A., Die wichtigste Angelegenheit für Europa. Leipzig 1791.

1792
P.P. Cloots, An., La république universelle. Paris, an 4 de la rédemption (= 1792 !).
.... Cloots, An., De algemeene republiek. Uit het Fransch vertaald door G. J. G. Bacot. Duinkerken 1792.
.... Le rêve d'un homme de bien réalisé. Par un républicain. An I (1792-93).
.... Projet d'instruction pour assurer la paix (par le comte de Caraman). Metz et Paris 1792.

1793
P.P. Cloots, An., Bases constit. de la république du genre-humain. Paris 1793, an II.
.... Delauney, Plan d'une pacification gén. en Europe. An II (1793-94).
P.P. Etrennes de l'orateur du genre-humain (An. Cloots). (Paris) 1793, An II.
P.P. Freimüthige Betrachtungen eines philos. Weltbürgers. 1793.

1794
.... Bouterwek, Friedr., Fünf cosmopolitische Briefe. Berlin 1794.
P.P. Cloots, An., Appel au genre humain (Paris, an II, 1794).
.... Condorcet, J. A. N. de, Esquisse d'un tableau hist. des progrès. Paris 1794/95.
.... Erasmus, Des., Antipolemus. London 1794.

1795
P.P. Epitre du vieux cosmopolite Syrach (= Kronowsky ?). Sarmatie 1795.
.... Erasmus, Des., Antipolemos. Boston 1795.
.... Erasmus, The complaint of peace. London 1795.
.... Herder, J. G., Briefe zur Beförd. der Humanität, Sammlung 5, 6. Riga 1795.
P.P. Kant, Imm., Zum ewigen Frieden. Königsberg 1795.
.... Kant, I., Projects de paix perpétuelle. Bern 1795.
.... Odes on peace and war by Whitehead, Hurd, Anstey, etc. London 1795.
.... Scenen aus der Zukunft. Görlitz bei Hausdorf 1795.
P.P. Sendschreiben des alten Weltbürgers Syrach (= Kronowsky ?). Sarmatien 1795.

.... **Williams,** J. H., War, the stumbling block of a Christian. London 1795.

1796

.... **Fichte,** J. G., (article sur „Zum ew. Frieden" de Kant dans :) **Philos. Journal** einer Gesellschaft teutscher Gelehrter. Neu Strelitz 1796.

.... **Gargas,** P. A., Contrat social. Toulon, an V (1796·97).

.... **Gargas,** P. A., Contrat social .... ou projet de decret. Toulon s.a.

.... **Gutehr,** Fr., Was ist das wichtigste für die Menschheit ? Kosmopolis 1796.

.... **Jacob,** L. H., (article sur „Zum ew. Frieden" de Kant dans :) **Annalen** der Philosophie hrsg. von Jacob, II Jahrg. Leipzig 1796, pag. 436.

P.P. **Justus Sincerus Veridicus** (= C. J. A. **Hofheim** ou **Hochheim**), Von der europäischen Republik. Altona 1796.

P.P. **Kant,** I., Zum ewigen Frieden. Frankfurt—Leipzig 1796.

.... **Kant,** I., Zum ewigen Frieden. Grätz 1796.

P.P. **Kant,** I., Zum ewigen Frieden. Neue verm. Auflage. Königsberg 1796.

.... **Kant,** I., Projet de paix perpétuelle (traduit par) Jansen et Peronneau. Paris, an IV (1796).

P.P. **Kant, Em.,** Projet de paix perpétuelle. Königsberg 1796.

P.P. **Kant,** I., Den evige Fred. I. Kjöbenhavn 1796.

P.P. **La Motte,** Lud. Al., Discutitur utrum pax perpetua pangi possit nec ne ? Stuttgardiae 1796.

.... **La paix** ! la paix ! la paix ! par un ami de son pays et de la paix (J. F. **Bourgoing**). 1796.

P.P. **Ohnmasgebliche Vorschläge** zum allg. litterarischen Frieden. Erfurt 1796.

1797

.... **Embser,** Valentin, Widerlegung des ewigen Friedensprojekts. Mannheim 1797.

P.P. **Fichte,** J. G., Grundlage des Naturrechts. 2. Theil. Jena u. Leipzig 1797.

.... **Herder,** J. G., Briefe zur Beförd. der Humanität. Sammlung 9, 10. Riga 1797.

P.P. **Imm. Kants philos. Entwurf** zum ew. Frieden. Fortgesetzt von Hermann **H(eyni)ch.** Germanien 1797.

P.P. **Julliot,** J. F., Essai moral .... sur la guerre, la paix, etc. Paris, an V, 1797.

.... **Kant,** I., Zum ewigen Frieden. Frankfurt und Leipzig 1797.

P.P. **Linde,** J. W., Irenäus über das Kriegsübel. Königsberg 1797.

.... **Stapfer,** Ph. A., De natura, conditore et incrementis reipublicae ethicae. Bernae 1797.

3

1798

.... **Friedensepistel** oder moralischer Versuch (von F. L. **Reischel**) München 1798.

.... **Goerres,** J., Der allg. Frieden ein Ideal. Koblenz, im IV. Jahre der fränk. Rep. (1798).

.... **Kants Essays** and treatises (ed. by A. F. M. Willich). London 1798.

.... **Muenscherus,** Til., An pax perpetua sit speranda ? Oratio acad. ipsis cal. Ianuariis 1798 habita.

1799

.... **Der Friedenskongress** zu Lagado im Königreiche Balnibardi, etc. Leipzig 1799.

P.P. **Sales,** J. (Delisle) de, Au gouvernement provisoire. Paris, an VIII (1799).

.... **Zouboff,** Platon, (Projet d'un nouveau partage de l'Europe afin de garantir la paix perpétuelle. En russe. Fin ·du XVIIIe siècle).

1800

P.P. **Delisle de Sales,** De la paix de l'Europe et de ses bases. Paris 1800.

.... **Gentz,** Fr. von, Ueber den ewigen Frieden (dans :) **Berliner** hist. **Journal,** Dec. 1800.

.... **Moser,** Ar.dr., Gesunder Menschenverstand über die Kunst Völker zu beglücken. (Bern 1800).

.... **Patriotische Beiträge** zum ewigen Frieden. Berlin (1800).

.... **Peace** and home preferred to war and travel. Glasgow (1800 ?).

1801

P.P. **Despinoy** (H. F. J.), Ode sur la paix. Paris, an X — 1801.

.... **Gratama,** Seerp, Oratio qua docetur .... populos ad justitiam esse natos. Groningae 1801.

1802

.... **Eschasseriaux** aîné, Tableau politique de l'Europe .... et moyens d'assurer la durée de la paix générale. Paris, Pluv. an X (1802).

.... **La paix,** système cosmopolite (par A. P. A. **Batain**). Cosmopolis (Paris) an XII (1802 !).

.... **The complaint** of peace (d'**Erasmus**). London 1802, the first year of general peace.

.... **Vision** sur la paix et la guerre par une jeune demoiselle anglaise (= Charl. **Seymour**). Londres 1802.

P.P. **Zachariä,** K. S., Janus. Leipzig 1802.

1803

.... **Malinovski,** B., (Dissertation sur la paix et la guerre. En russe) 1803 (?).

4

.... Triumvirat continental et paix perpétuelle
(par Ch. Fourier dans :) **Bulletin** de Lyon,
17 déc. 1803.

1804
.... **Christianity**, a system of peace. By T. **P(ar-
sons)**. 1804.
.... **Hints** respecting the lawfulness of self-defense.
By a Scotch dissenter. Edinburgh 1804.

1806
.... **Dean Tucker's reflections** on the terrors of
invasion. Reprinted 1806.
.... **Gaillard**, G. H., Mélanges académiques, Tome
I. Paris 1806 (p. 49 : Discours qui .... a
remporté le prix en janv. 1767).

1807
.... **Gilfillian**, S., An essay on brotherly love.
Edinburgh 1807.
.... **Peace** without dishonour. By an American
farmer. London 1807.
.... **Sainte-Marie**, L. de, Essais hist. sur l'effusion
contin. du sang humain par la guerre.
Paris 1807.

1808
.... **Du droit** public et du droit des gens (par J.
J. B. **Gondon**). 3 vols. Paris 1808.
.... **Fourier**, Ch., Théorie des quatre mouvements.
Lyon 1808.
.... **Gedanken** über die Wiederherstellung des
Gleichgewichts. Von einem Staatsmanne.
Leipzig 1808.
.... **Sermon**. The question of war with Great
Britain. Boston 1808.
P.P. **The warrior's looking-glass.** (Compiled) by G.
Beaumont. Sheffield 1808.
P.P. **Wal**, Gab. de, De conjunctione populorum.
Groningae 1808.

1809
.... **Paul**, Jean (= J. P. F. **Richter**), Dämmerungen
für Deutschland. Tübingen 1809.
.... **The mediator's kingdom** not of this world
(par D. L. **Dodge**. En Amérique) 1809.

1811
.... **De jure generis humani** .... seu de jure
gentium et cosmopolitico. (par E. F. **Georgii**). Stuttgartiae 1811.
P.P. **Krause**, K. Chr. Fr., Das Urbild der Menschheit. Dresden 1811.

1812
.... **Dodge**, D. L., War inconsistent with the
religion of Jesus Christ. (En Amérique
1812 ?).
.... **Holcombe**, Henry, The first fruits. Philadelphia 1812.

5

.... **The lawfulness** of defensive war. By a clergyman of the Church of Engl. 4th ed. London
1812.
.... **Wells**, John I., An essay on war, in two
parts. New York 1812.
.... **Worcester**, Noah, Abraham and Lot, a sermon. Concord, N. H. 1812.

1813
.... **Bogue**, Dav., On universal peace. (Discours
d'octobre 1813).
.... **Chalmers**, Thom., Thoughts on universal
peace. New York 1813.
.... **Christianity**, a system of peace. Bij T. **P(arsons)**. 2d ed. Stockport 1813.
.... **Constant de Rebecque**, Benj., De l'esprit de
conquête. Hanovre 1813.
.... **Erasmus**, Des., Plea against war. New York
1813.
.... **Parsons** (Thom.), Christianity, a system of
peace. Burlington, N. J. 1813.

1814
.... **A solemn review** of the custom of war (par
Noah **Worcester**). (En Amérique) 1814.
.... **Bell**, Benj., The evils of war and when only
it is lawful to go to war. Sangerfield, N. Y.
1814.
.... **Constant de Rebecque**, B., L'esprit de conquête. 3e éd. Paris 1814.
.... **Del Prato**, A., Dissertation sur la possibilité
d'une félicité universelle. Paris 1814.
.... **Krause**, K. C. F., Entwurf eines europ.
Staatenbundes, (dans :) **Deutsche Blätter**
IV, No. 135—174. Leipzig u. Altenburg
1814.
.... **Lathrop**, John, Discourse on the law of
retaliation. Boston 1814.
P.P. **Lips**, Al., Der allgemeine Friede. Erlangen
1814.
P.P. **Lips**, Al., Der allg. Friede. 2e Aufl. Erlangen
—Leipzig 1814.
.... **Mallinckrodt**, Arn., Was thun bey Deutschlands, bey Europa's Wiedergeburt ? Dortmund 1814.
.... **Moyen** de pacifier l'Europe ; par un *général
français* (1814).
P.P. **Paix** universelle et perpétuelle, par un *Cosmopolite*, né à Paris. Paris 1814.
P.P. **Saint-Simon**, C. H. de, et A. **Thierry**, De la
réorganisation de la société europ. Paris
1814.
.... **Smeekschrift** aan de Vereenigde Mogendheden. Leyden 1814.
.... **Traitteur**, Th. von, Europa im Frieden.
Mannheim 1814.
.... **Traitteur**, Th. von, Skizze zu einem Völkergesetzbuche. 1814.
.... **Vorschläge** zu einer organ. Gesetzgebung für
den europ. Staatenverein. Leipzig 1814.

6

1815
.... The Friend of peace. By *Philo Pacificus* (= Noah **Worcester**). Cambridge 1815 (Bulletin of the Massachusetts peace society).

P.P. A review of the arguments of Lord Kames. By *Philo Pacificus* (= N. **Worcester**). Cambridge 1815 (The friend of peace, no. II).
P.P. A solemn review of the custom of war (par N. **Worcester**). Cambridge 1815.
P.P. Adresse au congrès de Vienne par M. **de St. L.** Paris 1815.
.... **Cleveland**, A., The life of man inviolable. (En Amérique) 1815.
.... **Demonvel**, J. J. A., Lettre adressée au roi. Paris 1815.
.... **Dodge**, D. L., War inconsistent with the religion. New York 1815.
P.P. Essai sur les causes des guerres. Paris 1815.
.... **Euchel**, G., Til evig Fred. Kiöbenhavn 1815.
.... **Gayl**, Kas. Wilh. von, Ideen über Errichtung eines europ. .... Staatenbundes, (dans :) **Nemesis**, 5. Band, IV. Stück 1815, p. 449 s.
.... **Moyen** de paix perpétuelle. Par l'ami des bêtes (= **Menard**). Paris 1815.
.... **Moyen** de paix universelle (par J. M. **Dufour**). Paris 1815.
.... **Schram**, Jos., Kleiner Beytrag zum Weltfrieden. Elberfeld 1815.
.... **Wagner**, Joh. J., Der Staat. Würzburg 1815.

1816
.... **Adress**(es) and **Annual Report**(s) of .... **Peace Society**(ies) 1816.
.... The Friend of peace 1816 (voir 1815).

.... A circular letter (from the Massachusetts peace society) Cambridge 1816.
.... **Chalmers**, Thom., Thoughts on universal peace. Edinburgh 1816.
P.P. **Channing**, W. E., A sermon on war. Boston 1816.
.... **Observations** on the kingdom of peace. New York 1816.
P.P. **Sarrazin**, N. J., Le retour du siècle d'or. Metz 1816.
P.P. **Thoughts** on the practical advantages of .... peace. New York 1816.
.... **Welcker**, Fr. G., Ueber die Zukunft Deutschlands (dans :) **Kieler Blätter** II, 1816, p. 345 ss.
.... **Williams**, Thom., A discourse on the evils and the end of war. Providence 1816.
.... **Worcester**, Noah, The peace catechism. Boston 1816.

1817
.... **Address**(es) and **Annual report**(s) of ... **Peace Society**(ies) 1817.

P.P. **First ann. rep.** of the Soc. for the promotion of .... peace for 1817. London (1817).
.... The Friend of peace 1817 (voir 1815).

.... A solemn review of the custom of war (by Noah **Worcester**). Greenfield, Mass. 1817.
P.P. Circular letter in behalf of the Massach. peace soc. Boston 1817.
.... **Clarkson**, Thom., An essay on the doctrines .... of the early Christians. 2d. ed. London 1817 (Tract III of the *Peace soc.*).
.... **Demme**, H. G., Von einem allg. Friedensbund (dans :) **Allgem. Anzeiger** der Deutschen, No. 26, 1817.
.... **Letters** addressed to Caleb Strong (par *Philadelphus* = S. **Whelpley**). 2d ed. Philadelphia 1817.
P.P. **Observations** on the subject of war. By *Pacificator*. Ipswich 1817.
P.P. **Pictures** of war. By *Irenicus*. Edinburgh 1817.
P.P. **Scott**, J., War inconsistent with the doctrine .... of Jesus Christ. 2d ed. London 1817 (Tract II of the *Peace soc.*).
P.P. **Substance** of a pamphlet .... (by Noah **Worcester**). 4th ed. London 1817 (Tract I of the *Peace soc.*).
.... **Thoughts** on the practical advantages of .... peace. New York 1817.

1818
.... **Address**(es) and **Annual Report**(s) of .... **Peace Society**(ies) 1818.
.... The Friend of peace 1818 (voir 1815).

.... **Bogue**, Dav., Discourses on the millennium. London 1818.
P.P. **Dawes**, Thomas, An address to the Massachusetts peace society. Boston 1818.
.... **Dillwyn**, G., Occasional reflections. Burlington, London 1818.
.... **Elegy** supposed to be written on a field of battle. London 1818.
.... **Erasmus**, Extracts from the writings on war 3rd. ed. London 1818 (Tract IV of the *Peace soc.*).
P.P. **Letters** addressed to Caleb Strong (par *Philadelphus* = S. **Whelpley**). 3rd. ed. Providence 1818.
P.P. **Letters** addressed to Caleb Strong (par *Philadelphus* = S. **Whelpley**). London 1818.
P.P. **Paoli-Chagny**, de, Projet d'une organisation politique. Hambourg 1818.
.... **Scott**, J., War inconsistent with the doctrine. London 1818 (Tract II of the *Peace society*).
.... **Sketches** of the horrors of war .... selected by Evan **Rees**. London 1818 (Tract V of the *Peace society*).
.... The **lawfulness** of defensive war upon Christ. principles. By a clergyman of the Church of Engl. 4th. ed. Glasgow 1818.

1819

.... **Address(es)** and **Annual Report(s)** of . . . Peace Society(ies) 1819.

.... **The Friend of peace** 1819 (voir 1815).

P.P. **The Herald of peace.** Vol. I. London 1819 (Bulletin of the London Peace Soc.).

P.P. **A catalogue** of the officers . . . . of the Mass. peace soc. Cambridge 1819.

P.P. **Bogue,** Dav., On universal peace. London 1819 (Tract VI of the *Peace soc.*).

.... **Burder,** G., The tendency of Christianity. (London 1819).

P.P. **Constitution** of the Mass. peace soc. Cambridge 1819.

P.P. **Kimball,** Dan., A sermon. Boston (1819).

1820

.... **Address(es)** and **Annual Report(s)** of . . . . Peace Society(ies) 1820.

P.P. **Fourth annual report** . . . . of the Soc. for the promotion of . . . . peace for 1820. London (1820).

.... **The Friend of peace** 1820 (voir 1815).

.... **The Herald of peace.** Vol. II. London 1820.

.... **A catalogue** of the officers and members of the Mass. peace soc. 1820. Cambridge (1820).

.... **Blakslee,** S., An address before the East-Haddam branch of the Mass. peace soc. Middletown, Conn. 1820.

P.P. **Clarkson,** Th., An essay on the doctrines . . . . of the early Christians. 5th ed. London 1820 (Tract III of the *Peace soc.*).

.... **Clarkson,** Th., Essai sur les doctrines . . . . des premiers chrétiens. Londres 1820 (?).

P.P. **Erasmus,** Des., Extracts from the writings on war. 4th ed. London 1820 (Tract IV of the *Peace soc.*).

P.P. **Gallison,** John, Address, deliv. at the 4th anniversary of the Mass. peace soc. Cambridge 1820.

P.P. **Scott,** J., War inconsistent with the doctrine. 5th ed. London 1820 (Tract II of the *Peace soc.*).

P.P. **Sketches** of the horrors of war, selected . . . . by Evan Rees. 3rd ed. London 1820 (Tract V of the *Peace soc.*).

1821

.... **Address(es)** and **Annual Report(s)** of . . . . Peace Society(ies) 1821.

P.P. **Third annual report** of the . . . . Tavistock auxiliary peace soc. for 1820. Tavistock 1821.

.... **The Friend of peace** 1821 (voir 1815).

.... **The Herald of peace.** Vol. III. London 1821.

.... **Brooks,** Ch., An address deliv. before the Hingham peace soc. Boston (1821).

9

.... **Godwin,** B., A discourse on the signs of the times. Great-Missenden (1821).

.... **Narrative** of Thom. Lurting, formerly a seaman. 1821.

P.P. **Quincy,** Jos., Address deliv. at the 5th anniv. of the Mass. peace soc. Cambridge 1821.

P.P. **Schmidt-Phiseldek,** C. F. von, Der europ. Bund. Kopenhagen 1821.

P.P. **The substance** of a pamphlet . . . . (par Noah **Worcester**) 5th ed. London 1821 (Tract I of the *Peace society*).

1822

.... **Address(es)** and **Annual Report(s)** of . . . . Peace Society(ies) 1822.

.... **Journal** de la Société de la morale chrétienne 1822.

.... **The Friend of peace** 1822 (voir 1815).

P.P. **The Herald of peace.** New series, Vol. I. London 1822.

.... **Bailey,** Th., The carnival of death. London 1822.

.... **Barton,** B., Napoleon and other poems. London 1822.

.... **Bogue,** D., De la paix universelle. Londres 1822.

P.P. **Erasmus,** Des., Extraits des oeuvres sur la guerre. Londres 1822.

.... **Fourier,** Ch., Traité de l'assoc. domestique et agricole. 2 vols. Besançon, Paris 1822.

P.P. **Schmidt-Phiseldek,** C. F. von, Die Politik nach den Grundsätzen der heil. Allianz. Kopenhagen 1822.

P.P. **Scott,** J., La guerre en opposition avec la doctrine . . . . de Jésus-Christ. Londres 1822.

.... **Traduction espagnole** de quelques tracts de la Société anglaise de la paix. 1822 (?).

1823

.... **Address(es)** and **Annual Report(s)** of . . . . Peace Society(ies) 1823.

P.P. **Seventh ann. report** of the Soc. for the promotion of . . . . peace for 1823. London (1823).

.... **Journal** de la Soc. de la morale chrétienne 1823.

.... **The Friend of peace** 1823 (voir 1815).

P.P. **The Herald of peace.** New series, Vol. II. London 1823.

P.P. **An enquiry** into the accordancy of war . . . . (par Jon. **Dymond**). London 1823.

.... **Holcombe,** Henry, The martial Christian's manual. Philadelphia 1823.

P.P. **Mill,** James, Essays on government, jurisprudence, etc. London (1823 ?).

.... **Peace and war** : an essay. London 1823.

.... **Webber,** S., War, a poem. Cambridge (Mass. 1823 ?).

10

.... Williams, F. P., A true son of liberty. New York 1823

1824
.... Address(es) and **Annual Report**(s) of .... Peace Society(ies) 1824.
P.P. **Eighth ann. report** of the Soc. for the promotion of .... peace for 1824. London 1824.
P.P **Seventh ann. report** of the Rhode-Island .... peace soc. 1829. Providence 1829.
.... Journal de la Soc. de la morale chrét. 1824.
.... The Friend of peace 1824 (voir 1815).
P.P. **The Herald of peace.** New series, vol. III. London 1824.

.... An enquiry into the accordancy of war .... (par Jon. **Dymond**). 2nd ed. London 1824.
.... An enquiry into the accordancy of war .... (par Jon. **Dymond**). 3d ed. London 1824.
.... Ancillon, Fréd., Nouveaux essais de politique. Tome I. Berlin 1824 (p. 85 s. : Doutes sur de prétendus axiomes politiques).
P.P. Bigelow, Tyler, Address deliv. at the 8th anniv. of the Mass. peace soc. 1823. Boston 1824.
.... Dymond, Jon., Observations on the applicability of the pacific principles. London 1824 (Tract VII of the *Peace soc.*).
.... Ladd, William, Address deliv. at Portland, 1824, before the Peace soc. of Maine (1824).
.... Observations and reflections on various subjects. London 1824.
P.P. Sketches of the horrors of war, selected by Evan Rees. 5th ed. London 1824 (Tract V of the *Peace soc.*).

1825
.... Address(es) and **Annual report**(s) of .... Peace society(ies) 1825.
P.P. **Ninth ann. report** of the Soc. for the promotion of .... peace for 1825. London 1825.
.... Journal de la Soc. de la morale chrét. 1825.
.... The Friend of peace 1825 (voir 1815).
P.P. **The Herald of peace.** New series, Vol. IV. London 1825.

.... Hancock, Thom., The principles of peace exemplified .... London 1825.
.... Mill, James, Essays on government, etc. London 1825.
.... The essays of *Philanthropos* (= William Ladd) on peace and war. Portland, Maine 1825.
.... Thrush, Thom., A letter addressed to the king. London, York 1825.
.... Thrush, Thom., A letter addressed to the king. Cambridge, Mass. 1825.
P.P. Ware, John, Address deliv. before the Mass. peace soc. 1824. Boston 1825.

11

1826
.... Address(es) and **Annual report**(s) of .. Peace society(ies) 1826.
.... Journal de la Soc. de la morale chrét. 1826.
.... The Friend of peace 1826 (voir 1815).
.... The Herald of peace. London 1826.

.... Hancock Thom., The principles of peace exemplified .... 2d ed. London 1826.
P.P. Ladd, Will., Address deliv. at the 10th anniv. of the Mass. peace soc. Boston 1826.
P.P. **Nouveau projet** de paix perpétuelle. Paris 1826.
.... Thrush, Thom., A letter addr. to the editor of the Monthly Mag. York 1826.
P.P. Thrush, Thom., A letter addr. to the king. Providence 1826.

1827
.... Address(es) and **Annual report**(s) of .... Peace society(ies) 1827.
.... Journal de la Soc. de la morale chrét. 1827.
.... The Friend of peace 1827 (voir 1815).
.... The Herald of peace. London 1827.

.... Dymond, Jon., Observations sur l'application des principes pacifiques. Londres 1827.
P.P. Fuller, Tim., Address deliv. at the 11th anniv. of the Mass. peace soc. Boston 1827.
P.P. Peace society of Windham County. Brooklyn, Con. 1827.
P.P. The essays of *Philanthropos* (= W. Ladd) on peace and war. 2nd ed. Exeter, N. H. 1827.
.... Thrush, Thom., The apology of an officer .... York, London 1827.

1828
.... Address(es) and **Annual report**(s) of .... Peace society(ies) 1828.
.... Advocate of peace and Christian patriot. Philadelphia 1828.
.... Journal de la Soc. de la morale chrét. 1828.
.... The Harbinger of peace. Vol. I. New York 1828—29 (Bulletin of the American peace soc.).
.... **The Herald of peace.** London 1828.

P.P. Erasme, Extraits sur la guerre. 2e éd. Londres 1828
.... Hancock, Thom., An address deliv. at the 12th annual meeting of the Soc. for the promotion of .... peace. London 1828.
P.P. Hancock, Thom., The principles of peace. 3 parts. 3rd ed. London 1828 (Tract IX of the *Peace soc.*).
.... Jones, Address deliv. before the Peace soc. of Minot. Portland 1828.
.... Ladd, W., Pacific overtures for christian harmony. No. 1. 1828.
.... Mill, James, Essays on government, etc. London 1828 (?).

12

P.P. **Perkins,** E. B., Address deliv. before the Peace soc. of Windham County, 1828. Brooklyn 1828.

.... **Rogers,** I., Sermon before the Peace soc. of Temple. Portland 1828.

.... **Sellon** J. J. de, Lettres et discours.... de l'inviolabilité de la vie de l'homme. 1828.

.... **The essays** of *Philanthropos* (= W. **Ladd**) on peace and war. 1828.

.... **Thrush,** Thom., The causes and evils of war. London 1828.

.... **Thrush,** Thom., The apology of an officer.... London 1828.

P.P. **Welch,** J. A , Address deliv. before the Windham County peace soc., 1828. Brooklyn 1828.

P.P. **Worcester,** Noé, Coup d'oeil raisonné sur la guerre. Londres 1828.

P.P. **Worcester,** Sam., An address deliv. at the 12th anniversary of the Mass. peace soc., 1827. Cambridge, Mass. 1828.

1829

.... **Address(es)** and **Annual report(s)** of.... **Peace society(ies)** 1829.

P.P. **The third ann. report** of the Windham County peace soc. Brooklyn, Con. 1829.

.... **Journal** de la Soc. de la morale chrét. 1829.

.... **The Harbinger of peace,** vol. I. New York 1828—1829, vol. II 1829—1830.

.... **The Herald of peace.** London 1829.

P.P. **A solemn review** of the custom of war (par N. **Worcester**). Hartford 1829.

P.P. **Beschouwing** der beginselen.... Zutphen 1829.

P.P. **Bogue,** Dav., Paix universelle durant le millennium. Genève—Paris 1829.

.... **Dymond,** Jon., Essays on the principles of morality. 2 vols. London 1829.

.... **Erasme,** Extraits sur la guerre. 4e éd. Londres 1829.

P.P. **Examen** des principes.... par une *dame.* Londres 1829.

P.P. **Fragmens** extraits des Mémoires de Commines, etc. par J. J. de **Sellon** (p. 101—118 Fragmens des mémoires de Sully).

.... **Hancock,** Thom., The principles of peace exemplified. Philadelphia 1829.

.... **Stone,** T. T., Sermons on war. Boston 1829.

1830

.... **Address(es)** and **Annual report(s)** of.... **Peace society(ies)** 1830.

.... **Journal** de la Soc. de la morale chrét. 1830.

.... **The Harbinger of peace,** vol. II. New York 1829—1830, vol. III 1830—1831.

.... **The Herald of peace.** London 1830.

P.P. **An examination** of the principles.... by a *lady.* Stereotype ed. London 1830 (Tract VIII of the *Peace soc.*).

P.P. **Appeal** to Amer. Christians on the practice of war. New York 1830.

.... **Avis** prélim. et programme d'un concours. Genève 1830.

P.P. **Clarkson,** Th., An essay on the doctrines.... Ster. ed. London 1830 (Tract III of the *Peace soc.*).

P.P. **Dymond,** Jon., Observations on the applicability.... Ster. ed. London 1830 (Tract VII of the *Peace soc.*).

.... **Essai** sur la diplomatie, man. d'un *Philhellène* (Ad. **Czartoryski**), publié par M. Toulouzan. Marseille, Paris 1830.

P.P. **Kellogg,** E. B., War contrary to the gospel. Providence 1830.

.... **Peace** that is not peace, and true peace. Greenock 1830.

P.P. **Programme** (d'un concours ouv. par la Soc. de la paix de Genève). Genève 1830.

.... **Sellon,** J. J. de, Allocution adr. à la Soc. de la paix. (Genève) 1830.

P.P. **Sellon,** J. J. de, Lettre sur la guerre. Genève 1830.

.... **Sellon,** J. J. de, Voeux adr. au futur congrès. Genève 1830.

.... **Tit for tat.** Poems by *Q in the Corner.* London 1830.

.... **Wagner,** J. J., Organon der menschlichen Erkenntnis. Erlangen 1830.

1831

.... **Address(es)** and **Annual report(s)** of.... **Peace society(ies)** 1831.

P.P. **Archives** de la Soc. de la paix de Genève I, No. 1. 1831.

.... **Journal** de la Soc. de la morale chrét. 1831.

.... **The Calumet.** Vol. I. New series of the Harbinger of peace. New York 1831.

.... **The Harbinger of peace,** vol. III. New York 1830—1831.

.... **The Herald of peace.** London 1831.

.... **A brief illustration** of the principles of war and peace. By *Philanthropos* (= W. **Ladd**). Albany 1831.

P.P. **Bogue,** Dav., On universal peace. Ster. ed. London 1831 (Tract VI of the *Peace soc.*).

.... **Butte,** Wilh., Die Kriegsfrage. Berlin 1831.

P.P. **Davis,** G. F., Christ the prince of peace. Address.... Hartford County peace soc. Hartford 1831.

.... **De la guerre** (par **de la Gervaisais**). Paris 1831.

P.P. **Histor. illustrations** of the origin.... of war. By the author of „An examination". London 1831 (Tract X of the *Peace soc.*).

.... **L(emaître),** L(ouis), La guerre. Paris 1831.

.... **Lessore,** J. B. L., Appel des Français ....
pour l'entier désarmement. Paris 1831.

P.P. **Necker,** J., Reflections on the calamities of
war. London 1831 (Tract X I of the *Peace
soc.*).

P.P. **Règlement** de la Soc. de la paix de Genève.
Genève 1831.

P.P. **Scott,** J., War inconsistent with the doctrine ..
Ster. ed. London 1831 (Tract II of the
Peace soc.).

P.P. **Sellon,** J. J. de, Adresse aux amis de la paix.
Genève 1831.

P.P. **Sumner,** Br., An address deliv. at the 15th
anniv. of the Mass. peace soc. Boston 1831.

P.P. **The substance** of a pamphlet entitled A solemn
review .... (par N. **Worcester**). Ster. ed.
London 1831 (Tract I of the *Peace soc.*).

P.P. **Ueber Rechte** der Könige und Völker. Von
Freunden des Friedens.... Leipzig 1831.

1832

.... **Address(es)** and **Annual report(s)** of ....
Peace society(ies) 1832.

P.P. **Archives** de la Soc. de la paix de Genève,
no. 2, 1832.

.... **Journal** de la Soc. de la morale chrét. 1832.

.... **The Calumet.** New York 1832.

.... **The Herald of peace.** London 1832.

.... **A dissertation** on a congress of nations. By
Philanthropos (= W. **Ladd** ?) Boston 1832.

.... **Bogue,** Discours sur la paix universelle (avec
des notes du comte de **Sellon.** Genève)
1832.

P.P. **Bogue,** Dav., Extract from a discourse on
universal peace, 1813. (Brooklyn 1832).

.... **Chevalier,** Mich., De l'armée sous le rapport
d'amélioration morale .... (dans :) Le **Globe**
VIII, 35, 4 févr. 1832.

.... **Chevalier,** Mich., Des bruits de guerre (dans :)
Le **Globe** VIII, 9, 10 janv. 1832.

P.P. **Chevalier,** Mich., Politique industrielle (Religion Saint-Simonienne). Paris 1832.

.... **Chevalier,** Mich., Sur la guerre. (dans :) Le
Globe VIII, 11, 11 janv. 1832.

.... **Delaporte,** L., De l'application de l'armée aux
travaux publics .... (dans :) Le **Globe**
VIII, 63, 3 mars 1832.

.... **Delaporte,** L., De l'armée considérée sous le
rapport de l'amélioration du sort des
peuples. (dans :) Le **Globe** VIII, 69, 9 mars
1832.

.... **Delaporte,** L., La paix et la guerre. (dans :)
Le **Globe** VIII, 53, 22 févr. 1832.

.... **Delaporte,** L., Organisation pacifique de
l'armée. (dans :) Le **Globe** VIII, 66, 6 mars
1832.

P.P. **Dymond,** Jon., On the applicability of the
pacific principles .... 1st American from
the 2d London ed. Brooklyn 1832.

P.P. **Fragment** sur la paix, tiré d'un journal anglais
par (J. J. **de Sellon**). Genève 1832.

P.P. **Grimké,** Th. S., Address on the truth ....
of the principles of peace. Hartford 1832.

.... **Grimké,** Th. S., A letter to the people of
South-Carolina. Charleston 1832.

.... **Jefferson,** J., The unlawfulness of war. London 1832.

.... **Ladd,** Will., The hero of Macedon .... in the
light of the gospel. Boston 1832.

P.P. **Recueil** de lettres adr. aux archives de la
Soc. de la paix par (J. J. **de Sellon**). Genève
1832.

.... **Rochette,** P., Du désarmement de la France.
(dans :) Le **Globe** VIII, 44, 13 févr. 1832.

.... **Sellon,** J. J. de, Article .... à plusieurs
journaux. Genève 1832.

P.P. **Sellon,** J. J. de, Lettre à M.*** sur .... les
travaux des soc. de la paix. Genève 1832.

P.P. **Sellon,** J. J. de, Lettre .... à l'éditeur des
archives. Genève 1832.

1833

.... **Address(es)** and **Annual report(s)** of ....
Peace society(ies) 1833.

.... **Archives** de la Soc. de la paix de Genève
1833 (?).

.... **Journal** de la Soc. de la morale chrét.
1833.

.... **The Calumet.** New York 1833.

.... **The Herald of peace.** London 1833.

.... **Cahier** de lithographies rel. à la Soc. de la
paix de Genève (par J. J. **de Sellon**).
Genève 1833.

.... **Gurney,** J. J., An essay on war. London
1833.

P.P. **Hickok,** L. P., The sources of military delu-
sion. Hartford 1833.

P.P. **La guerre** est-elle une oeuvre chrétienne ?
(Par J. J. **de Sellon**.) Genève (1833).

P.P. **La guerre** est-elle une oeuvre favorable à
la civilisation ? (Par J. J. **de Sellon**. Genève
1833).

P.P. **Qu'est-ce que la Soc. de la paix ?** Publié
par un membre (= J. J. **de Sellon**). Genève
1833.

.... **Roberts,** Mary, Peace societies and the scenes .... within the last 60 years. London
1833.

.... **Sellon,** J. J. de, Lettre .... sur la séance du
1er déc. 1833. Genève 1833.

P.P. **Sellon,** J. J. de, Notice hist. sur la Soc. de
la paix. Genève 1833.

.... **Thrush,** Thom., The apology of an officer.
2d ed. London 1833.

.... **Worcester,** Noah, Friend of youth. 2d ed.
Boston 1833.

P.P. **Yale,** Cyrus, War unreasonable and unscrip-
tural. Hartford 1833.

1834

.... **Address(es)** and **Annual report(s)** of .... **Peace society(ies)** 1834.

.... **American Advocate of peace.** Hartford 1834.

.... **Archives** de la Soc. de la paix de Genève, no. 3, 1834.

.... **Journal** de la Soc. de la morale chrét. 1834.

.... **The Calumet.** New York 1834.

.... **The Herald of peace.** London 1834.

.... **A prize essay** on the evils of war. By a native of Herefordshire. Hereford 1834 (*Hereford-shire peace tract*).

.... **Adresse** du fondateur de la Soc. de la paix de Genève (**J. J. de Sellon**) aux chrétiens. Genève 1834.

.... **Dymond,** Jon., An inquiry into the accordancy of war .... with .... notes by **Grimké.** Philadelphia 1834.

P.P. **Henry,** C. S., Principles and prospects of the friends of peace. Hartford 1834.

P.P. **Linsley,** J. H., The first annual address .... Hartford peace soc. 1829. 2nd ed. Hartford 1834.

P.P. **Nassau,** H. J., Hist. proeve over den gunstigen invloed .... oorlogen der oude geschiedenis .... Groningen 1834.

P.P. **Reflections** on the nature and dignity of the enterprise .... 1834.

.... **Roberts,** Sam., Thoughts on war. London 1834.

P.P. **Veit,** Mor., Saint Simon und der Saintsimonismus. Leipzig 1834.

.... **War** unchristian. 1834 (Tract **J** of the *Connecticut peace soc.*).

P.P. **Ware,** Henry, The promise of universal peace. Boston 1834.

1835

.... **Address(es)** and **Annual report(s)** of .... **Peace society(ies)** 1835.

.... **American Advocate of peace.** Hartford 1835.

.... **Archives** de la Soc. de la paix de Genève 1835 (?).

.... **Journal** de la Soc. de la morale chrét. 1835.

.... **The Calumet.** New York 1835.

.... **The Herald of peace.** London 1835.

.... **Channing,** W. E., A sermon on war. Boston 1835.

P.P **Clarkson,** Th., An essay on the doctrines .... London 1835 (Tract III of the *Peace soc.*).

P.P. **Dissertation** sur la cause primitive des guerres .... par un Ami de l'humanité (= J. J. de Sellon ?). Genève 1835.

P.P. **Dymond,** Jon., An inquiry into the accordancy of war .... 4th ed. Philadelphia 1835.

P.P. **Mackintosh,** James, A discourse on the study of the law of nature and nations. Edinburgh 1835.

P.P. **Neale,** R. H., The 4th ann. address of the Connecticut peace soc. Hartford 1835.

.... **Notice sur** .... la Soc. de la paix de Genève (par J. J. **de Sellon** ?) Genève (1835).

P.P. **Récit** succinct de .... la séance de la Soc. de la paix de Genève du 10 juillet 1835. (Par J. J. **de Sellon.**) Genève 1835.

.... **Reflections** on the nature and dignity .... Hartford 1835 (Tract II of the *Conn. peace soc.*).

P.P. **Report** (of) the committee of the Senate (of Massachusetts on) the petition of **Thompson** and **Ladd** (concerning) the abolition of war. (1835).

.... **Sellon,** J. J. de, Lettre à M. les rédacteurs .... Genève 1835.

.... **Sellon,** J. J. de, Notice sommaire .... Genève 1835.

1836

.... **Address(es)** and **Annual report(s)** of .... **Peace society(ies)** 1836.

.... **American Advocate of peace.** Hartford 1836.

.... **Archives** de la Soc. de la paix de Genève 1836 (?).

.... **Journal** de la Soc. de la morale chrét. 1836.

.... **The Herald of peace.** London 1836.

.... **Kurzer Inbegriff** der Arbeiten des Grafen von Sellon. Genf 1836.

P.P. **Liste** raisonnée des écrits publiés par le comte de Sellon. Genève 1836.

P.P. **A solemn appeal** to Christians .... By *Philanthropos* (= W. **Ladd**). Ster. ed. Boston 1836 (Tract II of the *Amer. peace soc.*).

.... **Copie** d'une lettre autogr. de S. M. le *roi de Prusse* au Comte de Sellon. Berlin 1836.

P.P. **Dymond,** Jon., Essays on the principles of morality. 3rd ed. London 1836.

.... **Ladd,** Will., The history of the peace societies. Boston 1836.

P.P. **Programme** d'un concours ouv. par le fond. de la Soc. de la paix de Genève. (Genève 1836).

.... **Sigourney,** L. H., Olive buds. Hartford, Con. 1836.

.... **Stebbins,** R. P., Address on the subject of peace. Boston 1836.

P.P. **Upham,** Th. C., The manual of peace. New York 1836.

1837

.... **Address(es)** and **Annual report(s)** of .... **Peace society(ies)** 1837.

.... **Advocate of peace,** publ. by the American peace soc. Boston 1837.

P.P. **Archives** de la Soc. de la paix de Genève, no. 4, 1837.

.... Journal de la Soc. de la morale chrét. 1837.
.... The Herald of peace. London 1837.

.... Allen, Will., Defensive war. A letter to W. Ladd. (En Amérique 1837 ?).
.... Dissertation on the subject of a congress of nations. Bij *a friend of peace* (= Or. Bacheler). New York 1837.
.... Letters from an American (par *Philanthropos* = W. Ladd). London (1837).
P.P. Obstacles and objections to the cause of .... peace, by *a layman*. Boston 1837.
P.P. Sartorius, J. B., Organon des vollkommenen Friedens. Zürich 1837.

1838
.... Address(es) and Annual report(s) of .... Peace society(ies) 1838.
.... Advocate of peace. Boston 1838.
.... Journal de la Soc. de la morale chrét. 1838.
.... The Herald of peace. London 1838.

P.P. Actien-Verein zum Frieden, (dans :) Leipzig —Berlin—Dresdner Dampfwagen 1838, No. 4.
.... Chevalier, Mich., De ijzerbanen. Vrij gevolgd naar het Fransch. Rotterdam 1838.
.... Declaration of sentiments .... Peace convention in Boston (par W. L. Garrison). Boston 1838.
.... Flournoy, John J., An earnest appeal for peace. Athens, Georgia 1838.
P.P. Hancock, Th., The principles of peace exemplified. Ster. ed. London 1838 (Tract IX of the *Peace soc.*).
.... Hancock, Th., The principles of peace exemplified. Boston 1838.
P.P. Letters of *Lillian Ching* .... to which is added the apology of St. Thurston. Portland 1838.
P.P. Welcker, C. Th., Friede, Friedensstand, etc. (dans :) Staats-Lexikon hrsg. von v. Rotteck u. Welcker. Bd. VI. Altona 1838.
.... Whipple, Ch. K., Dialogues between Frank and William. Boston 1838.

1839
.... Address(es) and Annual report(s) of .... Peace society(ies) 1839.
.... Advocate of peace. Boston 1839.
.... Journal de la Soc. de la morale chrét. 1839.
.... The Herald of peace. London 1839.

.... Bolles, J. A., Essay on a congress of nations. Boston 1839.
P.P. Bonaparte, Nap.-Louis, Des idées napoléoniennes. Londres 1839.
.... Channing, W. E., Lecture on war. Boston 1839.

P.P. Gurney, J. J., An essay on war. Ster. ed. London 1839 (Tract XII of the *Peace soc.*).
.... Lord, John, An address deliv before the Peace soc. of Amherst college. Amherst 1839.
.... Pecqueur, C., Economie sociale. 2 vols. Paris 1839.
P.P. Principles of the Non-resistance society. Boston 1839.
P.P. Siñeriz, J. F., Constitucion europea. Madrid 1839.
P.P. The substance of a pamphlet, entitled A solemn review (par N. Worcester). Ster. ed. London 1839 (Tract I of the *Peace soc.*).
.... Whipple, Ch. K., Evils of the revolutionary war. Boston 1839.

1840
.... Address(es) and Annual report(s) of .... Peace society(ies) 1840.
.... Advocate of peace. Boston 1840.
.... Journal de la Soc. de la morale chrét. 1840.
.... The Herald of peace. London 1840.

P.P. All war antichristian. London 1840 (Tract I—XIII of the *Peace soc.*).
.... Bjerregaard, H., Er den evige fred en saadan chimaere. Randers 1840.
P.P. Considérant, V., De la politique générale. Paris 1840.
.... Eichthal, Gust. d', De l'unité européenne. Paris 1840.
.... Gurney, Jos. J., An address to ministers of the gospel. London—Norwich 1840.
.... Ladd, W., An essay on a congress of nations. Boston 1840.
.... Ladd, W., The duty of women. Boston 1840.
P.P. Obstacles and objections to the cause of .... peace. London 1840 (Tract XIII of the *Peace soc.*).
P.P. Prize essays on a congress of nations. Boston 1840.
.... Taparelli, Luigi, Saggio teoretico di diritto naturale. Palermo 1840.
.... The essays of *Philanthropos* (= W. Ladd) on peace and war. 1840.
.... Wagner, Joh. J., Der Staat. 2e Aufl. Ulm 1840.

1841
.... Address(es) and Annual report(s) of .... Peace society(ies) 1841.
.... Advocate of peace. Boston 1841.
.... Journal de la Soc. de la morale chrét. 1841.
.... The Herald of peace. London 1841.

.... Beckwith, G. C., Eulogy on Will. Ladd. Boston 1841.
.... Bouvet, Fr., Lettre à M. Guizot sur la paix. Nantua 1841.

.... **Durand,** Ferd., Des tendances pacifiques de la soc. europ. Paris 1841.

.... **Essay** on peace (par James **Richardson**). Malta 1841.

.... **Lamartine,** A. de, La Marseillaise de la paix. Mai 1841.

P.P. **Macnamara,** H. T. J., Peace, permanent and universal. London 1841.

.... **The unlawfulness** of all wars. (Signé par George **Stacey**.) London 1841.

1842

.... **Address(es)** and **Annual report(s)** of . . . . Peace society(ies) 1842.

.... **Advocate of peace.** Boston 1842.

.... **Journal** de la Soc. de la morale chrét. 1842.

.... **The Herald of peace.** London 1842.

P.P. **Bazan,** P., D'une paix universelle et permanente. Paris 1842.

P.P. **Coues,** Sam. E., War and Christianity. Boston 1842.

.... **Die Unvereinbarkeit** des Krieges . . . . mit den Lehren des Evangeliums. (Signé par George **Stacey**.) London 1842.

.... **Distribution** of prizes in . . . . Paris on the subject of peace. London 1842.

P.P. **Gurney,** J. J., Observations on the . . . . views and practices of the Soc. of Friends. A new ed. Norwich—London 1842 (pag. 367—403 On war).

P.P. **Jay,** Will., War and peace. New York 1842.

P.P. **Jay,** Will., War and peace. London 1842.

P.P. **Joubleau,** F., (Mémoire sur la paix perpétuelle. 1842. *Ouvrage manuscrit*).

.... **Judd,** Sylv., A moral review of the revolutionary war. Hallowell, Maine 1842.

P.P. **Marchand,** P. R., Nouveau projet de traité de paix perpétuelle. Paris 1842.

P.P. **Pecqueur,** C., De la paix. Paris 1842.

.... **Pecqueur,** C., Des armées dans leurs rapports avec l'industrie, etc. Paris 1842.

.... **The unlawfulness** of all wars. (Signé par G. **Stacey**.) London 1842.

.... **Upham,** Th. C., The manual of peace. Boston 1842.

1843

.... **Address(es)** and **Annual report(s)** of . . . . Peace society(ies) 1843.

.... **Advocate of peace.** Boston 1843.

.... **Journal** de la Soc. de la morale chrét. 1843.

.... **The Herald of peace.** London 1843..

.... **The Peace Advocate** and Correspondent. Series I. London—Newcastle-on-Tyne 1843.

.... **Bentham,** Jeremy, Works, ed. John Bowring. Edinburgh 1843 (Vol. II, p. 356 s. „A plan for an universal and perpetual peace").

21

.... **Blanchard,** J. P., Preparations for war. (London 1843).

.... **Congrès** de la paix, 1843.

P.P. **Dymond,** Jon., An inquiry into the accordancy of war . . . . 4th ed. London 1843.

P.P. **Peabody,** Andr. P., The nature and influence of war. Boston 1843.

.... **The cause** of the heavy burdens of Great Britain. London 1843.

P.P. **The proceedings** of the first gen. Peace Convention held in London. London 1843.

1844

.... **Address(es)** and **Annual report(s)** of . . . . Peace society(ies) 1844

.... **Advocate of peace.** Boston 1844.

.... **Journal** de la Soc. de la morale chrét. 1844.

.... **L'Olivier** ou résumé hist. des opérations des soc. de la paix. Paris 1844.

.... **The Christian Citizen,** ed. by El. **Burritt.** Worcester, Mass. 1844.

.... **The Herald of peace.** London 1844.

.... **The Peace advocate** and corr. London—Newcastle 1844.

P.P. **An address** to the Dutch public on the evils of war. Amsterdam 1844.

.... **Beckwith,** G. C., A universal peace society. Boston 1844.

P.P. **Channing,** Walter, Thoughts on peace and war. Boston 1844.

.... **Duncan,** Phil. B., The motives of war. London 1844.

P.P. **Fallati,** J. F., Die Genesis der Völkergesellschaft, (dans :) **Zeitschr.** f. d. ges. **Staatswiss.** I, 1844, p. 160 s.

.... **Hall,** Edw. B., Christians forbidden to fight. Providence 1844.

.... **Jewell,** Joseph, Peace pleading for peace and good will . . . . 1844.

.... **Kemper,** Jer. de Bosch, De publieke opinie als middel om den vrede te bewaren, (dans :) De **Tijdgenoot.** IV, 1844.

.... **Progress** of peace. Boston 1844.

P.P. **Report** . . . . on the petition of J. P. Andrews for the promotion of univ. peace. (Boston) 1844.

.... **Rice** Jr., Roswell, Orations on intemperance, war and the atonement. 1844.

.... **Ware,** Henry, Memoirs of the Rev. N. Worcester. Boston 1844.

1845

.... **Address(es)** and **Annual report(s)** of . . . . Peace society(ies) 1845.

.... **Advocate of peace.** Boston 1845.

.... **Journal** de la Soc. de la morale chrét. 1845.

.... **L'Olivier.** Paris 1845.

.... **The Christian Citizen.** Worcester, Mass. 1845.

.... **The Herald of peace.** London 1845.

22

.... The **Peace advocate** and corr. London—New-castle 1845.

.... **Comings,** A. G., The reign of peace. Boston 1845.

P.P. **Durand,** Ferd., Des tendances pacif. de la société europ. 2e éd. Paris 1845.

.... **Gannett,** E. S., Peace — not war. Boston 1845.

.... **Huntingdon,** Fr. D., The famine and the sword. Boston 1845.

.... **Incompatibilité** de la guerre.... (Signé par G. **Stacey.**) Londres 1845.

P.P. **Jay,** Will., An address deliv. before the American peace soc. Boston 1845.

.... **Langermann,** Lettre adr. à M. de Stassart. Bruxelles 1845.

.... **Sumner,** Ch., The true grandeur of nations. New York 1845.

P.P. **Taparelli,** Aloys, Versuch eines.... Natur-rechts. Aus dem Ital. Regensburg 1845.

P.P. **The book of peace.** Boston 1845.

.... **The unlawfulness** of all wars. (Signé par G. **Stacey.**) London 1845.

1846
.... **Address(es)** and **Annual report(s)** of.... Peace society(ies) 1846.

.... **Advocate of peace** and univ. brotherhood. Worcester, Mass. 1846.

P.P. **Bond of brotherhood.** Conducted by El. **Burritt.** London, Birmingham and Worcester, Mass. 1846.

.... **L'Olivier.** Paris 1846.

.... **The Christian Citizen.** Worcester, Mass. 1846.

.... **The Herald of peace.** London 1846.

.... **The Peace advocate** and corr. London—New-castle 1846.

.... **Ballou,** Adin, Christian non-resistance. Phi-ladelphia 1846.

P.P. **Bowring,** John, The polit. and commercial importance of peace. London (1846 ?).

P.P. **Hood,** E. P., An encyclopaedia of facts, etc. in support of.... perm. and univ. peace. Manchester, London 1846.

.... **Howitt,** Marie, Memoir of El. Burritt, (dans :) The **people's journal** 1846, p. 241—246.

.... **Huntingdon,** F. D., Peace, the demand of Christianity. Boston 1846.

.... **Jackson,** John, Reflections on peace and war. Philadelphia 1846.

.... **Parker,** Theod., A sermon on war. Boston 1846.

.... **Richard,** Henry, Defensive war ; extracted from a lecture. London 1846.

.... **Sharp,** Dan., Plea for peace. 2d ed. Boston 1846.

.... **Sumner,** Ch., The true grandeur of nations. London 1846.

.... **Wright,** Henry C., Defensive war proved to be a denial of Christianity. London 1846.

23

1847
.... **Address(es)** and **Annual report(s)** of .. Peace society(ies) 1847.

.... **Advocate of peace.** Boston 1847

P.P. **Bond of brotherhood.** London, Birmingham and Worcester, Mass. 1847.

.... **The Christian Citizen.** Worcester, Mass. 1847.

.... **The Herald of peace.** London 1847.

.... **The Peace advocate** and corr. London, New-castle 1847.

P.P. **Beckwith,** G. C., The peace manual. Boston 1847.

.... **Bjerregaard,** H., Er ikke en profetisk spaa-dom .... gaaet i opfyldelse ? Randers 1847.

.... **Burritt,** El., Sparks from the anvil. London 1847.

.... **Parker,** Theod., Speech deliv. at the anti-war-meeting 1847.

.... **Peace** (permanent and univ.) the law of Christ. London 1847.

.... **Sumner,** Ch., Fame and glory. An oration before.... Amherst College, Aug. 1847.

.... **Tilden,** W. Ph., All war forbidden by Christi-anity. Dover 1847.

1848
.... **Address(es)** and **Annual report(s)** of.... Peace society(ies) 1848.

.... **Advocate of peace.** Boston 1848.

P.P. **Bond of brotherhood.** London, Birmingham and Worcester, Mass. 1848.

.... **The Christian Citizen.** Worcester, Mass. 1848.

.... **The Herald of peace.** London 1848.

.... **The Peace advocate** and corr. London, New-castle 1848.

.... **Adresses** amicales du peuple anglais au peuple francais. Paris 1848.

P.P. **Ballou,** Adin, Christian non-resistance. Lon-don, etc. 1848.

.... **Blanchard,** J. P., Communications on peace. Boston 1848.

.... **Burritt,** El., Voices from the forge. London 1848.

.... **Channing,** W. H., Memoir of W. E. Chan-ning. 3 vols. Boston 1848.

P.P. **Cobden** und die Weltfriedensmänner. Augs-burg 1848. (Extrait du „Allg. Zeitung", 6 févr. 1848, p. 585).

P.P. **Considerations** respecting the lawfulness of war (par R. **Carpenter**). New York (1848).

.... **Dewey,** Orv., An address before the Am. peace soc. Boston 1848.

.... **Feugueray,** H., De la fédération européenne, (dans :) **Revue** nationale, 23 mars 1848.

.... **Gallatin,** Alb., War expenses. New York 1848.

.... **Hudson,** Ch., Non-resistance. Boston 1848.

24

.... **Mackay,** Charles, (Articles sur les Etats-Unis d'Europe dans :) **The London Telegraph,** mars et avril 1848.

.... **Manifestation** à Manchester en faveur de la liberté du commerce et de la paix. (dans :) **Journal** des économistes 1848.

P.P. **Nunes da Costa,** M. v., Coup-d'-oeil sur les événements, les voeux, ... d'établir une paix durable. (Amsterdam 1848).

.... **Parker,** Theod., A sermon on the Mexican war. 1848.

.... **Report** of the speeches .... at the conference and publ. meetings in London, Birmingham and Manchester (1848).

.... **Rolland,** Pauline, De l'esprit de paix et de fraternité humaine, (dans :) **Revue sociale,** janv. 1848.

.... **The Peace congress** at Brussels, sept. 1848 London 1848.

.... **Wagner,** J. J., Der Staat. 2e Ausg. Ulm 1848.

1849
.... **Address(es)** and **Annual report(s)** of .... Peace society(ies) 1849.

.... **Advocate of peace.** Boston 1849.

P.P. **Bond of brotherhood.** London and Worcester, Mass. 1849.

.... **The Christian Citizen.** Worcester, Mass. 1849.

.... **The Herald of peace.** London 1849.

.... **The Peace advocate** and corr. London, Newcastle 1849.

P.P. **Ballou,** Adin, Christian non-resistance. Questions answered. (Hopedale, Mass. 1849 ?)

.... **Berry,** Phillip, A review of the Mexican war on Chr. principles. Columbia, South Car. 1849.

.... **Boissenaux,** Des moyens de pacification générale. Paris 1849.

.... **Bridge,** J. D., The character of war. Worcester 1849.

.... **Chevalier,** Mich., Lettre au meeting de Londres, (dans :) **Journal** des économistes 1849, tome XXIV, pag. 434—436.

P.P. **Clairville et Saint-Yves,** Le congrès de la paix. A-propos en un acte. (Paris 1849).

.... **Concours** institué par les Soc. anglo-américaines de la paix au congrès de Bruxelles, 1848. Rapport des commissaires. Bruxelles 1849.

P.P. **Congrès** des amis de la paix univ., réuni à Bruxelles, en 1848. Bruxelles 1849.

P.P. **Desnoyer,** Ch., Le congrès de la paix. Vaudeville en un acte. (Paris 1849.)

.... **Dresser,** Amos, The bible against war. Oberlin 1849.

.... **Edmond,** Ch. (= Ch. E. **Choieçki**), La paix et la guerre. Paris 1849.

.... **Fleck,** F. F., Der Krieg und der ewige Frieden. Leipzig 1849.

P.P. **Gallic gleanings.** By a *lady.* London (1849).

.... **Gibbes,** G. M., A letter to the American peace soc. Paris 1849.

.... **Girardin,** E. de, Abolition de l'esclavage militaire. 1849.

.... **Girardin,** E. de, Etudes politiques. Nouv. éd. Paris 1849.

.... **Girardin,** E. de, Les 52. Paris 1849 et suiv. (Contient e.a. La politique de la paix).

.... **Hugo,** Victor, The united states of Europe. Speech at Paris peace congress, 1849. London (1849).

.... **Krig,** civilisationens, humanitetens, etc. fjende. (Par V. C. E. **Børgesen.**) København 1849.

.... **Martin,** Ch., Un grognement pour le congrès de la paix. Paris 1849.

.... **Mazzini,** Gius., La santa alleanza dei popoli. Torino 1849.

.... **Our wars** in India. (London 1849 ?)

.... **Pyne,** T., Britain's mission. (1849 ?)

P.P. **Report** of the proceedings of the 2d general peace congress, held in Paris, 1849. London 1849.

.... **Rupp,** Jul., Der ewige Friede (et autres articles dans :) **Volksbote,** Königsberg mai— décembre 1849.

.... **Sagra,** Ramon de la, Utopie de la paix. Extraits. Paris 1849.

.... **Sumner,** Ch., The war system of the commonwealth. Boston 1849.

.... **Suringar,** (F. W. N.) Discours prononcé le 23 août 1849 (au Congrès de la paix). Paris 1849.

P.P. **The question** of arbitration in the House of Commons. London (1849).

.... **The soldier's progress,** from designs by J. Gilbert .... with a few words on peace and war (par El. **Burritt**). London (1849 ?)

1850
.... **Address(es)** and **Annual report(s)** of .... **Peace** society(ies) 1850.

.... **Advocate** of **peace.** Boston 1850.

P.P. **Bond of Brotherhood.** London and Worcester, Mass. 1850.

.... **The Christian Citizen.** Worcester, Mass. 1850.

.... **The Herald of peace.** London 1850.

.... **Bastiat,** F., Lettre au président du Congrès de la paix à Francfort en 1850.

P.P. **Beckwith,** Geo. C., Peace and government. (Boston, Mass. 1850 ?)

.... **Biedermann,** Karl, Offener Brief an die Gesellschaft der Friedensfreunde. Leipzig 1850.

.... **Brialmont,** Eloge de la guerre ou réfutation des doctrines des amis de la paix. Bruxelles 1850.

P.P. **Congrès** des amis de la paix universelle réuni à Paris en 1849. Paris 1850.

P.P. **Considérant,** Victor, La dernière guerre et la paix définitive en Europe. Paris 1850.

P.P. Eine ernste Untersuchung über den Gebrauch Krieg zu führen.... (par Noah Worcester). Hannover 1850.

P.P. Gruenhagen, Friedrich, Ein Wort an und für die Friedensvereine. Königsberg 1850.

.... Hancock, Thomas, Die Grundsätze des Friedens, veranschaulicht.... London 1850.

.... La guerre (par Bortier). Paris 1850.

.... Labour, A., Les amis de la paix dans l'antiquité (dans :) Journal des économistes, I, 26, p. 84—88.

.... Livermore, Abiel Abbot, The war with Mexico reviewed. Boston 1850.

.... Morhange, Ed., Mémoire sur la paix universelle. Bruxelles 1850.

.... Reden, Frhr. von, Zuschrift an den Kongress der Friedensfreunde. Frankfurt a. M. 1850.

.... Report of the speeches and proceedings at the conference.... held in London Birmingham and Manchester. 1850.

P.P. Report of the proceedings of the 3rd General Peace Congress. London 1850.

.... Rupp, Jul., Der Friedenscongresz und die Presse (et autres articles dans :) Volksbote, Königsberg 1850.

.... Stone, A. L., Address before the American peace society 1850.

.... The sailor's progress.... exhibiting some of the horrors of war.... With a few words on peace and war (par Ch. Sumner). London (1850?).

.... Trois meetings des amis de la paix, à Londres .... Paris 1850.

1851

.... Address(es) and Annual report(s) of.... Peace society(ies) 1851.

.... Advocate of peace. Boston 1851.

P.P. Bond of Brotherhood. London and Worcester, Mass. 1851.

.... Der Völkerfriede (supplément du Volksbote, 4 nos). Königsberg 1851.

.... The Christian Citizen. Worcester, Mass. 1851.

P.P. The Herald of peace. London 1851.

.... Blanchard, J. P., To the members of the American peace society. Boston 1851.

.... Buckingham, J. S., An earnest plea for the reign of temperance and peace.... London 1851.

.... Burritt, El., Peace paper for the people. London 1851.

.... Dymond, Jon., Bemerkungen über die Anwendbarkeit der Friedensgrundsätze.... London 1851.

.... Dymond, Jon. Observations sur l'application des principes pacifiques.... Paris (1851).

.... Garnier, Jos., L'exposition universelle (de Londres en 1851) et la paix (dans :) Journal des économistes I, 29, p. 177—180.

.... Gasc, Ferd. E. A., Lettres à M. Ramon de la Sagra sur l'utopie de la paix. Paris 1851.

27

.... Girardin, E. de, Abolition de l'esclavage militaire. Paris 1851.

.... Gurney, Jos., Eine Abhandlung über den Krieg.... unter der Christl. Heilsordnung. London 1851.

.... Krause, K. C. F., Das Urbild der Menschheit. 2e Ausg. Göttingen 1851.

.... Peace (On universal peace). London 1851.

.... Report of the proceedings of the 4th General Peace Congress. London 1851.

.... Rupp, Jul., Das verschiedene Verhalten zum Kriegsdienst (et autres articles dans :) Volksbote. Königsberg 1851.

.... Simples réflections sur les séances du Congrès de la Paix, par le plus humble de ses membres. Francfort a.M. 1851.

.... Spiess, G. A., Gedanken über die Bildung von Friedens-Vereinen in Deutschland. Frankfurt a. M. 1851.

P.P. Verhandlungen des dritten allgemeinen Friedenscongresses.... 1850. Frankfurt a. M. 1851.

1852

.... Address(es) and Annual Report(s) of .... Peace society(ies) 1852.

.... Advocate of peace. Boston 1852.

P.P. Bond of Brotherhood. London and Worcester, Mass. 1852.

.... The Herald of peace. London 1852.

.... Burritt, El., The olive leaf movement. London (1852).

P.P. Dymond, Jon., Essays on the principles of morality. 5th ed. London 1852.

P.P. Girardin, E. de, La politique universelle. Bruxelles, etc. 1852.

.... Jay, Will., The Kossuth excitement : a letter. Boston 1852.

.... Mazzini, Gius., Europe, its condition and its prospects (dans:) Westminster Review, April 1852.

.... People-diplomacy (par El. Burritt). London (1852).

.... Petition on behalf of the religious society of Friends against the.... military bill. 1852.

1853

.... Address(es) and Annual Report(s) of .... Peace Society(ies) 1853.

.... Advocate of peace. Boston 1853.

P.P. Bond of brotherhood. London and Worcester, Mass. 1853.

P.P. The Herald of peace. London 1853.

P.P. Justus, Siegfr., Ueber die Bedeutsamkeit der heil. Stättenfrage und ihren Einfluss auf das Friedenssystem. Berlín 1853.

P.P. Kant, Emm., Éléments métaphys. de la doctrine du droit. Suivis d'un essai philos. sur la paix perpétuelle.... Traduit par Jules Barni. Paris 1853.

28

P.P. **Kant,** Emm., Principes métaphys. du droit suivis du Projet de paix perpét. 2me éd. en français. Paris 1853.

.... **Opinions** of modern philosophers and statesmen. (Tract of the *Peace Soc.*) 1853.

.... **Report** (of the proceedings at the peace conference in) Edinburgh 1853.

P.P. **Report** of the proceedings at the peace conference held in Manchester. Manchester 1853.

1854

.... **Address(es)** and **Annual Report(s)** of .... **Peace Society(ies)** 1854.

.... **Advocate of peace.** Boston 1854.

P.P. **Bond of brotherhood.** London and Worcester, Mass. 1854.

.... **The Herald of peace.** London 1854.

.... A **christian appeal** from the society of Friends to their fellow-countrymen. (Signé par Rob. **Forster.** London) 1854.

.... A **sermon** preached on the day of general .... prayer. Guildford (1854).

P.P. **Allen,** Will. H., Tendencies of the age to peace. Boston 1854.

.... An **address on peace.** Issued by the yearly meeting of Friends for New England. (1854.)

.... **Appel chrétien** de la Société des Amis à leurs concitoyens (signé Londres, Rob. **Forster**). 1854.

.... **Bright,** John, War with Russia. Speech in the House of Commons. London 1854.

.... **Burritt,** El., Thoughts of things at home and abroad. Boston 1854.

.... **Channing,** W. H., Memoir of W. E. Channing. Boston 1854.

.... **Corvaja,** G., La pace ossia l'impero delle cifre .... Malta 1854.

.... **Dodge,** D. L., Memorial consisting of an autobiography .... Boston 1854.

.... **Evans,** B., The duty of Christians in relation to war. London (1854).

.... **Girard,** J. de, Les bienfaits de la paix .... poème .... Paris 1854.

.... **Girardin,** E. de, La politique universelle. Paris 1854.

.... **Guthrie,** Thom., The war in some of its aspects. Edinburgh (1854).

.... **Harston,** Edw., The war in the East. A sermon. London 1854.

.... **Hervé,** Ed., Quelques réflexions sur la paix, ... (dans :) **Journal** des économistes, 1854, II, p. 57—65.

.... **Massié,** James W., The contrast : War and Christianity. London 1854.

.... **Mr. Bright's reply** to Lord J. Russell. Speech .... on the Foreign enlistment bill. London 1854.

.... **Prize essays** on a congress of nations. 2d ed. Boston 1854.

P.P. **Smith,** Gerrit, Speech on war in Congress. Washington, D.C. 1854.

.... **Some account** of a deputation .... to the Emperor of Russia. London 1854.

.... **Sturge,** Joseph, The Russian war. (Birmingham 1854.)

P.P. **Summer,** Ch., The war system of the commonwealth of nations. 2d ed. (Boston 1854 ?).

P.P. **The letter** of John Bright .... on the war verified .... London (1854).

.... **The York peace handbills.** York—London (1854).

.... **Wagner,** J., Erläuterungen zum Organon der menschlichen Erkenntnis. Nach dessen Vorträgen hrsg. Ulm 1854.

P.P. **Wie vermeidet man in Europa Kriege ?** (dans :) **Unterhaltungen** am häusl. Herd, II (1854), 22, pag. 350—352.

1855

.... **Address(es)** and **Annual Report(s)** of .... **Peace Society(ies)** 1855.

.... **Advocate of peace.** Boston 1855.

P.P. **Bond of Brotherhood.** London and Worcester, Mass. 1855.

.... **The Herald of peace.** London 1855.

.... A **few words** about war (par Eliza **Sharpless**). London (1855).

.... **Bartlett,** David, Modern agitators : or pen portraits .... New York 1855.

.... **Bouvet,** Francisque, La guerre et la civilisation. Paris 1855.

.... **Burritt,** El., The world's workingmen's strike against war. 1855.

.... **Burritt,** El., Year book of the nations. London 1855.

.... **Collier,** A., The right way or the Gospel applied .... (Prize Essay of the *American Tract Soc.*).

.... **Comte,** A., Appel aux conservateurs. Paris 1855.

P.P. **Contre la guerre !** Etudes historiques .... (par F. **Delhasse** et Th. **Thoré**). Bruxelles 1855.

.... **Edwards,** J. Passmore, The war, a blunder and a crime. London (1855).

.... **Evans** A. Bowen, War : its theology ; its anomalies. London (1855).

.... **Fry,** Edm., Peace Tracts. (1855).

P.P. **Für den Frieden** in Gottes Ordnungen. Berlin 1855.

.... **Girardin,** E. de, La paix. 2me éd. Paris 1855.

P.P. **Girardin,** E. de, Der Friede. Nach der 3ten Auflage aus dem Französischen. Dresden 1855.

.... **Girardin,** E. de, De vrede. Amsterdam 1855.

P.P. **Girardin,** E. de, La politique universelle. 3me éd. Paris 1855.

.... Gurney, J. J., An essay on war, and its lawfulness. London 1855.

P.P. History of the origin of the war with Russia
(par Henry **Richard**). London 1855.

.... Hoppin, Nich., The good news of peace. A sermon. Cambridge-Port 1855.

.... Jay, Will., The eastern war, an argument ....
Boston 1855.

.... Jemison, Will. H., The utility of standing
armies, (dans :) **Journal** of the **Dublin Sta-
tistical Soc.**, 1855, p. 73.

.... Jenkison, J., Does Christianity sanction war ?
London (1855).

.... Kaufmann, P., Die Idee .... einer Weltaka-
demie des Völker-Rechts. (Bonn 1855.)

.... Kell, Edm., Peace, the gift .... of our holy
redeemer. 3d ed. London 1855.

.... La paix par la justice (par D. P. A. de **Haerne**).
Bruxelles 1855.

P.P. Levi, Leone, The law of nature and nations
.... London 1855.

.... Liggins, John, Strictures on " Prayer and the
war". London (1855).

.... Mason, James, Peace or war. An answer to
" A Christian Appeal ...." London 1855.

.... Minute on Appeal on war (Printed minutes of
the meeting for sufferings) 1855.

.... Necessity of peace (dans :) **Living Age**, 48,
p. 433.

.... Short reflections upon "The Friends Appeal
.... on war". London 1855.

.... Smith, Gerrit, Speeches. New York 1855.

.... Speech of John **Bright** in the House of Commons on the war and the ministry. Manchester 1855.

.... Stokes, William, A prize essay on war. 4th
ed. London (1855).

.... Taparelli, Luigi, Saggio di diritto naturale.
Roma 1855.

.... The soldier and the Christian. London (1855).

.... Thoughts on war and warriors ; extracted
from the writings of William **Cowper** (par
William **Tatum**). Chatham 1855.

.... Words on the war : being lectures on life and
death. London (1855).

1856

.... Address(es) and **Annual Report**(s) of ....
Peace Society(ies) 1856.

.... Advocate of peace. Boston 1856.

P.P. Annual report of the American Peace Society.
(= Lessons of peace from the Crimean
War) Boston 1856.

P.P. Bond of Brotherhood. London 1856.

.... The Herald of peace. London 1856.

.... Alger, William R., Lessons of the late war in
the East. Boston—New York 1856.

.... Bartlett, David, Modern American agitators.
New York 1856.

.... Bernal, Calixto, Teoria de la autoridad ....
Madrid 1856.

P.P. Bouvet, Francisque, Introduction à l'établissement d'un droit public européen. 2me éd.
Paris 1856.

.... Burritt, El., Year book of the nations. New
York 1856.

.... Burton, Warren, Address delivered at ....
the American Peace Soc. 1856.

.... Cobden, Richard, What next, and next ?
London 1856.

.... Der Friede und seine Folgen vom Standpunkte
der Nationalökonomie. Heidelberg 1856.

.... Dymond, Jon., On the lawfulness of war
(*Ipswich series of Tracts*, 14). Ipswich 1856.

P.P. Ficquelmont, C. L., Zum künftigen Frieden.
Wien 1856.

P.P. Kauffmann, A propos de la paix. **Revue de
Paris**, XXXI, p. 401-423. 1856.

P.P. Larroque, Patr., De la guerre et des armées
permanentes. Paris 1856.

.... Longo, Ag., La pace sotto il punto di vista
economico. Catania 1856.

.... Macchi, Mauro, La pace. Genova 1856.

.... Molinari, G. de, La paix perpétuelle est-elle
une utopie ? (dans :) **Journal** des économistes, 2me série, XII, p. 33-56.

.... Montague, Bernard, On the growth of the
laws and usages of war. (dans :) **Oxford
Essays.** London 1856.

.... Observations on the .... appeal of the Society
of Friends .... (par Richard **Oblath**).
London 1856.

.... Passy, Frédéric, Maux naturels et maux arti-
ficiels. (Article dans ?) 1856.

.... Peace in War. (Cambridge) 1856.

.... Ralph Dixon, the converted soldier. (*London
Tract soc.*) 1856.

P.P. Vigil (Francisco de P. G.), Pax perpetua en
América. 2ª ed. Bogota ou Lima 1856.

.... What have I done to promote peace? London
1856.

1857

.... Address(es) and **Annual Report**(s) of ....
Peace Society(ies) 1857.

P.P. Bond of Brotherhood. London 1857.

.... The Advocate of peace. Boston 1857.

.... The Herald of peace. London 1857.

P.P. Molinari, G. de, L'Abbé de Saint-Pierre.
Paris 1857.

.... Robert Owen's Millennial gazette. 11, August
1st, 1857. (London 1857.)

.... Stebbins, R. Ph., Peace will triumph. Boston
1857. (Address before the *American Peace
Soc.*)

1858

.... Address(es) and **Annual Report**(s) of ....
Peace Society(ies) 1858.

31   32

.... **The Advocate of peace.** Boston 1858.
.... **The Herald of peace.** London 1858.

.... **A peace tract** from "the Times", May 12th 1858. London.
P.P. **Bastide,** Jules, La république française et l'Italie en 1848. Bruxelles 1858.
.... **Fülleborn,** F. L., Der Schlusssatz in Kant's Schrift "Zum ewigen Frieden". Berlin 1858.
.... **Gast,** C. M., Eine naturgemässe Friedensidee für alle Völker, Zürich 1858.
.... **Girardin,** E. de, Questions de mon temps. Paris, 1858. 12 vols.
.... **Miotti,** Paolo, Delle odierne velleità di guerra in Europa. 1858.
P.P. **Smith,** Gerrit, Peace better than war. (Address *American Peace Soc*) Boston 1858.
.... **Wars of the Boers** in South-Afrika. (Printed minutes of the meeting for sufferings.) 1858.
.... **Wurm,** Chr. F., Selbsthülfe der Staaten in Friedenszeiten. Hamburg 1858.

1859
.... **Address(es)** and **Annual Report(s)** of .... Peace Society(ies) 1859.
.... **The Advocate of peace.** Boston 1859.
.... **The Herald of peace.** London 1859.

.... **Cheever,** George B., Address delivered at .... the American Peace Soc. 1859.
.... **Est-ce la paix?** Est-ce la guerre? (par Louis Jourdan.) Paris (1859).
.... **Finanzgeschichtliche** volkswirtschaftliche Betrachtungen über den Krieg. (dans :) **Deutsche Vierteljahrsschrift,** 1859, pag. 1-60.
.... **Fox,** Ann., Thoughts on peace. 1859.
.... **George Fox** and his Friends as leaders in the peace cause (par William **Naish**). London 1859.
P.P. **Girardin,** E. de, L'empereur Napoléon III et l'Europe. Bruxelles 1859.
P.P. **Girardin,** E. de, L'empire avec la liberté. Paris 1859.
P.P. **Girardin,** E. de, L'équilibre européen. Paris 1859.
P.P. **Girardin,** E. de, La guerre. Paris 1859.
.... **Girardin,** E. de, Oorlog. Zalt-Bommel 1859.
P.P. **Girardin,** E. de, Le désarmement européen. 2me éd. Paris 1859.
.... **Girardin,** E. de, De ontwapening van Europa. Doesburg 1859.
.... **Goumy,** Ed., Etude sur la vie .... de l'Abbé de Saint-Pierre. Paris 1859.
.... **Helps,** Arthur, Friends in Council. 2nd series. London 1859.
.... **Helps,** Arthur, Peace and war (dans :) **Frazer's Magazine,** March 1859.
.... **La guerre.** Bruxelles 1859.

.... **Maccia,** Raim., La pace : brevi osservazioni. Torino 1859.
.... **Memorial** to the earl of Derby on war (Printed minutes of the meeting for sufferings. 1859.)
P.P. **Napoleon III,** das politische Project Heinrich's IV .... und der zukünftige europ. Areopag. Hamburg 1859.
.... **Parker,** Joseph, Peacemaking : a sermon. London (1859).
.... **Passy,** Frédéric, Guerres et congrès .... (dans :) **Economiste Belge,** 19 Nov. 1859.
P.P. **Programme** de la Sainte-Alliance des peuples. Bruxelles et Ostende 1859.
.... **Proposals** for peace. London 1859.
.... **Ribeyre,** Fel., La pace e l'opinione. Parma 1859.
P.P. **Schulz-Bodmer,** Wilh., Die Rettung der Gesellschaft. Leipzig 1859.
P.P. **Schulz-Bodmer,** Wilh., Entwaffnung oder Krieg. Leipzig 1859.
.... **Sigaud,** Pierre, Confédération européenne. Mémoire .... adressé à S. M. l'Emp. des Français. Paris 1859.
.... **The unlawfulness** of all wars. (Signé par George Stacey.) London 1859.
P.P. **Tyrwhitt,** R. St. John, Five sermons on war. Oxford—London 1859.
.... **Walker,** Amasa, Le monde : or, In time of peace prepare for war. London 1859.

1860
.... **Address(es)** and **Annual Report(s)** of ... Peace Society(ies) 1860.
.... **The Advocate of peace.** Boston 1860.
P.P. **The Herald of peace.** London 1860.

.... **A Christian address** .... on the subject of war. (Signé par Robert **Alsop.**) London 1860.
.... **Backhouse,** James. A reply to Canon Hey's letter vindicating defensive war. 1860.
.... **Backhouse,** James, Is war lawful for the Christian? York 1860.
.... **Bonaparte,** Nap. Louis **(Napoléon III),** Des idées napoléoniennes. Paris 1860.
.... **Bonaparte,** Nap. Louis **(Napoléon III),** Des idées napoléoniennes. Berlin 1860.
.... **Bonaparte,** Nap. Louis **(Napoléon III),** Napoleontische ideeën. Amsterdam 1860.
.... **Bourke,** Charles E., La France et l'Europe ou la paix du monde. Genève 1860.
.... **Burritt,** El., Peace papers for the people. New ed. London 1860.
.... **Cheever,** George B., A discourse on .... the late judge Jay. Boston 1860. (voir 1859).
.... **Conference** of progressive thinkers. With four sermons by Theodore **Parker.** London 1860.
.... **Félicité,** Joseph de, La régéneration du monde. 1860.
.... **Furness,** W. H., Put up thy sword. A discourse. Boston 1860.

P.P. Girardin, E. de, Conquête et nationalité. Paris 1860.
P.P. Girardin, E. de, L'empereur Napoléon III et l'Europe. Paris 1860.
.... Gurney, J. J., War is it lawful under the Christian dispensation? London 1860.
.... Lamennais, Fél. R. de, Paroles d'un croyant. (nouv. ed. 1860.)
.... Leslie, T. E. Cliffe, The future of Europe foretold in history. (dans:) **Macmillan's Magazine,** May 1860.
.... Loewenthal, Ed., Die soziale und geistige Reformation des 19. Jahrhunderts. Frankfurt a. M. 1860.
.... May, Sam. Jos. An address before the American Peace Society. Boston 1860.
.... Molesworth, Will. N., The prize essay on .... a close alliance between England and France. Manchester (Ireland) 1860.
.... Newman, F. W., The ethics of war. London 1860.
.... Richard, Henry, A letter addressed to ... bible and missionary societies. London 1860.
.... Richter, Friedrich, Zum Frieden Europa's. Hamburg 1860.
P.P. Sanz del Rio, Julian, C. Cr. Krause. Ideal de la humanidad para la vida. Madrid 1860.
.... Stokes, Will., A permanent European congress as a substitute for war. Manchester 1860. (voir 1861).
.... Stokes, Will., The olive branch. London 1860.
.... The Recruits; or facts about soldiers (par William Naish). London (1860).
.... The unlawfulness of all wars. (Signé par George Stacey.) London 1860.
.... Thonissen, J. J., La guerre et la philosophie de l'histoire. (Extrait des **Bulletins de l'Acad. de Bruxelles.** 1860).
.... Vacherof, Etienne, Démocratie. Paris 1860.
.... Vivien, Fréd., Un trait d'union entre la France et l'Angleterre. (1860?)
.... Wayland, Fra., Elements of moral science. London 1860.
P.P. Whipple, Ch. K., Non-resistance applied to the internal defence of a community. Boston 1860.
P.P. Wolowski, L., Le grand dessein de Henri IV. Paris 1860.
.... Wolowski, L., Le grand dessein de Henri IV (dans:) **Séances et travaux de l'Acad. des sciences morales et politiques** t. 54, 1860 III, p. 29-59.

1861

      Address(es) and Annual Report(s) of.... Peace Society(ies) 1861.
.... The Advocate of peace. Boston 1861.
P.P. The Herald of peace. London 1861.

.... Alger, William R., The relations of war to human nature. Boston 1861.

.... Bernal, Calixto, Théorie de l'autorité appliquée aux nations modernes. Paris 1861.
.... Bonaparte, Nap. Louis **(Napoléon III),** Des idées napoléoniennes. Londres 1861.
.... Burritt, El., Address delivered at the anniversary of the American Peace Soc. 1861.
.... Canepa, Pietro, Carta della pace europea: saggio. Torino 1861.
.... Desewffy, Marzel, Beiträge zu einer Doctrin des menschheitlichen Friedens. Pesth 1861.
.... Gratry, A., La paix. Méditations historiques et religieuses. Paris 1861.
.... La paix en Europe par l'alliance anglo-française. 1861.
.... Lamber, Julliette, Idées anti-Proudhonniennes .... (et) critique du livre: « La guerre et la paix ». Paris 1861.
P.P. Malardier, M., Solution de la question européenne. Confédération europ. Bruxelles et Leipzig 1861.
P.P. Pinguet, B. C., Invention de nouvelles armes de guerre imprenables et invincibles. Paris 1861.
P.P. Proudhon, P. J., La guerre et la paix. Paris et Leipzig 1861.
.... Reports of the peace congresses at Brussels, Paris, (etc.) in the years 1848(−1853). London 1861.
.... Rowntree, Will., War and Christianity. Carlisle (1861).
.... Rowntree, Will., ——. 2d ed. Carlisle (1861?)
.... Rowntree, Will., ——. 3d ed. London 1861.
.... Stokes, Will., A permanent European Congress in lieu of war. London 1861. (voir 1860.)
P.P. Villiaumé, N., L'esprit de la guerre. Paris 1861.

1862

      Address(es) and Annual Report(s) of .... Peace Society(ies) 1862.
.... The Advocate of peace. Boston 1862.
P.P. The Herald of peace. London 1862.

.... Backhouse, James, Magistracy and war. London 1862.
.... Backhouse, James, Magistracy and war. York 1862.
.... Barker, G., The expediency of principle. London 1862.
.... Bentzien, D., Programme du général Garibaldi à la nation anglaise. 1862.
P.P. Cobden, Richard, The three panics. 6th ed. London 1862.
.... Cobden, Richard, Les trois paniques. Paris 1862.
P.P. Dunant, Henri, Un souvenir de Solferino. Genève 1862.
.... Dunant, Henri, Un souvenir de Solferino. (2me éd.) Genève 1862.
.... Guinness, H. G., Tract on war. 1862.

.... Lebloys, E., Voulez-vous la paix et le désarmement général? Bruxelles 1862.
.... Love, Alfred H., An appeal in vindication of peace principles. Philadelphia 1862.
.... Malcom, Howard, Signs of the times favorable to peace. Boston 1862.
.... Nicholson, Will., The theory of a universal peace critically investigated. London 1862.
P.P. Noble, John, Arbitration and a congress of nations as a substitute for war. London 1862.
P.P. Sain de Boislecomte, E., De la crise américaine. Paris 1862.
.... The testimony of the early Christians. (*London Tract Assoc.*, Leaflet series, 16) 1862.
.... Walker, Amasa, Iron-clad warships. Speech before the American Peace Soc. May 26, 1862. Boston 1862.
.... Williams, Th., A discourse ; on the evils and the end of war. Providence 1862.

1863

      Address(es) and Annual Report(s) of .... Peace Society(ies) 1863.
.... Courier International (International Courrier). London 1863 (?)
.... Le Cosmopolite. (1863 ?)
.... The Advocate of peace. Boston 1863.
P.P. The Herald of peace. London 1863.

.... Ballou, Adin, Christian non-resistance defended
.   against Rev. Henry Ward Beecher. (1863 ?)
.... Brenneman, John M., Christianity and war. Chicago 1863.
.... Burton, John, War irreconcilable with Christianity. London 1863.
.... Chevalier, Michel, La guerre et la crise européenne. (1863 ?)
P.P. Dunant, J. Henry, Un souvenir de Solferino. 3me éd. Genève 1863.
P.P. Dunant, J. Henry, Eine Erinnerung an Solferino. Basel 1863.
.... Dunant, J. H., Solferino. De stem der menschheid op het slagveld. Den Haag 1863.
.... Ferber (ou bien Ferrer), Jean B. de, L'ère nouvelle. Nécessité d'un code international. Paris 1863.
.... Fortaelling on Thomas Lurting, forhen sømand under admiral Blake. Christiana 1863.
.... Funk, John F., Warfare. Its evils. Our duty. Chicago 1863.
.... Funk, John F., Warfare. Its evils. Our duty. Markham 1863.
.... Girardin, E. de, Paix et liberté. Questions de l'année 1863. Paris 1863.
.... Napoleon III en het congres. Rotterdam 1863.
.... Peto, S. Morton, Taxation : its levy and expenditure. London 1863.
.... Proceedings of the great Peace Convention held in New York city, June 3, 1863. 1863.

P.P. Proudhon, P. J., Du principe fédératif. Paris 1863.
.... Rowntree, Will., War and Christianity. London 1863.
P.P. Sumner, Ch., Our foreign relations. Boston 1863.
.... The testimony of the early Christians. (Leaflet series *Dublin Tract Assoc.*, 7). Dublin 1863.
.... Thomas, David, The American war. London (1863 ?).
.... Walker, Amasa, The suicidal folly of the war system. An address before the American Peace Soc. May 25, 1863. Boston 1863.

1864

      Address(es) and Annual Report(s) of .... Peace Society(ies) 1864.
.... Le Cosmopolite. (1864 ?)
.... The Advocate of peace. Boston 1864.
P.P. The Herald of peace. London 1864.

P.P. Boom, Corn. de, Une solution politique et sociale. Paris 1864.
.... Brenneman, John M., Das Christenthum und der Krieg. Lancaster, Pa. 1864.
P.P. Czartoryski, Adam, Essai sur la diplomatie. Paris 1864.
.... Feillet, Alph., Les antécédents historiques du Congrès. Paris 1864.
.... Fraternité et charité internationales en temps de guerre (par Henry Dunant). Paris (1864).
.... Garaude, abbé, La guerre considérée au point de vue philosophique. Paris 1864.
.... Girardin, E. de, Paix et liberté. Questions de l'année 1863. Paris 1864.
.... La paix universelle, idée napoléonienne devant l'histoire. Paris 1864.
.... Larroque, Patrice, De la guerre et des armées permanentes. 2me éd. Paris 1864.
P.P. Le Congrès de Genève, août 1864. 2me éd. (1864 ?)
.... Miles, Edw., The drafted Friends in the American war. London 1864.
.... Musser, Dan., Non-resistance assented. 1864.
.... Pelletan, Eugène, Qui perd gagne. Paris 1864.
P.P. Read, Charles, Paix perpétuelle (dans :) Dictionnaire général de la politique de Maur. Block, Paris 1864, tome II p. 449.
P.P. Richard, Henry, Memoirs of Joseph Sturge. London 1864.
.... Robbins, E. G., An impartial view of the war in America. London (1864 ?).
.... Robbins, E. G., England as a peacemaker. New York (1864 ?).
.... Sabatini, Vit., Sul dritto della pace. Napoli 1864.
P.P. Villiaumé, N., L'esprit de la guerre. 3me éd. Paris 1864.

1865

Address(es) and Annual Report(s) of ....
Peace Society(ies) 1865.
.... **Le Cosmopolite.** (1865?)
.... **The Advocate of peace.** Boston 1865.
P.P. **The Herald of peace.** London 1865.

P.P. **Avenel,** Georges, Anacharsis Cloots, l'orateur
du genre humain. Paris 1865.
.... **Bagny,** marquis de, La paix et la guerre.
Lyon 1865.
.... **Confédération européenne** (par F. **Pescantini**).
1865.
.... **Eichthal,** Gustave d', Les trois grands peuples
méditerranéens. Paris 1865.
.... **Engels,** Friedr., Die preussische Militärfrage.
Hamburg 1865.
.... **Lamartine,** A. de, Manifeste aux puissances.
Paris, 4 mars 1848 (dans :) **La France parle-
mentaire.** Paris 1865.
.... **Le moribond** de l'Europe. London (1865).
.... **Napoleonische Ideen** vom Prinzen N. L.
Bonaparte. Wien 1865.
.... **Passy,** Frédéric, La paix armée (dans :) **Jour-
nal** des Economistes, 2e série, tome 46. p.
221.
.... **Sanson,** André, Article sur les horreurs de la
guerre (dans :) **La Presse,** 25 juillet 1865.
.... **Setti,** Gius, L'abolizione della guerra. Bologna
1865.
.... **The Scripture testimony on peace.** Philadelphia 1865.
.... **Tolstoi,** L. N., Voïna i mir (= La guerre et
la paix). (dans:) **Rouskii Vestnik,** 1865—
1869.

1866

Address(es) and Annual Reports of ....
Peace Society(ies) 1866.
.... **Le Cosmopolite.** Anvers 1866.
.... **The Advocate of peace.** Boston 1866.
P.P. **The Herald of peace.** London 1866.

.... **Address** of the Universal Peace Society to all
Persons.... and Nations. 1866.
P.P. **Audiganne,** A., L'économie de la paix. Paris
1866.
.... **Chevalier,** Michel, La guerre et la crise euro-
péenne. 2me éd. Paris 1866.
P.P. **Chierici,** Luigi, La guerra per la pace. Bologna
1866.
P.P. **Cochut,** André, Des nationalités à propos de
la guerre. (dans :) **Revue des deux mondes,**
LXIV, p. 689.
.... **Cornelius** (K. A.), Der grosze Plan Heinrichs
IV. von Frankreich (dans:) **Münchener**
historisches **Jahrbuch** 1866.
.... **Correspondance cosmopolite.** Projet d'établissement d'un tribunal international (avec
suite dans :) **La Mutualité.** Paris 1866.

.... **Der** ohne Blut und Eisen **zu erringende natur-
gemässe Sieg** des sittlichen Fortschritts-
über das unsittliche Rückschrittsprincip.
Berlin 1866.
P.P. **Europa** : Wird es republikanisch oder kosa-
kisch? 2e Auflage. Leipzig 1866.
.... **Girardin,** E. de, Ce qu'a coûté la paix armée.
(dans :) **Journal** des Economistes, 3e série,
Ie année, III p. 435.
.... **Histoire des idées** au XIXe siècle. Emile de
Girardin (par **Odysse-Barot).** Paris 1866.
.... **International arbitration** (dans :) **North Ameri-
can Review** (reproduit dans le "Herald of
peace"). 1866.
P.P. **International policy.** Essays on the foreign
relations of England. London 1866.
.... **Kaufmann,** P., Die Wissenschaft des Welt-
friedens im Grundrisse. Bonn 1866.
.... **Kaufmann,** P., Die Wissenschaft des Welt-
friedens im Grundrisse. (2e Auflage). Bonn
1866.
.... **La démocratie** devant la guerre. Paris 1866.
.... **Love,** Alfred H., Address before the Peace
Convention held in Boston. Hopedale, Mass.
1866.
.... **Mangin,** E., (Article dans :) **Le Phare de la
Loire.** 1866.
.... **Maronier,** H., De oorlog, een vraagpunt des
tijds. Amsterdam 1866.
.... **Proceedings** of the Peace Conventions (of the
Universal Peace Society) held in Boston and
in Providence, 1866. Hopedale Mass. 1866.
.... **Reybaud,** Louis, L'économie politique et la
guerre (dans :) **Journal des économistes,**
3e série. Ie année, III. (1866). p. 5-12.
.... **The shepherd's sorrow;** or war at variance
with Christianity (par Cornelius **Hanbury).**
London 1866.
.... **Witnesses for peace** on Christian principles
(par W. L. **Bellows).** Gloucester 1866.

1867

.... Address(es) and Annual Report(s) of....
Peace Society(ies). 1867.
P.P. **Bulletin** du congrès de la paix à Genève,
1-11 sept. 1867. (Genève 1867).
.... **Les Etats-Unis** de l'Europe. Berne 1867.
.... **Premier Bulletin** de la Ligue internationale et
permanente de la paix. (Saint-Germain
1867).
.... **The Advocate of peace.** Boston 1867.
P.P. **The Herald of peace.** London 1867.

.... **A common-sense course** for diminishing the
evils of war (par William **Tallack).** London
1867.
P.P. **Arnd,** Karl, Die Friedenswünsche, Frankfurt
a. Main. 1867.
.... **Beaudemoulin,** L.A., La guerre s'en va. Paris
1867.

.... **Bonner,** W. H., The Chistian as a citizen. London 1867.
P.P. **Boom,** C. de, Unité européenne. Paix—décentralisation—émigration. Paris 1867.
.... **Borkheim,** Ma perle devant le Congrès de la paix à Genève, par un diplomate européen. Bruxelles 1867.
.... **Cavalieri,** Michele, La paix générale. Milan 1867.
.... **Ceneri,** Giuseppe, Relazione sul congresso della pace.... in Ginevra. Bologna 1867.
P.P. **Confédération européenne.** Paix universelle par *Gallus* (A. **de Bonnard**). Paris 1867.
.... **Demeur,** A., Le congrès de la paix à Genève (dans :) **Revue trimestrielle,** LVI, p. 214.
.... **Demeur,** A., Le congrès de la paix à Genève. Bruxelles 1867.
.... **Des livrets du mérite....** (par Ferd. **Féline**). Paris 1867.
.... **Dolgoroukow,** Pierre, Lettre à M. le président du soi-disant Congrès de la paix. Genève et Bâle 1867.
.... **Frantz,** Const., A European peace-institution (dans :) **The Chronicle,** août 1867.
.... **Girardin,** E. de, (Des articles dans le journal) **La Liberté** (de l'année) 1867.
.... **Girardin,** E. de, Pensées et maximes.... extraites par A. **Hétrel.** Paris 1867.
.... **Hugo,** Victor, Introduction (de) **Paris uide.** GParis 1867.
.... **Hugo,** Victor, Introduction (de) **Paris Guide.** 2e éd. Paris 1867.
P.P. **Hugo,** Victor, Friedensmanifest an die Völker Europa's. Berlin 1867.
.... **Kant,** Imm., Zum ewigen Frieden. Neue Ausgabe. Bern 1867.
P.P. **La Codre,** J. M. de, L'opinion publique et l'extinction de la guerre. Paris 1867.
.... **Le problème européen.** Paris (1867 ?).
.... **Lemonnier,** Ch., La paix perpétuelle. Paris 1867.
P.P. **Lemonnier,** Ch., La vérité sur le Congrès de Genève. Berne—Genève 1867.
.... **Ligue internationale** de la paix et de la liberté. Statuts revisés. Berne (1867).
.... **Ligue internationale** (et permanente) de la paix. Le comité à ses adhérents. 1867.
.... **Lorimer** (James), On the application of the principle of relative or proportional equality .... Edinburgh 1867.
P.P. **Marr,** W., Es musz alles Soldat werden. Abdruck aus dem **Kosmopolit,** 1867. Hamburg 1867.
P.P. **Passy,** Frédéric, Conférence sur la paix et la guerre. Paris 1867.
.... **Passy,** Frédéric, Conférence sur la paix et la guerre. Paris (1867).
.... **Passy,** Frédéric, Conférence sur la paix et la guerre. (Abbeville 1867).

P.P. **Peabody,** Andr. P., Lessons from our late rebellion. An address.... at.... the American Peace Soc. Boston 1867.
.... **Proceedings of the....** Universal Peace Society. New York 1867.
.... **Richard,** Albert, Te Deum laudamus. Genève 1867.
.... **Ross,** David, On an international High Court. A paper, read before the Social Science Association at Belfast, Sept. 1867.
.... **Ruge,** Arnold, Der Krieg und die Entwaffnung. Berlin 1867.
.... **Santallier,** F., L'union de la paix entre tous les peuples civilisés. Havre 1867.
P.P. **Santallier,** F., Friedens-Union zwischen allen civilisirten Völkern. Havre 1867.
.... **Saulais,** S., La paix universelle ou l'équilibre européen. Paris 1867.
.... **Schulze-Delitzsch,** Hermann, Promemoria an die „Ligue du désarmement", Potsdam 12 juillet 1867 (dans :) **Berliner Volkszeitung** 1867, No 177.
.... **Talbot,** Ed., L'Europe aux Européens. Paris 1867.
P.P. **Un programme** de paix européenne fondé sur le droit chrétien (par Leszek Dunin **Borkowski ?**). Leipsic 1867.
.... **Veyrat,** P. A. S. A. R., La riforma dei congressi politici. Oneglia 1867 (avec Appendice).
.... **Walcker,** C., Zur allgemeinen Entwaffnung der Europäischen Staaten (dans :) **Baltische Monatsschrift** XV. Riga 1867.
.... **Wars.** How brought about (par Charles **Smith**). Norwich (1867).
.... **White,** John J., Peace and other poems. Philadelphia 1867.

1868
Address(es) and Annual Report(s) of .... Peace Society(ies) 1868.
.... **Bulletin de l'Union de la paix.** Hâvre 1868.
.... **Bulletins de quinzaine** (de la Ligue internationale et permanente de la paix dans le Temps). 1868.
.... **Deuxième Bulletin de la Ligue internationale et permanente de la paix.** Versailles 1868.
.... **Die Vereinigten Staaten von Europa.** Bern 1868.
.... **Les Etats-Unis de l'Europe.** Berne 1868.
.... **The Advocate of peace.** Boston 1868.
.... **The Bond of peace.** 1868.
P.P. **The Herald of peace.** London 1868.

P.P. **Annales** du Congrès de Genève.... de la Ligue internationale de la paix et de la liberté. Genève 1868.
.... **Beaudemoulin,** L. A., Actualités. La guerre s'en va. (2e éd.) Paris 1868.
.... **Beckwith,** G. C., The peace manual, or, War and its remedies. Boston 1868.

.... **Börne,** Ludw., Menzel der Franzosenfresser (Gesamm. Schriften, Band VI). Wien 1868.

.... **Bogue,** Dav., On universal peace. 1868. (Tract VI of the *Peace Soc.*).

.... **Brenneman,** John M., Christianity and war. Elkhart, Indiana 1868.

.... **Brenneman,** John M., Das Christenthum und der Krieg. Elkhart, Indiana 1868.

.... **Bulletin sténographique** du deuxième congrès de la paix et de la liberté tenu à Berne, 1868.

.... **Castiglia,** Benedetto, Abolizione della guerra internazionale. Firenze 1868.

.... **Chevalier,** Mich., Discours prononcé.... sur la loi militaire. Paris 1868.

.... **Chevalier,** Mich., Exposition universelle.... Introduction. Paris 1868.

.... **Clarkson,** T., An essay on the doctrines and practice of the early Christians. London 1868. (Tract III of *the Peace Soc.*).

.... **Coolhaas van der Woude,** S., De oorlog en de Tien Geboden. Winschoten (1868).

.... **Coulanges,** H. de, Lettre d'un utopiste au Prince Humbert (dans :) **le Figaro,** 6 juin 1868.

P.P. **Der Krieg,** die Congressidee und die allgemeine Wehrpflicht.... von einem *Freunde der Wahrheit* (**Moritz Adler**). Prag 1868.

.... **Discours de M.** l'Abbé Gratry prononcé à sa réception à l'Académie française. Paris 1868.

.... **Dreuille,** L. de, Comment on pourrait réduire l'armée. Paris 1868. (*Bibliothèque de la paix,* 8.)

.... **Dubois,** Louis, Le congrès de la paix. Pièce en un acte. Genève 1868.

.... **Dymond,** J., Observations on the applicability of the pacific principle. London 1868 (Tract VII of the *Peace Soc.*).

.... **Examination** of the principles considered to support the practice of war. London 1868. (Tract VIII of the *Peace Soc.*)

.... **Extracts** from the writings of **Erasmus.** London 1868. (Tract IV of the *Peace Soc.*)

.... **Girardin,** E. de, Questions philosophiques. Paris 1868.

.... **Goegg,** Marie, Rede.... geh. am 26. Sept. 1868. Bern 1868.

.... **Gueroult,** A., L'utopie de la paix européenne. (6 articles dans :) **L'opinion nationale,** 4 mai-4 juin 1868.

.... **Guilhaumon,** M. F., La guerre et les épidémies. Paris 1868. (*Bibliothèque de la paix,* 3.)

.... **Gurney,** J. J., An essay on war. London 1868. (Tract XII of the *Peace Soc.*)

.... **Hancock,** T., The principles of peace. London 1868. (Tract IX of the *Peace Soc.*)

P.P. **Het Zwarte Boek** der Staatsgeheimen.... door den *Oud-Bankier* (H. **Martin**). Amsterdam 1868.

.... **Historical illustrations** of the origin and consequences of war. London 1868. (Tract X of the *Peace Soc.*)

P.P. **Im Thale der Thränen.** Wien 1868.

P.P. **Jähns,** Max, Krieg und Frieden. Berlin 1868.

.... **Jourdan,** Louis, La fédération européenne (dans :) **Le Siècle,** 18 avril 1868.

P.P. **La Guerre** par N(ottelle). (Paris) 1868.

.... **La Guerre** et les armées. Paris 1868.

.... **Labaume,** E., Sketches of the horrors of war. London 1868. (Tract V of the *Peace Soc.*)

.... **Landa,** Don Nicasio, Menschenliefde en oorlog. Rotterdam 1868.

P.P. **Larrieu,** A., Guerre à la guerre. Paris 1868. (*Bibliothèque de la paix,* 5.)

.... **Lavigne,** Georges, La politique de la paix. Bruxelles 1868.

.... **Le système** de guerre en Europe. Londres 1868.

.... **Leroy-Beaulieu,** Paul, Les guerres contemporaines (1853-1866). Paris 1868. (*Bibl. de la paix,* 1.)

.... **Leslie,** T. E. Cliffe, Nations and international law (dans :) **Fortnightly Review,** 1 juillet 1868.

.... **Loewenthal,** Ed., Friedensbetrachtung. (dans :) **Dresdener Kurier,** 27/IX, 1868.

.... **Loewenthal,** Ed., Der Krieg und die stehenden Heere. (dans :) **Dresdener Kurier,** 11/XI, 1868.

.... **Loewenthal,** Ed., Cultur oder Barbarei. (dans :) **Dresdener Kurier,** 25/XII, 1868.

.... **Munier,** Le congrès internat. de la paix à Genève. Genève 1868.

.... **Necker,** J., Reflections on the calamities of war. London (1868?). (Tract XI of the *Peace Soc.*)

.... **Nicoladzé,** N., Du désarmement et de ses conséquences. Paris 1868.

.... **Obstacles and objections** to the cause of peace By a *layman.* (Tract XIII of the *Peace Soc.*) 1868.

.... **Passy,** Fréd., La ligue internationale de la paix (dans :) **Journal des économistes** 3e série, 3e année, X, p. 233-240.

P.P. **Première assemblée** générale (de la Ligue internat. et perm. de la paix). 2e éd. Paris 1868.

.... **Richard,** Henry, On standing armies. London 1868.

.... **Röder,** Karl, Die Kriegsknechtschaft unserer Zeit (dans :) **Deutsche Vierteljahrschrift,** XXXI. 3.

.... **Scott,** J., War inconsistent with the doctrine of Jesus Christ. London 1868. (Tract II of the *Peace Soc.*)

P.P. **Seigneur,** Georges, La ligue de la paix. Paris 1868.

P.P. **Sem,** Victor, Quelques conséquences du principe des nationalités. Paris 1868.

.... **Spencer,** Nathan F., A narrative of the cruelties. London 1868.
.... **Strada,** J. de, l'Europe sauvée et la fédération. Paris 1868. •
.... **The substance** of a pamphlet (par Noah **Worcester**). éd. stéréot. London 1868. (Tract I of the *Peace Soc.*)
.... **Urquhart,** David, Appeal of a protestant to the pope. London 1868.
.... **Valmy,** le duc de, Du droit souverain de paix et de guerre (dans :) **Revue contemporaine,** juin 1868.
P.P. **Varella,** Hector Flor., Discurso no congreso da paz em Genebra. Rio de Janeiro 1868.
P.P. **Vreede,** G. G., Montesquieu et le désarmement général (dans :) **Le Conservateur,** I (1868), p. 280-284.
.... **Walker** (ou Walcker), Carl, Guérison des maux financiers.... par un désarmement général. St. Pétersbourg 1868.

1869

Address(es) and **Annual Report(s)** of.... Peace Society(ies) 1869.
.... **Bulletin officiel** du congrès de la paix et de la liberté. Lausanne 1869.
.... **Die Vereinigten Staaten von Europa.** Bern 1869.
.... **Les Etats-Unis d'Europe.** Berne 1869.
.... **l'Harmonie sociale.** Bruxelles 1869.
.... **The Advocate of peace.** Boston 1869.
.... **The Bond of peace.** 1869.
P.P. **The Herald of peace.** London 1869.

P.P. **Beaudemoulin,** L. A., La guerre s'en va. 2e éd. Paris (1869). (*Bibliothèque de la paix*, 5.)
.... **Bogue,** Dav., On universal peace. New Vienna, Ohio 1869.
.... **Burritt** El., Lectures and speeches. London 1869.
.... **Chalybaeus,** Th., Der Krieg und die Sanitätspflege (dans :) **Westermanns Monatshefte,** XXVI. (1869), S. 425.
.... **Chambouvet,** Le règne du canon. Paris 1869.
.... **Chase,** Thom., The churches of Christendom responsible. New Vienna, Ohio 1869.
.... **Chevalier,** Michel, Les Etats-Unis de l'Europe et la paix internationale (dans :) **Journal des économistes,** 3e série, 4e année (1869), XV, p. 76-91.
.... **Chevalier,** Michel, Die Weltindustrie des 19. Jahrhunderts. Stuttgart 1869.
.... **Chevers,** Norman, Humanity in war. Calcutta 1869.
.... **Coquerel** (fils), Athanase. La guerre. Discours, Paris 1869.
P.P. **Das Vertrauen** ist der Friede (par Wilhelm Rudolf **Schulze**?). Altenburg 1869.
.... **Deuxième Assemblée** générale de la Ligue int. et perm. de la paix. Paris 1869.

.... **Esmarch,** Ueber den Kampf der Humanität gegen die Schrecken des Krieges. Kiel 1869.
.... **Faivre,** B., Le respect mutuel. Conférence faite à Metz le 9 janvier 1869.
P.P. **Fayet,** A., De la paix perpétuelle. Moulins 1869.
P.P. **Gardane,** le comte de, La France libre et armée. Paris 1869.
.... **Gurney,** J. J., An essay on war. New York 1869.
.... **Helps,** Arthur, Friends in Council. London 1869.
P.P. **Junius,** F. J. J. A., De oorlog in verband met Christendom en beschaving. Tiel 1869.
.... **La bataille** et la retraite de Leipzic. Paris (1869). (*Bibliothèque de la paix*, 10.)
P.P. **La paix.** Discours prononcé par **Hyacinthe** (**Loyson**). Paris 1869.
.... **La paix** par la guerre (par Ed. **Gillon**). Strasbourg et Paris 1869.
P.P. **Laboulaye,** E., La médecine militaire en France.... (dans :) **Revue des deux mondes,** LXXXIV, pag. 841-884.
.... **Lange,** J. P., Vom Krieg und von Sieg. Bonn 1869.
P.P. **Larrieu,** A., Weg met den oorlog. Arnhem 1869.
P.P. **Lavergne,** L. de, L'abbé de Saint-Pierre. (dans :) **Revue des deux Mondes** LXXIX, p. 557-589 (aussi dans :) **Séances et travaux** de l'Académie des sciences morales et politiques 1869, t. 89, p. 217-239, 365-391.
.... **Lemonnier,** Ch., Bulletin de quinzaine. (dans :) **Le Phare de la Loire,** janvier 1869 (?).
.... **Lemonnier,** Ch., Rapport au congrès tenu à Lausanne : Déterminer les bases d'une organisation fédérale de l'Europe. Paris 1869.
.... **Leroy-Beaulieu,** Paul, Les guerres contemporaines. 3me éd. Paris 1869.
.... **Leroy-Beaulieu,** Paul, Contemporary wars (1853-1866). London 1869.
P.P. **Leroy-Beaulieu,** Paul, Recherches économiques, historiques et statistiques sur les guerres contemporaines (1853-1866). Paris (1869).
P.P. **Les maux de la guerre.** Réunion publique. Paris 1869.
.... **Littrow,** H. von, Die Torpedos. Graz 1869.
.... **Löffler,** G., Rückblicke auf die Humanität in den Kriegen. (dans :) **Allg. Militärzeitung,** 1869, 41, 42, 43.
.... **Macé,** Jean, L'Anniversaire de Waterloo. Paris 1869.
.... **Macé,** Jean, De bond des vredes en Waterloo. Amsterdam (1869). *De vriend van armen en rijken,* 259.
P.P. **Markgraf,** Herm. Ueber Georgs von Podiebrad Project eines Christl. Fürstenbundes (dans :) **Sybel's Historische Zeitschrift,** XXI, p. 245-304.
.... **Mennet,** François, Le crime de la guerre. 1e éd. Genève 1869.
.... **Morandi,** Luigi, La guerra. Discorso. Sanseverino 1869.

.... Peace, An address by father Hyacinthe (Loy-
son). London 1869.
P.P. Perraud, Charles, L'evangile de la paix.
Paris 1869. (*Bibliothèque de la paix*, 8.)
P.P. Piazza, Joseph, Suppression des armées per-
manentes. Paris 1869.
.... Plus de guerres, plus d'idolâtrie, plus de servi-
tudes! Lyon 1869.
.... Sabatini, Vitaliano, Epistola apologetica del
diritto naturale per la pace. Napoli 1869.
.... Semichon, Ernest, La paix et la trêve de Dieu
(au moyen age). Paris 1869.
.... Simon, Jules, Article dans le journal belge
„Le Progrès" du 16 mai 1869.
.... Stokes, William, British war history during
the present century. London 1869.
.... Stokes, William, British war taxation. 1869.
.... Symptômes d'une régéneration sociale et reli-
gieuse. Louviers 1869.
P.P. The Peace Society on the law of nations. Lon-
don 1869. (Extrait du) Diplomatic Review,
Oct. 1869.
.... Tolstoi, Leo, War and peace. 1869.
P.P. Urquhart, David, Ad summum pontificem,
ut jus gentium restauretur. Londini 1869.
.... Urquhart, David, Appel d'un Protestant au
Pape. Paris 1869.
.... War justified: An appeal to scripture and com-
mon sense. London 1869.
P.P. Wiskemann, H., Der Krieg. Preisschrift.
Leiden 1869.

1870
Address(es) and Annual Report(s) of ....
Peace Society(ies) 1870.
P.P. De Vredebond. Amsterdam 1870.
.... Les Etats-Unis d'Europe. Genève 1870.
P.P. l'Harmonie sociale. Bruxelles 1870.
.... Quatrième Bulletin de la Ligue internationale
et permanente de la paix. 1870.
.... The Advocate of peace. Boston 1870.
.... The Bond of peace. 1870.
P.P. The Herald of peace. London 1870.

.... A Crusade against war. London 1870.
.... A plea with ministers for the cause of peace.
1870.
.... Born, F., Oorlogskreet tegen den oorlog.
Joure 1870.
.... Bright, J., Non Intervention. Manchester
(1870).
.... Bulletin officiel du congrès (extraordinaire)
de la paix et de la liberté, tenu à Bâle, le
24 juillet 1870.
P.P. Caro, E., La morale de la guerre (dans :)
Revue des deux mondes, XC, p. 577-594.
.... Caro, E., Le principe du droit des gens d'après
Kant (dans :) Séances et travaux de l'Acad.
des sciences morales et politiques, XCIV
(1870), p. 361-377.

.... Chenu, J. C., De la mortalité dans l'armée.
Paris 1870.
.... Chéron, Jules, Guerre et civilisation. Paris
1870.
.... Clement, Ambr., La guerre (dans :) Journal
des économistes 3e série, 5e année, tome
XIX (1870) p. 169-187.
.... Conti, Alfred, L'armée et le travail. Amiens
1870.
.... Ethics and evils of war. Boston 1870.
P.P. Etienne, Louis, L'idée de la guerre au XVIIIe
siècle (dans :) Revue des deux Mondes, XC,
p. 702-715.
P.P. Garelli, A. S., La pace nell' Europa moderna.
Torino-Firenze (1870).
.... Gasparin, Agénor de, La déclaration de la
guerre. 2e éd. Paris (1870).
.... Gass, Wilh., Recht und Nothwendigkeit des
Krieges (dans:) Protestantische Kirchen-
zeitung, 49 et 51.
.... Girardin, E. de, La guerre fatale, prévue et
annoncée en 1868. Paris 1870.
P.P. Gossi, Max., La réconciliation de la France et
de l'Allemagne. 2e ed. Anvers 1870.
.... Harte, Rich., On the possibility of permanent
peace. London (1870).
.... Headley, T. G., The voice of a peacemaker.
London 1870.
.... Hill, B., Treatment of the sick and wounded.
London 1870.
.... Howell, J. W., Memorial of perfect peace.
New ed. London 1870.
P.P. Jottrand, L., Perspective de paix durable
(dans:) le Conservateur, II (1870), p. 67-101.
.... Kant, Imm., Zum ewigen Frieden. Berlin
1870. *Philos. Bibliothek*, XXXVII, 8, p.
147-205.
.... Kwartus, Vrede door strijd! Amsterdam 1870.
.... La guerre. Manifeste du Conseil général de
l'Assoc. internat. des travailleurs. Genève
(1870).
.... Lamartine, A. de, Marseillaise de la paix,
übers. von Freiligrath. Dichtungen. Stuttgart 1870.
P.P. Larroque, Patr., De la guerre et des armées
permanentes. 3e éd. Paris 1870.
P.P. Loewenthal, Ed., Der Militarismus als Ursache
der Massenverarmung in Europa. Potsch-
appel (1870).
.... L'Olivier, Emile, Appel au peuple. Bruxelles
1870.
.... Marcy, Leo, Salut national ou prospérité et
paix universelle.
.... Monod, Mme William, La mission des femmes
en temps de guerre. Paris 1870.
P.P. Neumann, Herm., Krieg dem Kriege. Breslau
1870.
.... Nieuwenhuis, F. Domela, Een vraagstuk van
internationaal belang (dans :) Onze Tijd,
V, 2, p. 324-336.

.... **No more war.** .... The problem solved by a politician. London 1870.

.... **Oorlog.** (Groningen) 1870.

.... **Oosterzee,** J. J. van, De oorlogsbode. Tijdpreek. 's-Gravenhage (1870).

.... **Paix ou guerre** (par Ch. J. **Duponchel).** Aix-les-Bains 1870.

.... **Paschoud,** Martin, Lettre à l'empereur des Français. Paris, 18 juillet 1870. (*Bibliothèque de la paix, ?*)

.... **Passy,** Fréd., La perpétuité de la guerre (?). (dans :) **la Revue du Christianisme libéral.** Paris 1870.

.... **Passy,** Fréd., Le 2e banquet annuel du Club Cobden (dans :) **Journal des économistes** 3e série, 5e année, tome XIX (1870), p. 290-295.

.... **Renan,** Ernest, Lettre à M. D. Strauss (dans :) **Journal des Débats,** 13 Sept. 1870. (réimprimé dans : **La Réforme intellectuelle et morale,** p. 150.)

P.P. **Renan,** Ernest, La France et l'Allemagne (dans :) **Revue des deux Mondes, LXXXIX,** p. 264-283.

P.P. **Richard,** Henry, Great Britain and the continental war. Speech in the House of Commons. (London) 1870.

.... **Richard,** Henry, Two speeches on the abolition of standing armaments. (London 1870.)

P.P. **Riko,** A. J., Menschenslachting en blinde vernieling. 's-Gravenhage 1870.

.... **Rogier,** Charles, Retour à la maison. Nouv. éd. Bruxelles 1870.

.... **Roussinet,** A., De la guerre dans la société. Paris 1870.

.... **Rouville,** L. M., Tu ne tueras point. Sermon 1869. Paris 1870.

.... **Rijnders,** J. W., Hoe komen wij tot een duurzamen vrede. 1870.

P.P. **Strauss,** Dav., Krieg und Friede. Zwei Briefe an Ernst Renan. Leipzig 1870.

P.P. **Sumner,** Charles, The duel between France and Germany. Lecture, Boston, 26 Oct. 1870.

.... **Tankar** om kriget (par Carl **Andersson).** Stockholm 1870.

.... **Thumser,** Schlagfertiger .... Uebergang .... zum Friedensheere. München 1870.

.... **Travailleur** (= H. M. **Werker),** Beschouwingen over den oorlog. Amsterdam 1870.

.... **Un meeting à Londres.** Paris 1870. (*Bibliothèque de la paix,* 11.)

.... **Urban,** Benno, Ueber Ideale, I. Die Abschaffung des Krieges. 2e Aufl. Königsberg 1870.

.... **Veit,** Der Krieg und der ewige Friede. Berlin 1870.

.... **Vermeil,** Louis-Lucien, Les douleurs de la guerre. Lausanne (?) 1870.

49

.... **Vincent,** Francis, Essay recommending the union of Great-Britain and her colonies .... and the final union of the world. 2d ed. Wilmington, Del. 1870.

.... **Vredebond** te 's-Gravenhage. 1870.

.... **Yriarte,** Ch., Les tableaux de la guerre. Paris 1870.

.... **Zeeman,** H., Mag de stelselmatige moord, die men oorlog noemt, blijven bestaan ? Amsterdam 1870.

1871

.... **Address(es)** and **Annual Report(s)** of .... **Peace Society(ies)** 1871.

P.P. **Bulletin officiel** du 5e congrès de la Ligue internationale de la paix et de la liberté. Lausanne 1871.

.... **Cinquième Bulletin** de la Ligue internationale et permanente de la paix. 1871.

P.P. **De Vredebond.** Amsterdam 1871.

P.P. **l'Harmonie sociale** (Organe de l'Association belge des amis de la paix). Bruxelles 1871.

.... **The Advocate of peace.** Boston and Chicago. 1871.

P.P. **The Herald of peace.** London 1871.

.... **A historic survey** of international arbitration. (London 1871).

.... **Är kriget ett nödvändigt ondt ?** (par Carl **Andersson.)** Stockholm 1871.

P.P. **Amberley,** Lord, Can war be avoided ? (dans :) **Fortnightly Review,** IX new series (1871), p. 614-633.

.... **Baltzer,** Ed., Unter dem Kreuze des Krieges. Nordhausen 1871.

P.P. **Bemmelen,** P. van, Middelen tot voorkoming van den oorlog. Utrecht 1871.

.... **Blessed are the peacemakers,** or peace and war. London 1871.

P.P. **Brandat,** Paul, et Fréd. **Passy,** La Colonne. Brest 1871.

.... **Caillat,** J., Réflexions sur la guerre et sur la religion. Paris 1871.

.... **Carneri,** Sittlichkeit und Darwinismus. Wien 1871.

.... **Cassel,** Paulus, Vom Frieden. Zwei Reden. Berlin 1871.

.... **Clavel,** Charles, Oeuvres diverses. Paris 1871.

.... **Colonna,** Ces., Dalla guerra alla pace. Palermo 1871.

.... **Congrès Universel** des amis de la civilisation. Paris 1871.

.... **Coninck,** Frédéric de, A l'assemblée nationale. Guerre ou paix, Hâvre 1871.

P.P. **Conversations on war** and general culture (par Sir Arthur **Helps).** London 1871.

P.P. **Cremer,** J. J., De oorlog een noodzakelijk kwaad ? Leiden 1871.

P.P. **Delmas,** L., Le crime de la guerre. 2e éd. La Rochelle 1871.

50

.... **Die preussische Kriegführung** im J. 1870 vom humanitären Standpunkt (dans :) **Militär. Wochenblatt** 1871, n° 62.

.... **Dudley,** Crews, Modern pleas for war. London 1871.

.... **Dymond,** Jon., Eine Untersuchung über die Uebereinstimmung des Krieges mit den Grundsaetzen des Christenthums. Elkhart, Indiana 1871.

.... **Emmanuel,** Appel aux mères. Toulouse 1871. (*Petite Bibliothèque des campagnes.*)

.... **Emmanuel,** Secret pour ne pas être soldat. Toulouse 1871. (*Petite Bibliothèque des campagnes.*)

.... **Flourens,** Gustave, Paris livré. Paris 1871.

.... **Guéronnière,** Alfrèd de la, Place au droit. Bruxelles 1871.

.... **Hanson,** Ed., The prevention of war. London 1871.

P.P. **Heinrichs,** Joseph, Gedanken über den Krieg (dans :) **Zur Lösung dreier Zeitfragen.** Prag 1871.

.... **Hodgkin,** Thomas, The duties of neutrality. London 1871.

P.P. **Howitt,** William, The mad war-planet. London 1871.

.... **Jurgensen,** Jules F. U., Le soir du combat. Poème. Genève 1871.

P.P. **Kemper,** J. de Bosch, De vredebeweging in Nederland. Toespraak. Amsterdam 1871.

.... **Krig og** Kristendom. En adresse. (signé par Joseph **Crosfield.**) London 1871.

.... **La paix** et un pouvoir fédéral européen (Par **A.Z.**) 1871 ?

.... **Lasson,** A., Prinzip und Zukunft des Völkerrechts. Berlin 1871.

.... **Laveleye,** E. de, Causes of war (dans :) **Fortnightly Review** 13, p. 149-153 (Febr. 1873).

.... **Levi,** Leone, Proposals for a plan of arbitration and mediation (dans :) Sessional Proceedings of the Social Science Association 1871.

.... **Lietar,** Bernard, Le nouveau monde. Bruxelles 1871.

P.P. **Loewenthal,** Ed., Das preussische Völker-Dressur-System. Zürich 1871.

.... **Loewenthal,** Ed., Zur Friedensagitation (dans :) **Neue Freie Zeitung** 20 VII, 1873.

P.P. **Lorimer,** J., Proposition d'un congrès international (dans :) **Revue de droit international et de lég. comp.,** III (1871) p. 1-11.

P.P. **Marcel,** Lara, Plus de guerre, plus d'idolâtrie. Conférence. Genève 1871.

.... **Möller,** Jul., Unser Fortschritt zum ewigen Frieden (dans :) **Altpreussische Monatschrift,** 8, 1871.

.... **Monnier,** Marc, Le congrès de la paix. Comédie de marionettes. Genève 1871.

.... **Naquet,** Gustave, L'Europe délivrée. Histoire prophétique. Paris 1871.

.... **Nelson,** John, The faithful Christian soldier (*Peace tract* 1871).

P.P. **Nieuwenhuis,** F. Domela, De vredebond. Amsterdam 1871. (*Bibliotheek van Volksvoordrachten,* II, 4.)

.... **Oppenheim,** H. B., Friedensglossen zum Kriegsjahr. Leipzig 1871.

.... **Paix ou victoire.** Pau 1871.

.... **Passy,** Fréd., Ce que coûte la paix armée. Paris 1871. (*Petite bibliothèque de la paix,* 1.)

.... **Passy,** Fréd., La barbarie moderne. Discours. Paris 1871.

P.P. **Passy,** voir aussi ci-dessus : **Brandat.**

.... **Peace and war.** London 1871.

.... **Pollard,** Will., Considerations .... on the peace question. London 1871.

.... **Potvin,** Ch., Le génie de la paix en Belgique. Bruxelles 1871.

P.P. **Projet** de ligue internationale pour la paix perpétuelle. Stockholm 1871.

.... **Report** of the special committee (of the Social Science Assoc.) ,,Wether some general scheme of International Arbitration ...."? 1871.

.... **Richard,** Henry, Speech.... in Committee on the army estimates. In the House of Commons. (1871.)

P.P. **Ritter,** Moritz, Die Memoiren Sullys. München 1871.

.... **Sauveur,** Anne-Marie, La délivrance. Toulouse 1871. (*Petite bibliothèque des campagnes.*)

.... **Sauveur,** Anne-Marie, Secret pour n'avoir plus de guerres. Toulouse 1871.

P.P. **Seebohm,** Fred., On international reform. London 1871.

.... **Seeley,** John Rob., On the abolition of war. London (1871?).

.... **Seeley,** John Rob., On the prevention of war. London (1871).

.... **Simon,** Ludwig, Polit. und intern. Recht .... Bericht an die Friedens-.... Liga. Bern 1871.

.... **Simpson,** J. H., A new crusade to put down wars. London 1871.

.... **Stevenson,** Thomas, The expense and folly of war. Reprint] from the **Christian World.**

.... **Torrens,** W. M., What are we waiting for ? Reprint from **Daily News.**

.... **Trevelyan,** Arthur, False glory. (1871.)

.... **Venables,** Gilbert, Is war unchristian ? London 1871.

.... **Vermeil,** L., Les douleurs de la guerre. 3e éd. Lausanne 1871.

P.P. **War and Christianity.** An address .... (signé par Joseph **Crosfield.** London 1871.)

.... **War** — is it lawful — is it justifiable — is it Christian ? An address. (Signé par Jos. **Crosfield.**) London 1871.

.... **Westlake,** W. C., International Peace (dans .) **The Friends' Quarterly Examiner,** April 1871:

.... **What is war ?** *Peace Tract,* 1871.

1872
.... Address(es) and Annual Report(s) of ....
      Peace Society(ies) 1872.
.... Almanach de la paix. Paris 1872.
P.P. Bulletin de la Soc. des Amis de la paix. Paris
      1872.
P.P. Bulletin officiel du 6me congrès de la Ligue
      internationale de la paix et de la liberté.
      Genève· 1872.
.... Les Etats-Unis d'Europe. Genève 1872.
.... The Advocate of peace. Boston 1872.
.... The Arbitrator. A journal .... of the Work-
      men's peace association. London 1872.
P.P. The Herald of peace. London 1872.
P P. The Voice of peace. Mystic, Conn. 1872.

.... A bas la guerre ! Dialogues en vers familiers.
      Bergues 1872.
P.P. Adviezen en beschouwingen over herziening
      van art. 56 der Grondwet (par :) P. van
      Bemmelen etc. 's-Gravenhage 1872.
P.P. Bara, Louis, La science de la paix. Bruxelles
      1872.
P.P. Barbault, Louis, Du tribunal international.
      Genève 1872.
.... Barni, Jules, Manuel républicain. Paris 1872.
.... Beaudemoulin, L. A., La guerre s'en va. Paris
      1872.
.... Beaussire, Emile, La guerre étrangère et la
      guerre civile. Paris 1872.
.... Beecher, Henry Ward, War and peace. New
      York 1872.
P.P. Bellaire, Henry, Etude historique sur les
      arbitrages. Suivi du discours prononcé par
      Fréd. Passy. Paris 1872.
•... Burritt, Elihu, Bearing each other's war
      burdens.
P.P. Castex, B. Sernin, Le tribunal des nations.
      Paris 1872.
.... Clavel, Charles, Oeuvres diverses. Paris 1872.
.... Dameth, H., Les bases naturelles de l'écono-
      mie sociale. Genève 1872.
P.P. Douay, Edmond, Catéchisme de la paix. Paris
      1872.
P.P. Dumesnil, Henri, La guerre. Etude philoso-
      phique. Paris 1872.
.... Durand—Savoyat, Max, A propos de l'armée.
      Genève 1872.
P.P. Facts and illustrations in reference to war,
      peace and international arbitration. (Lon-
      don) 1872.
.... Field, D. Dudley, Draft outlines of an interna-
      tional code. New York 1872.
.... Fromentin, R., Le crime de la guerre. Sedan
      1872.
.... Goblet d'Alviella, E., Désarmer ou déchoir.
      Bruxelles 1872.
.... Hälschner, Hugo, Der deutsch-französ. Krieg
      und das Völkerrecht (dans :) Deutsche
      Blätter von Füllner. Gotha 1872.

53

.... Hemmenway, John, The Apostle of peace.
      Memoir of William Ladd. Boston 1872.
.... Henry, Léon, Le crime international. Paris
      1872.
.... Historic Survey of Internat. Arbitration. Re-
      print from North Am. Review.
.... Holtzendorff, F. von, Eroberungen und Ero-
      berungsrecht. Berlin 1872.
P.P. Kemper, J. de Bosch, Discours d'ouverture
      de la première assemblée .... des sociétés
      de la paix. La Haye 1872.
.... La Codre, J. M. de, Le principe de moralité.
      Paris 1872.
.... Laveleye, E. de, On the causes of war. London
      1872. (aussi dans :) Cobden Club Essays,
      2nd series, 1871-1872.
P.P. Le crime de la guerre dénoncé à l'humanité.
      Rapport. Paris 1872.
.... Le respect de la vie. Paris (1872). (*Bibliothèque
      de la paix*, 12.)
P.P. Lemonnier, Ch., Les Etats-Unis d'Europe.
      Paris 1872. (*Bibliothèque démocratique*.)
.... Letter to working men on national armaments.
      (1872.)
.... Lucas, Charles, Nécessité d'un congrès scien-
      tifique internat. relatif à la civilisation de
      la guerre (dans :) Compte-rendu de l'Acad.
      des sciences morales et politiques, XCIX,
      p. 131-158.
P.P. Mézières, M. L., De la polémomanie. Paris
      1872.
P.P. Möller, J., Zwei Vorträge. Elbing 1872.
.... Montagu, Lord Robert, Arbitration instead of
      war. London 1872.
P.P. Morin, Ach., Les lois relatives à la guerre selon
      le droit des gens moderne. Paris 1872.
P.P. Münnich, H. W., Kriget och den beväpnade
      freden. Stockholm (1872).
P.P. Nieuwenhuis, F. Domela, Een krachtig plei-
      dooi voor de internationale vredezaak.
      Amsterdam (1872).
.... Passy, Fréd., Revanche ou relèvement. Paris
      1872.
.... Passy, Fréd., Un souvenir et une espérance.
      (dans :) L'offrande à l'Alsace.
.... Rapport présenté à la loge des Amis philan-
      thropes sur la question de la paix. Bruxelles
      1872.
.... Ratel, Henry, La mort de deux ennemis.
      Paris 1872.
.... Richard, Henry, Speech on .... the military
      forces localisation bill in the House of Com-
      mons, July 15th 1872.
.... Richard, Henry, Speech on international ar-
      bitration, delivered in Dublin, 1872.
.... Richard, Henry, (other speeches).
.... Robinson, Vincent, Henry Horace. London
      1872.
.... The collapse of the great milit. powers of the
      continent. (1872.)

54

.... **Tissot, Victor,** Le congrès de la paix et de la liberté. Genève 1872.
.... **Tolstoï** (L. N.), Voina i. mir. 1872. 4 vol.
.... **Varigny,** C. de, Dépenses de deux guerres. Paris 1872.
.... **Whitfield,** Richard, Woman and war (dans :) **Woman,** 1872.

1873
.... **Address(es) and Annual Report(s) of.... Peace Society(ies)** 1873.
.... **Almanach de la paix.** Paris 1873.
P.P. **Bulletin de la Société des Amis de la paix.** Paris 1873.
P.P. **Bulletin officiel des Assemblées** (de La Ligue internationale de la paix et de la liberté) tenues à Genève, 1873. Genève 1873.
P.P. **Jaarboekje van het Nederlandsche Vredebond.** 's-Gravenhage 1873.
.... **Les Etats-Unis d'Europe.** Genève 1873.
.... **The Advocate of peace.** Boston 1873.
.... **The Arbitrator.** A journal.... of the **Workmen's peace association.** (London) 1873.
P.P. **The Herald of peace.** London 1873.
P.P. **The Voice of peace.** Mystic, Conn. 1873.
.... **The Woman's peace festival.** Boston 1873.

P.P. **Berialle,** H. (= H. Bellaire), La politique de Jacques Bonhomme. Paris 1873.
.... **Bill,** Arp, Peace papers. New York 1873.
.... **Burdon,** John, War : A lecture. Monmouth 1873.
.... **Discorso del deputato Mancini** sugli arbitrati internazionali. Roma 1873.
P.P. **Dupasquier,** Henri, Le crime de la guerre. Paris 1873.
P.P. **Field,** D. Dudley, Plan d'un code international. Paris 1873.
.... **Grès,** A., Pourquoi la guerre ? Marseille 1873.
.... **Heerwesen und National-Oekonomie.** (par) C. J. 1873.
.... **Henry,** Léon, Le crime des crimes. Paris 1873.
P.P. **Henry Richard in Nederland.** Leiden 1873.
.... **Hyde,** J., International arbitration. London 1873.
P.P. **International arbitration.** Debate in the House of Commons on the motion of Henry **Richard.** London 1873.
P.P. **Internationales Schiedsgericht.** Die Debatte über den Antrag Henry **Richard's.** London—Leipzig (1873 ?).
.... **Kant und Richard.** (dans :) **Die Wage** 1873, p. 132.
P.P. **Krigets Bundsförvandter** (par Carl **Andersson).** Stockholm 1873.
P.P. **La Motion Mancini** sur l'arbitrage international. Roma 1873.
.... **Lammers,** A., Staat und Krieg. (dans :) **Vierteljahrschr. für Volkswirtsch. und Culturgesch.,** XXXIX (1873).

P.P. **Laporte,** Michel-E., L'Alsace reconquise. Paris 1873.
.... **Laveleye,** E. de, Causes of war. (dans :) **Fortnightly review,** XIII, pag. 149—153.
P.P. **Laveleye,** E. de, Des causes actuelles de guerre. Bruxelles—Paris 1873.
.... **Lemonnier,** Ch., De l'arbitrage international et de sa procédure. Genève 1873.
.... **Loewenthal,** Ed., Zur Friedensagitation (dans :) **Neue Freie Zeitung,** 20 Juli 1873.
.... **Lucas,** Ch., De la substitution de l'arbitrage à la voie des armes (dans:) **Compte-Rendu** de l'Acad. des Sciences morales et politiques, C, p. 415—478.
.... **Lucas,** Ch., La cause de l'arbitrage international. (dans :) **Revue critique** de législation, août 1873.
P.P. **Lucas,** Ch., Le droit de légitime défense. Paris 1873.
P.P. **Lucas,** Ch., Les deux rêves de Henri IV. Discours, Pau, 1873. (Extrait du) **Compte-Rendu** du congrès scient. de l'Institut des provinces, XXXIXe session.
.... **Lucas,** Ch., Lettre du 3 juillet 1873 au peuple anglais sur l'arbitrage international.
.... **Lucas,** Ch., Nécessité d'un congrès.... pour la civilisation de la guerre. (dans :) **Compte-Rendu** de l'Acad. des Sciences mor. et pol., XCIX, p. 131—158.
.... **Lucas,** Ch., Observations.... sur.... la substitution de l'arbitrage à la voie des armes. (dans :) **Compte-Rendu** de l'Acad. des sciences mor. et pol. C, p. 695—712.
.... **Lucas,** Ch., Quelques mots sur le concours de l'action collective.... pour le progrès du droit des gens. Août 1873.
P.P. **Lucas,** Ch., Un voeu de civilisation chrétienne. Paris 1873. (Extrait de la) **Revue Chrétienne,** juin 1873.
.... **Motion of Henry Richard** for an address to the Crown. 1873.
P.P. **Nieuwenhuis,** F. Domela, De wereld op haar malst. Amsterdam 1873. (Extrait de) **Onze Tijd.**
.... **On the profession of a soldier.** Manchester 1873.
.... **Prins,** A., Le mouvement pour l'amélioration des rapports internat. Bruxelles 1873. (Extrait de) **La Revue de Belgique.**
.... **Rogers,** James E. Thorold, Cobden and modern political opinion. London 1873.
P.P. **Seebohm,** Fred., De la réforme du droit des gens. Paris 1873.
.... **Thonissen,** J. J., Mélanges d'histoire de droit et d'économie politique. Louvain 1873.

1874
.... **Address(es) and Annual Report(s) of ....Peace Society(ies)** 1874.
.... **Almanach de la paix.** Paris 1874.

55

56

P.P.   **Bulletin de la Société des Amis de la paix.**
       Paris 1874.
....   **Bulletin officiel des assemblées** tenues (de la
       Ligue internat. de la paix et de la liberté).
       Genève—Paris, 1874.
P.P.   **Jaarboekje van het Nederlandsche Vredebond.**
       's-Gravenhage 1874.
....   **Les Etats-Unis d'Europe.** Genève 1874.
....   **The Advocate of peace.** Boston 1874.
....   **The Arbitrator.** A journal .... of the Work-
       men's peace assoc. London 1874.
P.P.   **The Herald of peace.** London 1874.
....   **The Voice of Peace.** Philadelphia 1874.
....   **The Woman's peace festival.** Boston 1874.

....   **Burritt,** El., Ten-minute talks on all sorts
       of topics. Boston 1874.
....   **Der Krieg** gegen den Krieg (par J. C. **Brunner**).
       Aarau 1874.
....   **Eschenauer,** A., La morale universelle. Paris
       1874.
....   **Fauvety,** Charles, Assemblée de la Ligue inter-
       nationale de la paix. Genève 1874.
P.P.   **Field,** D. Dudley, Prime linee di un codice
       internazionale. Napoli 1874.
....   **Fontanès,** Ernest, La guerre. (dans :) **le Christia-**
       nisme libéral. Paris 1874.
....   **Friedländer,** L., Vom ewigen Frieden. (dans :)
       Altpreussische Monatschrift, XI, 3 (1874).
....   **Goff,** Dinah Wilson, Guddommelig beskyttelse.
       Kristiania 1874.
....   **Harris,** John, Peace papers for the people.
       (1874 ?)
....   **La guerre** et ses conséquences (par F. **Le**
       Doyen). Saint-Omer 1874.
....   **Lawrence,** Edw. A., The progress of peace
       principles. (dans :) **The Law Magazine,**
       Dec. 1874.
P.P.   **Lawrence,** W. B., Note .... à propos de
       l'étude historique de H. Bellaire (voir
       1872) sur les arbitrages dans les conflits
       internat. (dans :) **Revue de droit internat.,**
       VI, p. 117—129.
....   **Le Berquier,** Jules, Les ligues de la paix et
       les lois de la guerre. Paris 1874. (Extrait
       de :) **Revue des deux mondes** XLIV,
       p. 155—174.
P.P.   **Lemonnier,** Ch., Formule d'un traité d'arbi-
       trage entre nations. Genève 1874.
....   **Loewenthal,** Ed., Grundzüge zur Reform und
       Codification des Völkerrechts. Berlin 1874.
....   **Loewenthal,** Ed., Weltpolitik und Weltjustiz.
       (1874 ?) (Extrait de la revue) **Pionier.**
....   **Loewenthal,** Ed., Zur internationalen Frie-
       denspropaganda. Berlin 1874.
P.P.   **Lucas, Ch.,** La conférence .... sur les lois
       et coutumes de la guerre. Paris 1874.
P.P.   **Mancini,** P. S., Internationale arbitrage.
       Dordrecht 1874.

....   **Miles,** James B., Le tribunal international.
       Paris 1874.
....   **Monteil,** Edgar, Le congrès de Bruxelles (1874).
....   **Neumann,** Leop., Vom ewigen Frieden. (dans :)
       Zeitschrift für das Privat- und öffentl. Recht
       der Gegenwart, I, p. 570—583.
....   **Orelli,** Aloys v., Die Lehren der Wiener Welt-
       ausstellung. (Extrait du) **Illustrierte Schweiz,**
       1874.
....   **P(ictet) de S(ergy),** (D.) J., Union et paix.
       Genève 1874.
....   **Pozzoni,** Ces., L'Europa e la pace. Roma 1874.
P.P.   **Richard,** Henry, The gradual triumph of law
       over brute force. London 1874.
P.P.   **Sensuyt le testament,** de la guerre qui regne
       a présent sur la terre (par Jehan **Molinet** ?
       Fac-simile). Paris 1874.
....   **Tennyson,** Alfred, Maud and other poems.
       London 1874.
....   **The Italian parliament** and arbitration. Lon-
       don (1874).
P.P.   **The principles** and objects of the peace party.
       (London 1874.)
....   **The Times** on the armaments of Europe.
       (Tract of the *Peace soc.* 1874.)
P.P.   **Torres Asensio,** J., Le droit des Catholiques
       de se défendre. Paris 1874.
P.P.   **Turcotti,** Aurelio, Introduzione al nuovo
       codice di diritto delle genti. Torino 1874.
....   **Une vie de dévouement.** Joseph Sturge. Paris
       (1874).
....   **Valton,** Cyprien, Combattons ! Guerre à la
       guerre. Turin 1874.
P.P.   **War** and its consequences (par F. **Le Doyen**).
       Boulogne-sur-Mer 1874.
P.P.   **Waxel,** Platon de, L'armée d'invasion et la
       population. Leipzig 1874.

1875

....   **Address(es) and Annual Report(s)** of .... **Peace**
       Society(ies) 1875.
P.P.   **Bulletin de la Société des Amis de la paix.**
       Paris 1875.
....   **Bulletin officiel des assemblées et meeting**
       (de la Ligue internat. de la paix et de la
       liberté). Genève 1875.
P.P.   **Jaarboekje van het Nederlandsche Vredebond.**
       's-Gravenhage 1875.
....   **L'avenir des nations.** Marseille 1875.
....   **Les Etats-Unis d'Europe.** Genève 1875.
....   **The Advocate of peace.** Boston 1875.
....   **The Arbitrator.** A journal .... of the Work-
       men's peace assoc. London 1875.
P.P.   **The Herald of peace,** London 1875.
....   **The Voice of peace.** Philadelphia 1875.

P.P.   **Beelaerts van Blokland,** C. H., Internationale
       arbitrage. 's-Hage 1875.

P.P. **Beer Poortugael,** J. C. C. den, Réponse au questionnaire de Mr. Rolin Jaequemyns. 1875. (Manuscrit.)

P.P. **Bredius,** J. P., Over de internationale arbitrage in de Tweede Kamer. (Extrait de :) **De Tijdspiegel,** Februari 1875.

.... **Catéchisme de la paix** (par F. **Le Doyen**). Saint-Omer 1875.

P.P. **Dupasquier,** Henri, Le crime de la guerre. 2e éd. Paris 1875.

.... **Earl Russell** on the Crimean war. (Pamphlet of the *Peace soc.*) (1875 ?)

.... **Field,** D. Dudley, Association pour la réforme et la codification du droit des gens. Paris 1875.

P.P. **Fischhof,** Ad., Zur Reduction der continentalen Heere. Wien 1875.

P.P. **Fischhof,** Ad., On the reduction of continental armies. London 1875.

.... **Gurney,** Cath., Woman's work for peace. (1875 ?)

.... **Hemmenway,** John, The daily remembrancer on peace and war. New Vienna, Ohio 1875.

.... **Holtzendorff,** F. von, Die Streitfrage des neueren Völkerrechts. (dans :) **Deutsche Rundschau** von Rodenberg, II, 1 (Oct. 1875).

.... **La Codre,** J. M. de, La science du Bonhomme Félix. (1875 ?)

P.P. **L'arbitrage international.** Proposition faite à la Chambre des représ. de Belgique par A. **Couvreur** et J. **Thonissen.** Bruxelles 1875.

P.P. **Larroque,** Patr., De la création d'un code de droit international. Paris 1875.

P.P. **Lawrence,** Edw. A., The progress of peace principles. Boston 1875.

.... **Loewenthal,** Ed., Aufruf zur Einberufung eines Weltparlaments (dans :) **der Geisel** 19/IX, 1875.

.... **Lucas,** Ch., Les actes de la conférence de Bruxelles. (Extrait du) **Compte-rendu** de l'Acad. des Sciences mor. et pol., CIV (1875 II).

.... **Lucas,** Ch., Rapport sur la publication des actes de la conférence de Bruxelles. (dans :) **Compte-rendu** de l'Acad. des sciences mor. et pol., CIII (1875 I), p. 50—58.

P.P. **Miles,** James B., Association for the reform and codification of the law of nations. Paris 1875.

P.P. **Miles,** James B., Association pour la réforme et la codification du droit des gens. Paris 1875.

.... **Miles,** James B., A paper prepared for the Conference of the Assoc. for the reform and codif. of the law of nations. (*An international tribunal,* 2.) Boston 1875.

P.P. **Miles,** James B., Mémoire préparé pour la conférence de l'Assoc. pour la réforme et la codif. du droit des gens. (*Un tribunal international,* 2.) Paris 1875.

.... **Morin,** Pierre, L'armée de l'avenir. 1875.

.... **Neumann,** Léop., De la paix perpétuelle. 1875.

P.P. **Paretti,** Mauro, Degli arbitrati internazionali. Torino 1875.

.... **Reknil-Eilé** (= E. **Linker**), Die Begründung des europäischen Friedens. Wien 1875.

P.P. **Richard,** Henry, The limits of international arbitration. London 1875.

P.P. **Richard,** Henry, Le triomphe progressif de la loi sur la force (voir 1874). Paris 1875.

.... **Rocks ahead** ; or great armies and military conscription. (Pamphlet of the *Peace soc.*)

P.P. **Taparelli d'Azeglio,** Essai théorique de droit naturel. 2e éd. Paris 1875.

.... **Thompson,** Joseph P., The armament of Germany. 1875.

P.P. **Tideman,** B., Jzn, De vredesbeweging en de openbare meening in Nederland. (Extrait de **Onze Tijd,** Jan. 1875.)

.... **Wilson,** John J., Construction and destruction. Birmingham (1875 ?).

.... **Zecchini,** S. P., Dio, l'universo e la fratellanza di tutti gli esseri nella creazione. Torino 1875.

1876

.... **Address(es)** and **Annual Report(s)** of.... Peace Society(ies) 1876.

P.P. **Bulletin de la Société des Amis de la paix.** Paris 1876.

P.P. **Bulletin officiel des assemblées** (de la Ligue internat. de la paix et de la liberté). Genève 1876.

P.P. **Jaarboekje van het Nederlandsche Vredebond.** 's-Gravenhage 1876.

.... **L'Avenir des nations.** Marseille 1876.

.... **Les Etats-Unis d'Europe.** Genève 1876.

.... **The Advocate of peace.** Boston 1876.

.... **The Arbitrator.** A journal.... of the **Workmen's peace assoc.** London 1876.

P.P. **The Herald of peace.** London 1876.

.... **The Voice of peace.** Philadelphia 1876.

.... **Bellaire,** Henry, L'échange et la fraternité à la Soc. des amis de la paix. (dans :) **Journal des économistes,** t. 41, p. 454—457.

.... **Bellaire,** Henry, Note sur l'arbitrage international. Paris 1876.

.... **Cardona,** Enrico, L'abolizione della guerra. 1876.

.... **Cavalli,** Giov., Sulla pace universale. Torino 1876.

P.P. **Creasy,** Edw., First platform of international law. London 1876.

106   *1876-1877*

.... **Diaz,** Abbie M., Neighbourhood talks. New Vienna, Ohio 1876.
.... **Europe** crushed by armaments. (Tract of the *Peace Soc.*) (1876.)
.... **Farrer,** J. A., War and Christianity. London 1876.
P.P. **Field,** D. Dudley, Outlines of an international code. 2nd ed. New York-London 1876.
.... **Frommel,** Max, Weltreich und Gottesreich. 2. Aufl. Frankfurt a. M. 1876.
.... **Heinrich IV,** Christliche Republik Europa. (dans :) **Die Wage** 1876, p. 625.
.... **Hornby,** E., Constitution d'un tribunal international. Berne (1876 ?).
.... **Janney,** Sam. M., Peace principles exemplified. Philadelphia 1876.
.... **La guerre** au point de vue du Christianisme (par Jon. **Dymond**). Paris 1876.
.... **La guerre** et ses conséquences (par F. **Le Doyen**). Saint-Omer 1876.
P.P. **Lacombe,** Paul, Mémoire sur l'établissement d'un tribunal international. (dans :) **Marcoartu,** Internationalism.
.... **Lawrence,** Edw. A., A confession of faith in peace principles. Philadelphia 1876.
.... **Le Doyen,** F., Triomphe de la civilisation par l'extinction de la guerre. Saint-Omer 1876.
.... **Leeds,** Josiah W., The primitive Christians' estimate of war. New Vienna, Ohio 1876.
.... **Levi,** Leone, Peace the handmaid of Commerce. London 1876.
P.P. **Marco,** Pietro di, Degli arbitrati internazionali e dei dritti di guerra. Palermo 1876.
P.P. **Marcoartu,** Art. de, Internationalism. London 1876.
.... **Monteil,** Edgar, Le congrès de Bruxelles. Paris 1876.
.... **Nottelle,** Est-ce la fraternité ou l'échange qui amènera la paix ? (dans :) **Journal des économistes,** 1876, III, t. 42, p. 251—257.
.... **Peace or war ?** An appeal to the women of Great Britain and Ireland (par Miss **Pierce**). London 1876.
.... **Petersen,** Aleksis, Om det internationale Voldgiftssystem. København 1876. (Extrait du) **Nationaloekonomisk Tidsskrift.**
.... **Petriccioli,** Gius., Hymnus paci — L'inno alla pace. Parma 1876.
P.P. **Remonstrance** aux françois (1576). Paris 1876.
.... **Richard,** Henry, Increase of army expenditure. London 1876.
.... **Richard,** Henry, The gradual triumph of law over brute force. 2d ed. London 1876.
P.P. **Sprague,** A. P., The codification of public international law. (dans :) **Marcoartu,** Internationalism.
.... **The profession** of a soldier. Manchester (1876).
.... **Thiaudière,** D. A. E., La dernière bataille. 1876.

61

1877
.... **Address(es)** and **Annual Report(s)** of.... **Peace Society(ies)** 1877.
P.P. **Bulletin de la Soc. des amis de la paix.** Paris 1877.
P.P. **Bulletin officiel des conférence et assemblées** (de la Ligue internat. de la paix et de la liberté). Genève 1877.
P.P. **Jaarboekje van het Nederlandsche Vredebond.** 's-Gravenhage 1877.
P.P. **Les Etats-Unis d'Europe.** Genève 1877.
.... **The Advocate of peace.** Boston 1877.
.... **The Arbitrator.** A journal.... of the Workmen's peace assoc. London 1877.
P.P. **The Herald of peace.** London 1877.

.... **Address** (of the Peace Soc.) to their subscribers and friends. London 1877.
.... **Briggs,** Th., The peacemaker. London 1877.
.... **Britten,** J., Perpetual peace in five years. London 1877.
.... **Buchanan,** Rob., The shadow of the sword. 1877.
.... **Considérations** sur les propositions prés. par le Dr. **Thompson** à la conférence de Brême du 25 sept. 1876. (La Haye 1877.)
P.P. **Garrett,** Phil. C., Ein Staat ohne Krieg. Antwerpen 1877.
.... **Girardin,** Emile, Le dossier de la guerre de 1870. Paris 1877.
.... **Hornung,** J. M., Fédération brittannique, continentale et générale. Neufchâtel 1877.
.... **How to stop war** among civilized nations ? By a Birmingham Tradesman. 1877.
.... **Langbridge,** The war fever. Manchester 1877.
P.P. **Lorimer,** J., Le problème final du droit international. (dans :) **Revue de droit internat. et de lég. comp.,** IX (1877), p. 161—206.
.... **Lucas,** Ch., La civilisation de la guerre. 1877.
.... **Mackay,** Charles, Forty year's recollections of life. 2 vols. London 1877.
.... **Monteil,** Edgar, Catéchisme du libre-penseur. Anvers 1877.
.... **Pintos,** Luis Telmo, Liga internacional americana. Buenos Aires 1877.
.... **Programma** per la pace universale. Palermo 1877.
.... **Reknil-Eilé** (= E. **Linker**), Die Begründung des Europäischen Friedens. Wien 1877.
.... **Remarks** chiefly upon a sermon by Canon Mozley (par) **M. L. D.** Birmingham (1877).
.... **Résolutions** votées par les dix premiers congrès (de la Ligue internat. de la paix et de la liberté). Genève 1877.
.... **Richard,** Henry, On the application of Christianity to politics. London 1877.
.... **Richard,** Henry, The obligation of treaties. Antwerp (1877).

62

.... **Richard**, Henry, The relations of the temporal and spiritual power. London 1877.
P.P. **Rouard de Card**, E., L'arbitrage international dans le passé, le présent et l'avenir. Paris 1877.
.... **Salvatier-Laroche**, Etudes morales. Auxerre 1877.
.... **Tayler**, Maria, Women and war! London 1877.
.... **The war system** of Europe. (Tract 99 of the *Peace Soc.*) (1877.)
P.P. **Virchow**, (Rud.), Krieg und Frieden. Berlin (1877).
P.P. **Wiede**, F., Der Militarismus. Zürich 1877.
.... **Zur Lösung** der Sozialen Frage. (1877.)

1878
.... **Address** (es) and **Annual Report**(s) of .... **Peace Society**(ies) 1878.
P.P. **Bulletin de la Soc. des amis de la paix.** Paris 1878.
.... **Bulletin officiel des assemblées** (de la Ligue intern. de la paix et de la liberté). Genève 1878.
P.P. **Jaarboekje van het Nederlandsche Vredebond.** 's-Gravenhage 1878.
P.P. **Le Devoir.** Guise (Aisne).
P.P. **Les Etats-Unis d'Europe.** Genève 1878.
.... **The Advocate of peace.** Boston 1878.
.... **The Arbitrator.** A journal .... of the **Workmen's peace assoc.** London 1878.
P.P. **The Herald of peace.** London 1878.

.... **An Appeal** .... on war issued by the Society of Friends. London 1878.
.... **Appel**.... à propos de la guerre addressé par la Société des Amis. (1878.)
.... **Bluntschli**, J. C., Die Organisation des europäischen Staatenvereines. (dans :) **Die Gegenwart** 1878.
.... **Bright**, John. On sunday-school teachers and war. London 1878.
.... **Cervo**, Fil., Storia del codice di alleanza delle nazioni. (Opera.) Napoli 1878.
.... **Cobden**, Rich., Speeches and writings. London 1878.
.... **Die Armeen** gegenüber der Socialdemokratie. (dans :) **Die Gegenwart**, XIV, 1878.
.... **Droysen**, J. G., Über die Schrift Anti-St. Pierre. (Berlin 1878.) (Extrait de) **Monatsberichte** der K. Akad. der Wissensch. zu Berlin.
.... **Harvey**, Thom., On the proper attitude of the Christian Church with regard to war. Leeds 1878.
.... **Lajous**, Ad. de, Les rondes de la paix et du travail. Paris 1878.
.... **Lemonnier**, Ch., Conférence sur le droit internat. Paris 1878. (Extrait de) **Comptes rendus** .... du comité.... des congrès et conférences de l'exposition univ. internat.

P.P. **Lemonnier**, Ch., Formule d'un traité d'arbitrage entre nations. Paris 1878.
.... **L'union des peuples** par le conseil non politique des nations civilisées (par Jules **Polo**). Paris 1878.
.... **Mancini**, P. S., Trattato di commercio colla Francia. Discorsi. Roma 1878.
.... **Marzorati**, Egidio, Guerra e pauperismo. Milano 1878.
.... **Moffat** (John **Smith**), (Quotation of a heathen chief.) 1878. (*Peace Soc.*)
P.P. **Nieuwenhuis**, F. Domela, In het belang der vredezaak. Haarlem (1878). (Extrait du) **Banier**, III, 4.
.... **Peace or war** : the new moral law and the new treaty law. London 1878.
.... **Pye-Smith**, J., Address on behalf of peace to ministers of Christianity. (1878.)
.... **Reichenau**, Von, Ewiger Frieden und Abrüstung. 2. Aufl. Berlin-Leipzig 1878. (*Milit. Zeit- und Streitfragen*, 29.)
.... **Richard**, Henry, Standing armies a chief source of the social evil. (1878.) (Pamphlet of the *Peace soc.*)
.... **Richard**, Henry, The principle and the policy of peace. London 1878.
.... **Richardson**, Henry, Moralisings in verse. (1878.)
.... **Santo Agostino**, Aurelio, Sermone della virtu della pace. Faenza 1878.
.... **Sellon**, Valentine de, Congrès internat. de la paix. Discours. Paris 1878.
.... **Sellon**, Valentine de, Feuilles éparses. Paris 1878.
.... **Simmons**, James P., Peace on earth. Boston 1878.
.... **Türr**, (Stephan), Aux amis de la paix. Paris 1878.
.... **Valton**, Cip., Combattiamo ! guerra alla guerra. Torino 1878.
.... **Venables**, Gilb., Is war unchristian ? 2d ed. London 1878.

1879
.... **Address**(es) and **Annual Report**(s) of .... Peace Society(ies) 1879.
P.P. **Bulletin de la Soc. des amis de la paix.** Paris 1879.
.... **Bulletin officiel des meeting, conférence et assemblées** (de la Ligue internat. de la paix et de la liberté). Genève 1879.
P.P. **Jaarboekje van het Nederlandsche Vredebond.** 's-Gravenhage 1879.
P.P. **Le Devoir.** Guise (Aisne) 1879.
P.P. **Les Etats-Unis d'Europe.** Genève 1879.
.... **The Advocate of peace.** Boston 1879.
.... **The Arbitrator.** Organ of the **Workmen's peace assoc. and internat. arbitration league.** London 1879.
P.P. **The Herald of peace.** London 1879.

.... **Ballou,** Adin, Christian non-resistance. (1879).
.... **Cobby,** Eleanor F., The autobiography of war. Bognor (Suss.) (1879).
.... **Fischer de Chevriers,** Ph., Etudes sur la paix. Paris 1879.
.... **Franck,** Ad., Le parti de la paix. (dans :) Journal des économistes, 1879, IV, t. 6, p. 258—263.
.... **Gooch,** Rich., Boyle's ghost. London 1879.
.... **Harris,** John, The two giants. London 1879.
P.P. **Leslie,** E. Cliffe, Essays in political and moral philosophy. Dublin-London 1879.
.... **Letters to Christian women,** 2 : The army and navy, why so popular ? (1879).
.... **Monge y Puga,** L. M. de, La razón de la guerra. Madrid 1879.
.... **Passy,** Fréd., L'arbitrage international. Paris (1879).
.... **Paterson,** James, War and civilisation. Glasgow (1879).
P.P. **Richard,** Henry, International reduction of armaments. London (1879).
.... **Ruskin,** John, Women's responsibility for war. (1879).
P.P. **Salières,** A., La guerre. Ses causes. Ses résultats. Paris 1879.
.... **Sellon,** Valentine de, Congrès international de la paix. Firenze 1879.
.... **Severus,** Oorlog een slag in het aangezicht der beschaving. Wildervank 1879.
.... **Shaw,** G. Irving, The philosophy of peace versus the powers that be. London (1879).
.... **Sørensen,** N. J., Ved vinterens hjerte. Frederiksstad 1879.
.... **The military Trades Union.** (Appeal of the *Peace Soc.*) (1879).
.... **War :** or who would not be a conqueror. (Tract of the *Peace Soc.*) (1879).
.... **William Penn.** (Tract of the *American Peace Soc.*) (1879).
.... **Worms,** E., L'économie politique devant les congrès de paix. (Paris 1879.) (Extrait des Séances et Travaux de l'Acad. des sciences mor. et pol., CXI.)
.... **Wynne,** J. A., De groote en de kleine plannen van Hendrik IV. (dans :) De Gids, XLIII. (3e serie, XVII), II, p. 421—456.

1880
.... **Address(es) and Annual Report(s) of**.... Peace Society(ies) 1880.
P.P. **Bulletin de la Soc. des amis de la paix.** Paris 1880.
.... **Bulletin officiel des assemblées** (de la Ligue internat. de la paix et de la liberté). Genève 1880.
P.P. **Jaarboekje van het Nederlandsche Vredebond.** 's-Gravenhage 1880.
P.P. **Le Devoir.** Guise (Aisne) 1880.
P.P. **Les Etats-Unis d'Europe.** Genève 1880.
.... **The Advocate of peace.** Boston 1880.

.... **The Arbitrator.** Organ of the Workmen's peace assoc. etc. London 1880.
P.P. **The Herald of peace.** London 1880.

P.P. **Amos,** Sheldon, Political and legal remedies for war. London 1880.
P.P. **Bertolini,** Aless., La guerra e i mezzi di evitarla. Oneglia 1880.
P.P. **Congrès internat.** des sociétés des amis de la paix, tenu à Paris 1878. Paris 1880.
P.P. **Dr. J. H. MacLean's peacemakers.** New York 1880.
.... **Dymond,** Jon., Morality and private and political rights of mankind. London (1880).
.... **Euthys** (Éd. **Droit**), Le désarmement progressif. Paris 1880.
.... **Franck,** Ad., Les auxiliaires des amis de la paix. (dans :) Journal des économistes, 1880, IV, t. 10, p. 124—129.
P.P. **Hahn,** Otto, Ueber Mittel und Wege den Krieg abzuschaffen. (Reutlingen 1880).
P.P. **Kant,** Emm., Essai philosophique sur la paix perpétuelle. Paris 1880.
.... **La Codre,** (J. M. de), Ontologie pratique. Paris (1880).
P.P. **Levi,** Leone, Peace the handmaid of commerce. 3d ed. London (1880).
P.P. **Libertà,** fratellanza e pace. Atti della Lega italiana. Milano 1880.
.... **Lodyjensky,** Proiecty vetchnavo mira i ikh znatchenië (= Projets de paix perpétuelle et leur importance). Moskva 1880.
.... **Osseg,** Ann., Der europäische Militarismus. Amberg 1880.
.... **Reduction** of European armaments. The debate .... on the motion of Mr. Henry Richard for an address to the Crown. London (1880).
.... **The past decade** and peace (issued by the *Peace Soc.*). (1880).
.... **Tolstoï,** L. N., La guerre et la paix. St.-Pétersbourg 1880.
P.P. **Walterskirchen,** Rob. von, Zur Abrüstungsfrage. Wien 1880. (*Sammlung* öffentl. Vorträge und Reden, IV.)

1881
.... **Address(es) and Annual Report(s) of**.... Peace Society(ies) 1881.
.... **Almanach de la Soc. française des amis de la paix.** Paris 1881.
P.P. **Bulletin de la Soc. des amis de la paix.** Paris 1881.
.... **Bulletin officiel des assemblées** (de la Ligue internat. de la paix et de la liberté). Genève 1881.
P.P. **Jaarboekje van het Nederlandsche Vredebond.** 's-Gravenhage 1881.
P.P. **Le Devoir.** Guise (Aisne) 1881.
P.P. **Les Etats-Unis d'Europe.** Genève 1881.
.... **The Advocate of peace.** Boston 1881.

.... The Arbitrator. Organ of the Workmen's peace assoc. etc. London 1881.
P.P. The Herald of peace. London 1881.
.... The Olive Leaf. A monthly journal of the women's peace and arbitration assoc. London 1881.

.... Boer, L. M. de, Stemmen der natuur en des harten. Groningen 1881.
.... Bühler, v., Krieg oder Frieden. Stuttgart 1881.
.... Chauvet, Emm., Sur la paix perpétuelle. Discours. Caen 1881.
.... De aeldste Kristnes Vidnesbyrd imod Krig. London-Copenhague 1881.
P.P. Field, D. Dudley, Projet d'un code international. Paris-Gand 1881.
.... Gasparin, Agénor de, Trois paroles de paix. Paris 1881.
.... Géraud, P., L'unitéisme, religion universelle. Paris 1881.
.... Green, Thom., The duties of Christian ministers.... in relation to war. Manchester 1881.
.... Guerre ou paix. Strasbourg 1881.
.... Hvorledes skulle kristne handle i krigstid? Stavanger 1881.
.... Jay, John, The inefficacy of war. (1881 ?)
.... Kamarowsky, Leonid, Le tribunal international (en russe). 1881.
P.P. Kant, Imm., Zum ewigen Frieden. Hgb. von Karl Kehrbach. Leipzig (1881).
.... Krieg oder Frieden. Stuttgart 1881.
.... Lemonnier, Ch., Nécessité d'une juridiction internationale. Conférence. Genève (1881).
P.P. Le Play, Pierre-Fréd., La constitution essentielle de l'humanité. Tours 1881.
P.P. Levi, Leone, War and its consequences. London 1881.
.... Lucas, Charles, Observations sur les lois de la guerre. (1881.)
.... Planck, K. Ch., Das Testament eines Deutschen. Tübingen 1881.
.... Poinsot de Chansac, La France et l'Europe. Paris 1881.
.... Rhamon, S., Völkerrecht und Völkerfrieden. Leipzig 1881.
P.P. Richard, Henry, Speech in the House of Commons on the power to make war. London (1881).
P.P. Richard, Henry, The gradual triumph of law over brute force. 3rd ed. London 1881.
.... Richard, Henry, The recent progress of international arbitration. (Paper read at Cologne, 1881.)
.... Stokes, Will., Dare we take human life. (Tract edited bij Miss Peckover.) 1881.
P.P. Tatham, Will. S., War : its opposition to the.... Lord's Prayer. Prize essay. 1881.
.... The enormous evils of military establishments (signé : Edw. Butler). Manchester 1881. (*Peace Conference papers*, 4).

.... The war system of Europe. 1881. (Tract of the *Peace Soc.*)
.... War and the Bible. 1881. (Tract of the *Peace soc.*)
.... Watson, R. S., The Anti-Christian nature and tendency of war. 1881. (Pamphlet of the *Peace Soc.*)

1882
.... Address(es) and Annual Report(s) of.... Peace Society(ies) 1882.
.... Bulletin de la Soc. des amis de la paix. Paris 1882.
.... Bulletin officiel des assemblées et conférence (de la Ligue internat. de la paix et de la liberté). Genève 1882.
P.P. Jaarboekje van het Nederlandsche Vredebond. 's-Gravenhage 1882.
P.P. Le Devoir. Guise (Aisne) 1882.
P.P. Les Etats-Unis d'Europe. Genève 1882.
P.P. Peace and Goodwill. A sequel to The Olive Leaf. London-Wisbech 1882.
.... The Advocate of peace. Boston 1882.
.... The Arbitrator. Organ of the Workmen's peace assoc. etc. London 1882.
P.P. The Herald of peace. London 1882.

P.P. Är den sig så kallande kristna staten kristlig (par Carl Andersson). Enköping 1882.
.... Antydningar om den kristna kyrkans heliga kall (par Carl Andersson). Enköping 1882.
.... Blancard, Jules, Les lauréats-voyageurs. Valréas 1882.
.... Brace, C. L., Gesta Christi. 1882.
.... Burt, Th., Working men and war. (dans :) Fortnightly Review, Dec. 1882.
.... Conversations on war. (Pamphlet) 1882.
.... Davies, J. Llewellyn, Progressive goodwill amongst the nations. 1882.
.... Eschenauer, A., La morale universelle. 2me éd. Paris 1882.
.... Foltz, Jaulmes, G., et Fuzier, P., Articles (dans :) La Chrétienté au XIXe siècle.
.... Frank and William : dialogues illustrating the principles of peace. London 1882.
P.P. Holtzendorff, Franz von, Die Idee des ewigen Völkerfriedens. Berlin 1882. (*Sammlung gemeinverst. wiss. Vorträge*, 403/404).
.... Il testamento di Garibaldi (par E. T. Moneta). 1882. (*Manualetti* per il popolo, 6.)
.... Il vangelo el la democrazia (par E. T. Moneta). 1882. (*Manualetti* per il popolo, 9.)
.... Lemonnier, Ch., Du principe de neutralité et de ses applications. Genève 1882.
P.P. Mission actuelle des souverains par l'un d'eux (par A. Saint-Yves d'Alveydre). 2me éd. Paris 1882.
.... Montgrédien, Wealth creation. 1882.
.... Neumann, Léop., De la paix perpétuelle. Paris 1882.

.... N(ottelle), Le problème de la guerre. Paris
1882.
.... Om möjligheterna för och emot våldsrettens,
.... (par Carl Andersson). Enköping 1882.
(*I Mensklighetens lifsfrågor*, 7).
.... Richard, Henry, The Egyptian crisis. Speech
.... in the House of Commons. (London
1882.)
.... Withers, James, The Messiah King. London
(1882).

1883
.... Address(es) and Annual Report(s) of.... Peace
Society(ies) 1883.
P.P. Bulletin de la Soc. des amis de la paix. Paris
1883.
.... Bulletin officiel des assemblées et conférence
(de la Ligue internat. de la paix et de la
liberté). Genève 1883.
.... Freden. Organ for Foreningen til Danmarks
Neutralisering. København 1883.
P.P. Jaarboekje van het Nederlandsche Vredebond.
's-Gravenhage 1883.
P.P. Le Devoir. Guise (Aisne) 1883.
P.P. Les Etats-Unis d'Europe. Genève 1883.
P.P. Peace and Goodwill. London-Wisbech 1883.
.... The Advocate of peace. Boston 1883.
.... The Arbitrator. Organ of the Workmen's
peace assoc. etc. London 1883.
P.P. The Herald of peace. London 1883.
.... The Peacemaker and Court of Arbitration.
Philadelphia 1883.

.... Address by the women of France.... on behalf
of peace and international arbitration.
London 1883.
P.P. Arnoldson, K. P., Fredsarbetet och dess
motståndare. Stockholm 1883. (*Freds-
föreningens Skrifter*, 1).
.... Borgomaneri, Gaspare, Guerra all' anarchia
internaz. e pace cristiana universale.
Milano 1883.
.... Brasch, Moritz, Die Idee des ewigen Friedens.
(Extrait de : Auf der Höhe? 1883.)
.... Delafutry, Prosper, La paix universelle. Paris
1883.
P.P. Discourse on the shedding of blood (par
Robert Monteith). London 1883 (= 1885 ?).
.... Gasparin, Agénor de, Trois paroles de paix.
Paris 1883.
P.P. Godin, (J. B. A.), Le gouvernement.... et le
vrai socialisme en action. Paris 1883.
.... Hersant, Julien, Temple de la paix. 1883.
P.P. Latsio, G. (= J. M. van Stipriaan Luïscius),
Bellum delebile. Hagae Comitis 1883.
.... Meyer, J. B., Die Nothlüge. (dans :) Vom
Fels zum Meer, Stuttgart 1883/1884.
.... Molkenboer, Herm., Geschichtsunterricht in
Volksschulen und Soldatenwesen. Leipzig
1883.

69

.... Morris, W., Er Krig i Overensstemmelse med
det Ny Testamentes Laere ? (1883.)
.... Morris, W., Om Krigen i aeldre og nyere
Tider. (1883.)
.... Moscheles, F., Patriotism as an incentive to
warfare. London 1883.
.... Newman, F. W., A Christian Commonwealth.
London 1883.
.... Neymarck, Afred, Ce que coûte la paix en
Europe. (dans :) Journal des économistes,
1883, IV. t. 24, p. 94—98.
.... Olivi, L., Sull' indole della guerra. Firenze
1883.
P.P. Procès verbal de la Conférence internat. tenue
à Bruxelles, oct. 1882 ; convoquée par
l'Assoc. internat. de l'arbitrage et de la
paix de la Grande Bretagne (etc.). Londres
1883.
P.P. Richard, Henry, The recent progress of international arbitration. London (1883).
.... Richard, Enrico, Ulteriori progressi del princi-
pio d'arbitrato. Milano 1883.

1884
.... Address(es) and Annual Report(s) of....
Peace Society(ies) 1884.
.... Bulletin de la Soc. des amis de la paix. Paris
1884.
.... Bulletin officiel des assemblées et conférence
(de la Ligue internat. de la paix et de la
liberté). Genève 1884.
.... Freden. København 1884.
.... International arbitration and peace associa-
tion monthly journal. London 1884.
P.P. Jaarboekje van het Nederlandsche Vredebond.
's-Gravenhage 1884.
P.P. Le Devoir. Guise (Aisne) 1884.
P.P. Les Etats-Unis d'Europe. Genève 1884.
P.P. Peace and Goodwill. London-Wisbech 1884.
.... The Advocate of peace. Boston 1884.
.... The Arbitrator. Organ of the Workmen's
peace association etc. London 1884.
P.P. The Herald of peace. London 1884.
.... The Peacemaker and Court of Arbitration.
Philadelphia 1884.

.... Catford, Henry, How the taxes have been
spent (Coloured diagram). (1884).
.... Chiapperini, Fr., La guerra e l'arbitrato inter-
nazionale. Bergamo 1884.
P.P. Deynaud, S., L'arbitrage international. Guise
1884.
.... El internacionalismo (de A. de Marcoartu).
Dictamenes de las Academias de ciencias
morales y politicas de España y Francia.
Madrid 1884.
.... El internacionalismo (de A. de Marcoartu).
Informe leido ante la Real academia de
ciencias morales y politicas (par Fr. de
Cardenas et Casa-Valencia). Madrid 1884.

70

P.P. **Erwin** (= H. **Holtzmann**), Hundert Gedanken über den Krieg. Zürich 1884.

.... **Kamarovsky, L.**, Ob idee mira mejdou narodami (= De l'idée de paix entre nations). (1884.)

.... **Kant, Imm.**, A philosophical treatise on perpetual peace (transl. by J. D. **Morell**). London (1884).

.... **Lacey, W. J.**, Folly of war. (Tract of the *Peace Soc.*) (1884.)

.... **Lacey, W. J.**, War in its true colours. (Tract of the *Peace Soc.*) (1884.)

.... **Loewenthal, Ed.**, A bas les armes. (dans :) Paris-Rome, 14 Sept. 1884.

.... **Lysaght, S. R.**, War, its cost to the producing classes. (Tract of the *Peace Soc.*) (1884.)

P.P. **Mabille, P.**, La guerre, ses lois, son influence. Paris 1884.

.... **Mac Evoy, B.**, Arbitration the best way of settling disputes. (Tract of the *Peace Soc.*) (1884.)

.... **Morris, W.**, Fredsliv i krigstid. Efter **Hancock**: „Fra det irske Oprör". Vejle 1884.

.... **Norsa, Cesare**, I progressi dell' arbitrato internaz. in Italia. Torino 1884.

.... **Opinions** of eminent statesmen and jurists in favour of internat. arbitration. (Paper of the *Peace Soc.*) (1884.)

.... **Passy, Fréd.**, Union des femmes de France.... Conférence. Reims 1884.

.... **Peace** in the pulpit. (Tract of the *Peace Soc.*) (1884.)

.... **Proved practicability** of internat. arbitration. (issued bij the *Peace Soc.*) (1884.)

.... **Pumphrey, S. L.**, All men are brothers. (Tract of the *Peace Soc.*) (1884.)

.... **Robinson, Will.**, The white feather of peace. (Tract of the *Peace Soc.*) (1884.)

.... **Saint-Yves d'Alveydre, Alex.**, Mission actuelle des souverains. 3me et 4me éd.?) Paris 1884.

.... **Sessions, Fred.**, A slave for many years. (Tract of the *Peace Soc.*) (1884.)

.... **Sessions, Fred.**, War and Christianity. (Tract of the *Peace Soc.*) (1884.)

.... **Sessions, Fred.**, Working men and war. (Tract of the *Peace Soc.*) (1884.)

.... **The military profession**: is it a calling for a Christian? Leominster 1884.

.... **Yoxhall, J. B.**, The confessions of a soldier. (Tract 6 of the *Peace Soc.*) (1884).

1885

.... **Address(es)** and **Annual Report(s)** of.... Peace Society(ies) 1885.

.... **Bulletin** de la Soc. des amis de la paix. Paris 1885.

.... **Bulletin officiel des assemblées** (de la Ligue internat. de la paix et de la liberté). Genève, Paris 1885.

.... **Freden.** København 1885.

.... **Fredsvännen.** Månadsblad för Freds- och Skiljedomsföreningen. Stockholm 1885.

P.P. **Internat. arbitration and peace assoc.** monthly journal. London 1885.

P.P. **Jaarboekje van het Nederlandsche Vredebond.** 's-Gravenhage 1885.

.... **Journal de Correspondance** en vue de la fondation d'un conseil perm. et internat.d 'éducation 1885.

P.P. **Le Devoir.** Guise (Aisne) 1885.

P.P. **Les Etats-Unis d'Europe.** Genève 1885.

P.P. **Peace and Goodwill.** London 1885.

.... **The Advocate of peace.** Boston 1885.

.... **The Arbitrator.** London 1885.

P.P. **The Herald of peace.** London 1885.

P.P. **The Peacemaker and Court of Arbitration.** Philadelphia 1885.

.... **A word** to English women. (Tract of the *Women's auxiliary of the Peace Soc.*) (1885.)

.... **An earnest appeal** to all women everywhere. (Tract of the *Women's Auxiliary of the Peace Soc.*) (1885.)

.... **Arbitration** and the public mind. (Pamphlet of the *Peace Soc.*) (1885.)

.... **Blandignère, Adrien**, La soeur de charité. 2me éd. Toulouse 1885.

.... **Bleibender Internazionaler Erziehungsrat** (Niederlande). Bonn (1885).

.... **Bonde, Karl**, En rejsende Officer. Sangspil. 1885.

P.P. **Brasch, Moritz**, Die Idee des ewigen Friedens. (dans :) **Brasch**, Gesammelte Essays und Charakterköpfe I. Leipzig 1885.

.... **Chase, Thom.**, The churches of Christendom responsible for the continuance of war. (Tract of the *Peace Soc.*) (1885.)

.... **Cobden, Richard**, The three panics. (Reprint.) London 1885.

.... **Conseil permanent et international d'éducation** (Pays Bas). Bonn (1885).

.... **Contre la guerre.** Paris 1885.

.... **Discourse** on the shedding of blood (par Robert **Monteith**). London 1885?

.... **Fabre des Essarts**, Humanité. Paris 1885.

.... **Farrer, J. A.**, Military manners and customs. London 1885–1887.

.... **Farrer, J. A.**, Military manners and customs. New York 1885.

.... **Farrer, J. A.**, War and Christianity (dans :) Gentleman's Magazine, 1885. (Aussi pamphlet of the *Peace Soc.*)

.... **Første nordiske fredsmøde**, 17—19 August 1885. Beretning. Kingsted 1885.

.... **Foote, G. W.**, The shadow of the sword. London 1885.

.... Garaude, François, Dissertation philosophique et religieuse sur la paix. Tulle 1885.
.... Guyot, Yves, Lettres sur la politique coloniale. Paris 1885.
.... Hompesch, Adolphe de, Paupérisme et militarisme. Maestricht 1885.
.... Jones, Will., Italy and militarism. (London 1885.)
.... Kant, Em., Per la pace perpetua. Milano 1885.
.... Klingenberg, B. J., Krigsaarsager og fredsbestraebelser. Bergen 1885.
P.P. L'acte général de la conférence africaine de Berlin jugé par la Ligue internat. de la paix et de la liberté. Bâle—Genève 1885.
P.P. Le contrat international (par Guillaume Pays). Paris 1885.
.... Levallois, J., La vérité sur l'arbitrage. Paris 1885.
.... Loewenthal, Ed., La revanche (dans :) La revanche antiguerrière, Mars 1885.
P.P. Lorimer, J., Le désarmement proportionnel (dans :) Revue de droit internat., XVII (1885), p. 50—54.
.... Passy, Fréd., Les conflits internationaux, et la politique internationale (dans :) Journal des économistes, 1885, IV, t. 32, p. 119—121.
.... Richard, Henry, The work of the Peace society, in the past and future. London (1885).
.... The Root principle of peace (Tract of the *Peace Soc.*) (1885.)
.... Tolstoï, L.N., La guerre et la paix. Paris 1885.
.... Tolstoï, L. N., Skazka ob Ivane-dourake (= Le conte d'Ivan le fou). 1885.
P.P. Velio Ballerini, G., Il problema della pace perpetua. Torino 1885.

1886
.... Address(es) and Annual Report(s) of .... Peace Society(ies) 1886.
.... Bulletin de la Soc. des amis de la paix. Paris 1886.
.... Bulletin officiel des assemblées (de la Ligue internat. de la paix et de la liberté). Genève, Paris 1886.
.... Fredsvännen. Veckotidning för fred och broderskap. Stockholm 1886.
P.P. International arbitration and peace association monthly journal. London 1886.
P.P. Jaarboekje van het Nederlandsche Vredebond. 's-Gravenhage 1886.
P.P. Journal de Correspondance, en vue de la fondation d'un conseil permanent.... d'éducation. 1886.
P.P. Le Devoir. Guise (Aisne) 1886.
P.P. Les Etats-Unis d'Europe. Genève 1886.
P.P. Peace and Goodwill. London-Wisbech 1886.
.... The Advocate of peace. Boston 1886.
.... The Arbitrator. London 1886.
P.P. The Herald of peace. London 1886.

73

P.P. The Peacemaker and Court of Arbitration. Philadelphia 1886.

.... Appleton, Lewis, The military and financial condition of Europe. (2d ed.) London 1886.
.... Bajer, Fred., Fredsrejsebreve. København 1886.
.... Bajer, Fred, Om Krigs Forebyggelse. 1886.
.... Berg, F., Hermann Molkenboer. Skolan och fredssaken. Stockholm 1886.
.... Discours sur l'effusion du sang des hommes (par Robert Monteith). (Paris 1886).
.... Fischer, Marie, Pax humanitate. Havre 1886.
.... Freemantle, W. H., A pleading against war. 2. ed. London 1886.
P.P. Geiser, Bruno, Die Ueberwindung des Kriegs durch Entwicklung des Völkerrechts. Stuttgart 1886.
P.P. Geiser, Bruno, Die Ueberwindung des Kriegs. 2. Auflage. Stuttgart 1886.
.... Granjon, F., La fraternité universelle. Saint-Etienne 1886.
P.P. Hompesch, Ad. de, Paupérisme et militarisme. 's-Gravenhage 1886.
.... List of societies in Europe and America for the promotion of internat. concord. London 1886.
.... Mellini, La soluzione giuridica delle controversie internazionali. 1886.
.... Musser, Dan., Non-resistance asserted. Lancaster 1886.
.... Passy, Fred., Discours.... prononcé dans la Chambre des Députés, 22 déc. 1885. Paris 1886. (Extrait du Journal Officiel du 23 déc. 1885.)
.... Pays, Guillaume, Le contrat international. La paix. Paris 1886. (Edition de titre de 1885 ?)
.... Pollard, Will., Peace at any price. Manchester. 1886. (aussi dans : Fraser's Magazine.)
.... Réfutation de la guerre et de la paix de Proudhon. Paris 1886.
.... Richard, Henry, Parliament and war. Speech. London (1886).
.... Seventy years of peace societies, 1816—1886. London (1886).
P.P. Stieler, Karl, Durch Krieg zum Frieden. Stuttgart 1886.
.... Tempia, Il problema del diritto internazionale e la guerra. Firenze 1886.
.... Tolstoï, L. N., War and peace. New York 1886.
.... Vigano, Fr., Confederazione delle Società della pace e dell' arbitrato. Milano 1886.
P.P. War an unnecessary evil, forbidden by Scripture. (Providence 1886.)

1887
.... Address(es) and Annual Report(s) of.... Peace Society(ies). 1887.

74

.... **Bulletin de la Soc. des amis de la paix.** Paris 1887.
.... **Bulletin officiel des assemblées** (de la Ligue internat. de la paix et de la liberté). Genève, Paris 1887.
P.P. **Concord.** The journal of the International Arbitration and Peace Assoc. London 1887.
.... **Fredsvännen.** Stockholm 1887.
P.P. **Jaarboekje van het Nederlandsche Vredebond.** 's-Gravenhagé 1887.
P.P. **Journal de Correspondance** en vue de la fondation d'un conseil permanent.... d'éducation. 1887.
P.P. **L'Arbitre.** Organe du Comité de Paris de la fédération internationale de l'arbitrage et de la paix. 1887.
P.P. **Le Devoir.** Guise (Aisne) 1887.
P.P. **Les Etats-Unis d'Europe.** Genève 1887.
P.P. **Peace and Goodwill.** London-Wisbech 1887.
.... **The Advocate of peace.** Boston 1887.
.... **The Arbitrator.** London 1887.
P.P. **The Herald of peace.** London 1887.
P.P. **The Peacemaker and Court of Arbitration.** Philadelphia 1887.

.... **A good war.** (Tract of the *Peace Soc.*) (1887.)
.... **A plea for peace.** (dans :) **Edinburgh Review,** 166, p. 547—571.
.... **An address....** of the Soc. of Friends for Pennsylvania.... on the subject of war. Philadelphia 1887.
.... **Appeal** to the peoples of Europe (issued by the *Peace Soc.*). 1887.
.... **Bajer,** Fred., Zum künftigen Frieden zwischen Deutschland und Scandinavien. 1887.
.... **Björklund,** Gustaf, Om nationernas sammanväxning. Stockholm 1887.
.... **Black,** Léon, La paix ou la guerre ? Paris 1887.
.... **Bright,** John, (Speech delivered at a meeting of the Peace Soc. at Westminster). 1887.
.... **Defourny,** P., La déclaration de guerre. Paris 1887.
P.P. **Delvico** (= **Van der Wyck**), La pacification européenne. 2ᵐᵉ éd. Bruxelles 1887.
P.P. **Erasme,** Extraits sur la guerre. Nîmes 1887.
.... **Extraits** du rapport annuel (de l'Assoc. de l'arbitrage et de la paix de la Grande Bretagne et de l'Irlande). London (1887).
.... **Fabre des Essarts,** La loi militaire et le service agraire. Paris 1887.
.... **Fischer-Lette,** Marie, Kriegsbilder. Sondershausen 1887.
.... **Guerra,** civiltà et politica coloniale (signé par : Franc. P. **Contuzzi**). (Firenze) 1887.
.... **Hetzel,** (H.), Neuere deutsche Theologen und Philosophen über den Krieg. (dans :) **Protestantische Kirchenzeitung** 1887, p. 711 (etc.).
.... **International Peace.** (dans :) **Nation,** XLV, p. 350—351 (Nov. 3, 1887).
.... **John Bright,** M.P. and the Peace Soc. London 1887.

P.P. **Kamarowsky,** L., Le tribunal international. Paris 1887.
P.P. **Kamarowsky,** L., Quelques réflexions sur les Armements croissants de l'Europe (dans :) **Revue de droit internat.,** XIX (1887), p. 479—486.
.... **Kant,** Imm., Zum ewigen Frieden. Leipzig (1887).
P.P. **L'arbitrage international** devant les parlements. (dans :) **Journal du droit internat. privé,** XIV (1887), p. 417—430.
P.P. **Lavollée,** Renée, Les unions internationales (dans :) **Revue d'histoire diplomat.,** I (1887), p. 331—362.
.... **Lemonnier,** Ch., The problem of European peace : and its progressive solution.... London 1887.
P.P. **Levi,** Leone, International law with materials for a code of internat. law. London 1887.
.... **Levi,** Leone, War and its consequences. London 1887.
.... **Loewenthal,** Ed., L'union européenne de l'avenir. (dans :) **Etendard,** XVI, 2, 1887.
.... **Lopez,** José F., Das internationale Friedensgericht. (Hamburg 1887.)
P.P. **Lorimer,** J., La question du désarmement. (dans :) **Revue de droit internat.,** XIX (1887), p. 472—478.
.... **Lijst** der eerste deelnemers aan de oprichting van een permanenten internat. Raad van opvoeding. (Bonn 1887.)
.... **Mackenzie,** W. Douglas, Christianity and war. Extracts from a sermon, delia. 1887.
.... **Mazzini,** Gius., Europe, its condition and prospects. (dans :) **Mazzinis Essays,** London 1887, p. 261—298.
.... **Proposition** de résolution tendant à l'amélioration du droit internat., présentée par Fréd. **Passy** (etc.). (Paris 1887.)
.... **Rapport** du Comité central (de la Ligue internat. de la paix et de la liberté). De l'établissement d'un tribunal internat. permanent. Genève 1887.
.... **Richard,** Henry, Europe putting on its war paint. (Pamphlet of the *Peace Soc.* 1887.)
P.P. **Richard,** Henry, Papers on the reasonableness of internat. arbitration. London (1887).
P.P. **Rocholl,** Heinr., Ewiger Friede, Abrüstung, Krieg. Magdeburg 1887.
P.P. **Rolin-Jaequemyns,** G., Limitation conventionelle des dépenses et des effectifs militaires. (dans :) **Revue de droit internat.,** XIX (1887), p. 398—407.
.... **Sanitation** v. militarism. (Tract of the *Peace Soc.*) 1887.
.... **Secrétan,** Charles, Folkenes ret til fred. Høvik 1887. (*Bibliothek for de 1000 hjem.*)
.... **Tolstoï,** L. N., Oorlog en vrede. Arnhem 1887.
.... **Unione Lombarda** per la pace e l'arbitrato internazionale. Milano (1887).

.... **Viganò,** F., Confederazione delle società della pace e dell' arbitrato. 2ª ed. Milano 1887.
.... **Where** have the millions gone ? (Tract of the *Peace Soc.*) 1887.

1888

.... **Address(es)** and **Annual Report(s)** of.... **Peace Society(ies)** 1888.
.... **Bulletin de la Soc. des amis de la paix.** Paris 1888.
.... **Bulletin officiel des assemblées** (de la Ligue internat. de la paix et de la liberté). Genève, Paris 1888.
P.P. **Concord.** London 1888.
.... **Fredsvännen.** Stockholm 1888.
P.P. **Jaarboekje van het Nederlandsche Vredebond.** 's-Gravenhage 1888.
P.P. **Journal de Correspondance** en vue de la fondation d'un conseil permanent.... d'éducation. 1888.
P.P. **L'Arbitre** (voir 1887). 1888.
P.P. **Le Devoir.** Guise (Aisne) 1888.
P.P. **Les Etats-Unis d'Europe.** Genève 1888.
P.P. **Peace and Goodwill.** London-Wisbech 1888.
.... **The Advocate of peace.** Boston 1888.
.... **The American Arbitrator.** Philadelphia 1888.
.... **The Arbitrator.** London 1888.
P.P. **The Herald of peace.** London 1888.
P.P. **The Peacemaker and Court of Arbitration.** Philadelphia 1888.

.... **A handy reference list....** relating to internat. peace and arbitration. London 1888.
.... **Anderson,** Carl, Ett inlägg i den sociala frågan. Sala 1888.
.... **Aporti,** Pirro, Delle cause di guerra. Milano 1888. (*Manualetti per il popolo,* 9.)
.... **Bethune-Baker,** J. F., The influence of Christianity on war. Cambridge 1888.
.... **Buisson,** Ferdinand, Conférences et causeries politiques. Paris 1888.
.... **Charbonnier,** Pacifiques et belliqueux. Bruxelles 1888.
.... **Destrem,** Hipp., Les théoriciens de la paix universelle. (dans :) **Nouvelle Revue** (internationale ?), 1 août 1888.
.... **Fèvre,** Henry, Les beautés du militarisme (dans :) **La Révolte,** 23 déc. 1888.
P.P. **Fischer-Lette,** Marie, Entstehung.... der Friedensgesellschaften nebst einer Liste. Leipzig 1888.
P.P. **Fischer-Lette,** Marie, Friede auf Erden. (Sondershausen 1888.)
.... **Fremantle,** W. H., The excellence of arbitration. London 1888.
P.P. **Hertz,** Ed., Der Abbé de Saint-Pierre. (dans :) **Preussische Jahrbücher,** LXII, p. 465—496, 553—573.

P.P. **Hetzel,** H., Leiden und Thaten der Frauen im Kriege. Hamburg 1888. (*Sammlung gemeinverständl. wissenschaftl. Vorträge,* N. F. III, 59.)
.... **Il tempio** della pace. (dans :) **Cuore e critica,** gennaio 1888.
.... **Isocrate,** De pace. Firenze 1888.
.... **Italy** and international peace. London 1888.
.... **Lachmann,** J. J., Er fredsbestraebelserne utopi ? København 1888.
.... **Le droit de la guerre.** Rapport.... de la Ligue internat. de la paix et de la liberté. Genève 1888.
P.P. **Lemonnier,** Ch., Formule d'un traité d'arbitrage permanent entre nations. 2me éd. Genève-Paris (1888).
.... **Moneta,** E. T., La morte dell' imperatore Guglielmo. L'utopia di Mazzini e la pace. Milano 1888. (*Manualetti per il popolo,* 8.)
.... **Peace versus war :** the principle and precedent of combination. London 1888.
.... **Relazione** all' assemblea generale (dell' Unione Lombarda per la pace e l'arbitrato). Milano 1888.
P.P. **Résolutions** votées par les 21 premiers congrès (de la) Ligue internat. de la paix et de la liberté. Genève 1888.
.... **Rougier,** La teoria soziale per l'abolizione della guerra. Milano 1888.
.... **Schiff,** Paolina, L'influenza della donna sulla pace. Milano 1888.
P.P. **Sinigaglia,** Giorgio, Del concetto della pace nei pensatori antichi e nei moderni. Milano 1888.
.... **Stötzer,** E., Des Menschen Wert. Salzburg 1888.
P.P. **Sundblad,** Carl, Hvarför bilda vi fredsforeningar. (Stockholm 1888.)

1889

.... **Address(es)** and **Annual Report(s)** of.... **Peace Society(ies)** 1889.
P.P. **Almanach de la paix.** Paris 1889.
.... **Bulletin officiel des assemblées** (de la Ligue internat. de la paix et de la liberté). Genève 1889.
P.P. **Concord.** London 1889.
.... **Folkens Framtid.** 1889.
P.P. **L'Arbitre** (voir 1887). 1889.
.... **La Revue libérale.** 1889.
P.P. **Le Désarmement.** Paris 1889.
P.P. **Le Devoir.** Guise (Aisne) 1889.
.... **Leggetemi.** Almanacco illustrato. Milano 1889.
P.P. **Les Etats-Unis d'Europe.** Genève 1889.
.... **Pacific Banner.** Winthrop Centre, Maine 1889.
P.P. **Peace and Goodwill.** London—Wisbech 1889.
.... **The Advocate of peace.** Boston 1889.
.... **The American Arbitrator.** Philadelphia 1889.
.... **The Arbitrator.** London 1889.
P.P. **The Herald of peace.** London 1889.

.... **The Messiah's Kingdom.** Organ of the Christian Union for promoting international concord. London 1889.

P.P. **The Peacemaker and Court of Arbitration.** Philadelphia 1889.

.... **A key to the deliberations** of the annual peace congresses. (1889.)

.... **Androcles** (= Constant **de Vos),** Anathème à la guerre. 2me éd. Bruxelles 1889.

P.P. **Aperçu historique** du mouvement en faveur de la paix. (Paris 1889.)

.... **Appleton** (Lewis), Memoirs of H. Richard, the apostle of peace. London 1889.

P.P. **Atti del congresso** di Roma per la pace e per l'arbitrato internaz. (12—16 maggio 1889). Città di Castello 1889.

.... **Bajer,** Fred., Til Dansk fredsforenings medlemmer ! København 1889.

.... **Baker,** J. F. B,, The influence of Christianity on war. New York 1889. Voir aussi 1888 **Bethune.**

.... **Cariolato,** Dom., La propaganda per la pace. Vicenza 1889.

P.P. **Congrès internat.** de la paix. Compte rendu sommaire des séances. Paris 1889.

.... **Darby,** W. Evans, A league of peace. A paper. June 25, 1889. London.

.... **Deyo,** Amanda, Fondation d'une société d'arbitrage. Poissy (1889).

P.P. **Die Ursachen der Kriege** und die Wege zum Frieden. Leipzig 1889.

.... **Dudley,** Crews, The ultimate problem. London 1889.

P.P. **Dymond,** Jon., War : its causes, consequences etc. An essay. Manchester, London (1889).

.... **Dymond,** Joh., War, etc. 3d ed. New York (1889?).

.... **Federation** vs war. (dans :) **Westminster Review,** 131, p. 1—7 (Jan. 1889).

.... **Fernandez Prida,** Joaquin, La paz armada. Sevilla 1889.

P.P. **Fischer-Lette,** Marie, Frieden durch Erziehung. (Sondershausen 1889.)

.... **Garchine,** Vsevolod, La guerre. Paris 1889.

.... **Geetruyen,** Edm. van, Le problème de la paix. Roma 1889.

P.P. **Hersant,** Julien, Le temple de la paix. Paris 1889.

P.P. **Horrida bella ;** an impeachment of the war system. (par William **Catchpool ?)** London 1889.

.... **Howard,** R. B., The new sympathy of the nations. 1889.

P.P. **Kant,** Imm., Den evige fred. (Christiania 1889.) (*Bibliothek for de tusen hjem,* 191—193.)

.... **Kaye,** D., Militarism and aggressive war. Glasgow 1889.

P.P. **Klerck,** R. A., Enkele beschouwingen over vredebonden en arbitrage. 's-Gravenhage 1889.

.... **La fraternité** des peuples. Quimperlé 1889.

.... **La pace** e le cause della guerra. Roma 1889. (Estratto della **Rivista militare italiana,**1889.)

.... **La Société américaine** de la paix. Statuts et liste des membres. Cambridge, Mass. (1889).

.... **Lachmann,** J. J., L'oeuvre de la paix est-elle une utopie ? Copenhague 1889.

.... **Latchmore,** Jos., The Soc. of Friends and the American civil war. (Tract of *the Peace Soc.* 1889.)

.... **Le congrès interparlementaire** de la paix. (dans :) **Journal** des économistes, 1889, IV, t. 47, p. 84—90.

P.P. **Lemonnier,** Charles, Entwurf eines bleibenden Schiedsgerichts-Vertrages zwischen den Völkern. Genève, Sondershausen (1889 ?).

.... **Les Amis de la paix** du Puy-de-Dôme. Statuts et documents divers. Clermont-Ferrand 1889.

.... **Lockwood,** Belva A., Discours prononcé en séance plénière du Congrès internat. de la paix. (Paris 1889.)

.... **Moneta,** E. T., Del disarmo e dei modi pratici per conseguirlo. 1889.

.... **Moneta,** E. T., Il governo e la nazione. Discorso. Milano 1889.

.... **Neergaard,** N., Frihandels- og Fredsvennen Richard Cobden. 1889.

.... **Nourry,** Claudius, Paix. Poème. Paris 1889. (*Anthologie universelle,* 68.)

.... **Outlay certain.** — Defences uncertain. (Tract of *the Peace Soc.* 1889.)

.... **Passy,** Fréd., (Discours d'ouverture au Congrès international de la paix dans :) **Revue libérale** (1889), p. 335—348.

.... **Ponvosin,** E., L'exposition et la paix. Paris 1889.

.... **Powerful undercurrents** in relation to war. (Tract of *the Peace Soc.* 1889.)

.... **Questionnaire,** note (de la) comm. d'étude pour.... un Bureau internat. de la paix. Versailles (1889).

.... **Résolutions proposées** par la 2me commission sur la neutralisation. Paris 1889.

.... **Résolutions votées** à Paris (par divers congrès en 1889). Genève 1889.

.... **Résolutions votées** par le Congrès de Gothenbourg, le 17—19 août 1885. Copenhague 1889.

.... **Rovere,** Alberto, Lingua e città internazionale. Casale 1889.

.... **Scandinavian peace associations** with extract of report of the 1st united peace meeting at Gothenbourg 1885. Wisbech 1889.

.... **Séances des 29 et 30 juin 1889** (de la) 1ère conférence interparlementaire. Paris 1889.

.... **Sessions,** Fred., We dare not fight ; Christ forbids. (1889.)

.... **The new naval panic.** An address from the Peace Soc. (1889.)

P.P. The Paris peace congress.... Response of
America to the world's demand for leader-
ship. Boston 1889.
.... Tolstoï, L. N., Krieg und Frieden. 2. Aufl.
Berlin 1889.
P.P. Tolstoï, (Leo) de, La guerra y la paz. Madrid 1889.
.... Tolstoï, L. N., War and peace. New York 1889.
.... Umano, (= C. Meale), La fine delle guerre
nella federazione dei popoli. Milano 1889.
P.P: Valbert, G. (= V. Cherbuliez), L'arbitrage
internat. et la paix perpétuelle. (dans :) Revue
des deux mondes, XCII (1889), p. 184—210.
.... Wachenhusen, Hans, Wird's noch Kriege
geben ? (dans :) Schorer's Familienblatt,
1889, p. 692—698.
.... War panics and war doings. Manchester (1889).

1890
.... Address(es) and Annual Report(s) of.... Peace
Society(ies) 1890.
P.P. Almanach de la Paix. Paris 1890.
.... Bulletin de la Soc. française pour l'arbitrage
entre nations. Paris 1890.
.... Bulletin officiel des assemblées (de la Ligue
internat. de la paix et de la liberté). Genève,
Paris 1890.
P.P. Bulletin trimestriel de l'assoc. des jeunes amis
de la paix. Nîmes 1890.
P.P. Concord. London 1890.
P.P. Jaarboekje van het Nederlandsche Vredebond.
's-Gravenhage 1890.
.... L'Amico della pace. Almanacco illustrato.
Milano 1890.
.... La Libertà e la Pace. Palermo 1890.
.... La Paix. Paris 1890.
.... Le Courrier de l'Europe. London 1890.
.... Le Désarmement. Paris 1890.
P.P. Le Devoir. Guise (Aisne) 1890.
P.P. Les Etats-Unis d'Europe. Genève 1890.
.... Pacific Banner. Winthrop Centre, Maine 1890.
.... Peace Almanac (prepared by the Lancashire
Friends). 1890.
P.P. Peace and Goodwill. London—Wisbech 1890.
.... The Advocate of peace. Boston 1890.
.... The Arbitrator. London 1890.
.... The Christian Arbitrator and Messenger of
peace. Richmond, Ind. 1890.
P.P. The Herald of peace. London 1890.
.... The Messiah's Kingdom. London 1890.
P.P. The Peacemaker and Court of Arbitration.
Philadelphia 1890.

.... Abbott, H., War under new conditions. (dans :)
Forum, IX, p. 13—23 (March 1890).
.... Androcles, Anathème à la guerre. 2me éd.
Paris 1890.
.... Arbitration treaties and tribunals. (London
1890).
P.P. Arnoldson, K. P., Är världsfred möjlig ?
Stockholm (1890).

.... Arnoldson, K. P., Fredsarbeidet og dets mod-
standere. Bergen 1890.
P.P. Arnoldson, K. P. Lov — ikke krig mellem
folkene. Fagerstrand pr. Høvik (1890 ?).
(*Bibliothek for de tusen hjem* [439—444].)
.... Bajer, Fred., Den Dansk-Amerikanske Vold-
giftssag. (Extrait de : Tilskueren.) 1890.
.... Bajer, Fred., Interparlamentariske Konfe-
rencer. København 1890.
P.P. Bar, L. von, Friedensbürgschaften. (dans :)
Die Nation, VII, 50 (13 Sept. 1890).
.... Benham, Will., The Christmas song a reality.
London 1890.
.... Boardman, G. D., Disarmament of nations.
Address. (Washington) 1890.
.... Bonghi, Rug., La Pace. (dans :) Nuova Antho-
logia di Firenze, 4 sept. 1890.
.... Boys' brigades. (par W. E. Darby ? Tract of
the *Peace Soc.*) 1890.
.... Carrier, Felix, Le désarmement. Bourg-en-
Bresse 1890.
P.P. Cassel, Paulus, Völkerfrieden und Sozialdemo-
kratie. Berlin 1890.
.... Concorso Moneta. Relazione della commis-
sione esaminatrice. Milano 1890.
.... Cramer, S., De Doopsgezinden en het heden-
daagsche antimilitarisme. (dans :) De doops-
gez. Zondagsbode 1890.
.... Cramer, S., J. B. Zwaardemaker-Visscher,
G. J. Boekenoogen, De weereloosheid onzer
vaderen. (dans :) De doopsgez. Zondags-
bode 1890.
.... Dalla vera pace. La vera gloria (par A. Tachard).
Berne 1890. (Extrait de „Il secolo," 20—21
ottobre 1889.)
.... Darby, W. E., Military drill in schools. (Pamphlet of the *Peace Soc.*) (1890 ?)
.... Delivet, Emile, L'exagération des charges
militaires. Havre 1890.
.... Denis, Ernest, Georges de Podiebrad. Paris
1890.
.... Depraz, Ch., Les congrès de la paix et les anni-
versaires socialistes. Turin 1890.
.... Ducommun, Elie, Résumé d'un discours
prononcé à Grenoble. Genève 1890.
.... Ducommun, Elie, Skizze einer in Grenoble
gehaltenen Rede. Biel 1890.
.... Du Puy, Ch. M., How can Europe disarm with
safety. London (1890).
.... Dymond, Jon., War : its causes, consequences
(etc.). London 1890.
P.P. Dyserinck, J., De weerloosheid volgens de
Doopsgezinden. (dans :) De Gids 1890, I.
P.P. Europa vor der Frage : Abrüstung oder Krieg ?
2. Aufl. Kassel 1890.
P.P. Fiore, Pasquale, Un appel à la presse (etc.).
Paris 1890.
.... Francisci, Annibale, Fra sogni e utopie. Milano
1890.

.... **Gledstone,** J. P., Boy soldiers. (Pamphlet of the *Peace Soc.*) 1890.

P.P. **Hamaker,** H. J., Redevoering in de alg. vergadering van het Prov. Utrechtsch Genootschap. Utrecht 1890.

P.P. **Harden,** Max., Ein Kultur-Roman. (dans :) **Die Nation,** VII, 22, 1. März 1890.

.... **Hedin,** A., En oväntad indvändning mot mellemfolklig skiljedom. Stockholm 1890. (Extrait du **Aftonbladet.**)

.... **Heringa,** K., S. **Wartena** Jr., A. C. **Leendertz,** H. **Vrendenberg** Cz., De weerloosheid der oude Doopsgezinden. (dans :) De doopsgez. **Zondagsbode** 1890.

.... **Hilty,** Carl, Der ewige Friede, seine Wünschbarkeit. Frauenfeld 1890 (Extrait du : **Schweiz. Monatschrift für Offiziere,** II, 1—2.)

.... **Historical** outline of the modern peace movement. (par W. E. Darby ?) London (1890).

.... **Holland,** H. Scott, The redemption of war. 1890. (*Christian Union Paper,* 6.)

.... **Holland,** S. L., International arbitration (dans :) **Westminster Review,** 133, p. 240—252 (March 1890).

.... **Howard,** R. B., A battle as it appeared to an eye-witness. (1890 ?).

.... **Howard,** R. B., Peace in London. (dans :) **Our Day,** VI, p. 329.

.... **Howard,** R. B., Peace in London. (dans :) **Unitarian Review,** XXXIV, p. 244.

.... **Howard,** R. B., Progress and prospects of peace. Annual report of the American Peace Soc. Boston 1890.

.... **Hymans—Hertzveld,** E., Ten oorlog. (dans :) De doopsgez. **Zondagsbode** 1890.

.... **Kamarowsky,** L., La question du désarmement. (dans :) Trois essais, Moscou 1890, p. 18—24.

.... **Kamarowsky,** L., Sur les tendances des peuples à la paix. (dans :) Trois essais, Moscou 1890.

.... **Kamarowsky,** L., Ueber die Friedensbestrebungen der Völker (etc.). Moskau 1890.

P.P. **Katscher,** L., Frieden ! Frieden ! Frieden ! Dresden—Leipzig 1890.

.... **King,** Alex., The cry of Christendom for a divine eirenikon. 2me éd. London 1890.

.... **Kottié,**von, Die Gefahren des Krieges.Graz 1890.

P.P. **Krause,** K. Ch. F., Grundlage des Naturrechtes. Leipzig 1890.

.... **Löwenberg,** J., Vor dem Feind. Trauerspiel. Altona—Leipzig 1890.

.... **Mead,** Lucia A., Great thoughts for little thinkers. 1890.

P.P. **Meurer,** Chr., Völkerrechtliche Schiedsgerichte. Würzburg 1890.

.... **Molkenboer,** H., De permanente internationale Raad van opvoeding. Amsterdam 1890.

P.P. **Montluc,** L. de, Le congrès de la paix de Londres de juillet 1890. (dans :) Revue de droit internat., XXII (1890), p. 366—370.

.... **Notham,** Paul, La paix de l'Europe. Paris (1890 ?).

P.P. **Nys,** E., Histoire littéraire du droit international. (dans :) **Revue de droit internat.,** XXII (1890), p. 371—384.

.... **Omberg,** J. M., Irene. En samling fredssånger. Stockholm 1890.

.... **Opinions** on international arbitration. (Tract of the *Peace Soc.*) 1890.

.... **Passy,** Fréd., Congrès monétaire internat. de 1889. Paris 1890. (*Bibliothèque* des Annales économiques.)

.... **Passy,** Fréd., Le Congrès de la paix et la Conférence interparlementaire. (dans :) **Journal des économistes,** V, t. 3, p. 236—239.

.... **Pax vobiscum.** 2nd ed. London 1890.

.... **Pemjean,** Lucien, La paix nécessaire. Paris 1890.

.... **Per la pace** e l'arbitrato internazionale. Torino 1890. (Supplemento alla **Gazzetta Piemontese.**)

.... **Perez,** Fr. P., L'arbitraggio e la pace universale. Palermo 1890.

P.P. **Proceedings** of the (2nd) Universal Peace Congress. (London) 1890.

P.P. **Rapport** de la commission d'examen à l'Union lombarde pour la paix. Modène 1890.

P.P. **Reiswitz,** W. v., B. v. Suttner und der ewige Frieden. (dans :) **Das Magazin** für die Literatur des In- und Auslandes LIX, 39, p. 601—603.

.... **Resolutions** of the Paris Peace Congress of 1889. London 1890.

.... **Richard,** Henry, Defensive war. London 1890.

.... **Romance** and reality in war. (Tract of the *Peace Soc.*) 1890.

P.P. **Saint-Georges d'Armstrong,** Th. de, Principes généraux du droit internat. public. Paris 1890.

P.P. **Scarabelli,** Ignazio, Cause di guerra in Europa. Ferrara 1890.

.... **Schiff,** Paolina, La pace gioverà alla donna ? Milano 1890.

.... **Sessions,** F., Duties of ministers of religion with regard to peace. (Tract of the *Peace Soc.*) 1890.

.... **Suttner,** Bertha von, Die Waffen nieder. Dresden—Leipzig 1890.

.... **Sveistrup,** Poul, Fredsvennernes Katekismus. København 1890.

.... **The cost** of recent wars. (Tract of the *Peace Soc.*) 1890.

.... **The curse** of conscription. (Tract of the *Peace Soc.*) 1890.

.... **The illustrated** peace almanac. Birmingham 1890.

.... **Thomas Carlyle** on war (Tract of the *Peace Soc.*) 1890.

P.P. **Thomas,** Reuen, The universal peace congress. Sermon. London 1890.

.... **Thomas,** Reuen, The war system. Boston 1890.
.... **Tschernuschensko,** D., (Bestrebungen nach Frieden. En russe.) Charkow 1890.
.... **Umano** (= C. **Meale),** La fine delle guerre. Ed. popolare. Milano 1890.
.... **Umano** (= C. **Meale),** The end of war. London 1890.
.... **Wagstaff,** Horace H., War: is it justifiable? London 1890.
P.P. **Watson,** R. S., The anti-Christian nature and tendency of war. Manchester 1890.
.... **What is war?** (Tract of the *Peace Soc.*) 1890.
.... **Wolff,** Adolphe, Discours .prononcé.... à la séance d'ouverture (du Congrès univ. de la paix à Londres). (Londres 1890.)
.... **W(ood),** L. C., The Haydocks testimony. Philadelphia 1890.
.... („on a scheme for securing universal peace" dans :) Shih Pao (journal chinois), 1890.
.... (on the Philadelphia Christian arbitration and peace soc. dans :) **The Washington Post,** March or April 1890.

1891
.... **Address(es) and Annual Report(s)** of.... **Peace** Society(ies) 1891.
P.P. **Almanach de la paix.** Paris 1891.
.... **Bulletin officiel des assemblées** (de la Ligue internat. de la paix et de la liberté). Genève, Paris 1891.
P.P. **Bulletin trimestriel de l'Assoc. des jeunes amis de la paix.** Nimes 1891.
P.P. **Concord.** London 1891.
.... **Dansk Fredsforenings Medlemsblad.** København 1891.
.... **Fred paa Jorden.** En Julebog for Fredsvenner København 1891.
P.P. **Jaarboekje van het Nederlandsche Vredebond.** 's-Gravenhage 1891.
.... **L'Amico della pace.** Milano 1891.
.... **La Libertà e la Pace.** Palermo 1891.
.... **La Pace.** Torino 1891.
P.P. **Le Devoir.** Guise (Aisne) 1891.
P.P. **Les Etats-Unis d'Europe.** Genève 1891.
.... **Pacific Banner.** Winthrop Centre, Maine 1891.
P.P. **Peace and Goodwill.** London—Wisbech 1891.
P.P. **Progress by Peace.** Annual report of the American Peace Soc. Boston 1891.
.... **The Acorn.** 1891.
.... **The Advocate** of peace. Boston 1891.
.... **The Arbitrator.** London 1891.
.... **The Christian Arbitrator.** Richmond, Ind. 1891.
P.P. **The Herald** of peace. London 1891.
.... **The Messiah's Kingdom.** London 1891.
P.P. **The Peacemaker and Court of Arbitration.** Philadelphia 1891.

.... **Adam,** Paul, Pour la guerre. Paris 1891.
.... **Adelsköld,** C., L'Espero. (Hymne en Esperanto.) 1891.

.... **Aguanno,** G. d', L'abolizione della guerra. Milano 1891.
P.P. **Albicini,** C., Le utopie del diritto internazionale. Bologna 1891.
P.P. **Am Vorabend des Weltkrieges.** Kassel 1891.
.... **Amberly,** Lord, Can war be avoided? (dans :) **Fortnightly Review,** XV, p. 614—633 (May 1891).
.... **Appel** de la Société des Amis. Londres—Paris 1891.
P.P. **Arnoldson,** K. P., Kain, hjälten för dagen. Falun (1891). *(Sma väckare, 1.)*
.... **Arnoldson,** K. P., Sma väckare. Falun 1891.
.... **Bajer,** Fred., Danske og norske smaaskrifter om fredssagen. København 1891.
.... **Bajer,** Fred., Fredsvennernes krigsplan. København 1891.
.... **Bajer,** Fred., Piano di guerra. (1891).
.... **Bajer,** Fred., Plan de guerre. Paris 1891.
.... **Bajer,** Fred., Tactics for the friends of peace. Wisbech (1891?).
.... **Barth,** (Articles dans :) **Die Nation.** Berlin 1891.
.... **Bjoernson,** B., L'oratorio de la Paix. 1891.
.... **Bonner,** C., The cruelty of war. (Tract of the *Peace Soc.*) 1891.
.... **Burritt,** El., A word to boys. (Tract of the *Peace Soc.*) 1891.
.... **Burroughs,** S. M., Two great factors for peace. 1891.
.... **Carducci,** G., La guerra. Bologna 1891.
.... **Carducci,** G., La guerra. 2ª ed. Bologna 1891.
.... **Compagnoni-Natali,** G. B., Reminiscenze del 1878. Montegiorgio 1891.
.... **Cyon,** E. de, La guerre ou la paix? Paris 1891.
.... **Defourny,** Le militarisme. Rapport.... (dans :) **Revue catholique** du droit, mars 1891.
.... **Dehorter,** A., Réformes pédagogiques. Mémoire. Guise 1891.
.... **Demolins,** Ed., La guerre ou la paix. (dans :) **La science morale.** XI, p. 281.
.... **Demophilos,** (= Ed. **Müller),** Le lendemain de la guerre à venir. Bruxelles 1891.
.... **Den parlamentariske fredskongres** i London. Kristiania 1891.
.... **Die europäische Angst** und die neue Politik. Dresden—Leipzig 1891.
.... **Eternal peace,** views of a statesman. San Francisco 1891.
.... **Extrait des procès-verbaux** (de la IIIe Conférence interparlementaire). Rome 1891.
.... **Extraits d'Erasme** sur la guerre. (Tract of the *Friends' Tract Assoc.*) 1891.
.... **Fèvre,** Henry, Les beautés du militarisme. (dans :) **La Révolte,** janv. 1891.
.... **Fischer,** Marie, Die Entstehung und Entwickelung der Friedensgesellschaften. Frankfurt a. M. 1891.
.... **Fischer—Lette,** Marie, Die Versammlung zu Rom. Frankfurt a. M. 1891.

.... **Forbes**, A., Warfare of the future. (dans :) **Nineteenth Century**, XXIX, p. 782—795.

.... **Fredsforeningernes Sangbog**. Thisted 1891.

.... **Galeppi**, Gugl., Sulla pace. Biella 1891.

.... **Gobat**, (A ?), Die interparlementarische Konferenz in Rom. Bern 1891.

.... **Gray**, J. G., Peacemakers the sons of God. London 1891.

.... **Gray**, J. G., The universal peace congress. 1891.

.... **Harmening**, E., Das Recht der Völker auf Frieden. Breslau 1891.

.... **Hélio** (= Mort. **Gronou**), La dernière saignée. Paris 1891.

P.P. **Hetzel**, H., Die Humanisierung des Krieges. Frankfurt a. O. 1891.

.... **Howard**, R. B., Topics for essays and discussions. 1891 (*American Peace Soc. Publications.*)

.... **Huberti**, Frieden und Recht. (dans :) **Deutsche Zeitschrift für Geschichtswissensch.** II, 1.

.... **Indberetning** fra de norske delegerede angaaende.... freds-og voldgiftskongressen. (Kristiania 1891.) (*Stortingsdokument* 101, 1891).

.... **Indberetning** fra de norske delegerede. Kristiania 1891. (Bilag til „**Dagbladet**".)

.... **Jodl**, Fr., Morals in history (dans :) **Internat. Journal** of Ethics, Jan. 1891, p. 18.

P.P. **Kant**, Imm., Principles of politics, including his essay on perpetual peace. Edinburgh 1891.

.... **Krieg**, Friede und Erziehung. Leipzig 1891.

P.P. **La Fontaine**, Henri, Essai de bibliographie de la paix. Bruxelles 1891.

.... **La guerre** et le Christianisme. London—Paris 1891. (*Friends' Tract Assoc.*)

.... **La paix**. Etude de l'esprit politique. (par J.-L. W.) Lyon 1891.

.... **Lacey**, W. J., The folly and mistakes of war. (Tract of the *Peace Soc.*) 1891.

.... **Lacey**, W. J., War in its true colours. (Tract of the *Peace Soc.*) 1891.

.... **Lannes de Montebello**, M., L'armée, la question sociale. Paris 1891.

.... **Lansdale**, Hale, The war-game. (dans :) **Nineteenth Century**, N° 168.

.... **Limousin**, Ch. M., Causerie. (dans:) **Bulletin** des Sommaires, 1891, p. 678.

.... **Lockwood**, Belva A., La création d'un bureau internat. de la paix. Washington 1891.

.... **Lorini**, Eteocle, Pro pace. Torino 1891.

P.P. **Love**, Alfred H., A brief synopsis of.... the Universal peace union. (Philadelphia) 1891.

.... **Luce**, S. B., Benefits of war. (dans :) **North Americ. Review** 153, p. 672—683.

.... **Lysaght**, S. R., War, its cost. (Tract of the *Peace Soc.*) 1891.

.... **Mac Evoy**, B., Arbitration the best way of settling disputes. (Tract of the *Peace Soc.*) 1891.

.... **Macphail**, James M., A soldier is not a free man. (Tract of the *Peace Soc.*) 1891.

.... **Mazzini**, Gius., Lettera al Congresso per la pace, in Ginevra 1867. Roma 1891.

.... **Mazzoleni**, Ang., L'Italia nel movimento per la pace. Milano 1891.

P.P. **Melander**, E., Fredsdrömmar. Stockholm 1891.

.... **Mémorandum** de la Pologne au congrès de la paix à Rome. Roma 1891.

P.P. **Molkenboer**, H., Die internazionale Erziehungs-Arbeit. Flensburg 1891.

.... **Morin**, Gaston, (Article sur la paix internationale dans :) **Revue libérale** 1891.

.... **Ned med vaabnene** (par B. von **Suttner**). Kristiania 1891.

.... **Nelson**, Heinrich, Zum Weltfrieden. Berlin 1891.

.... **Neymarck**, A., La fortune mobil. franç. et la paix europ. (dans :) **Bulletin** de l'Inst. internat. de statistique, VI, p. 222

.... **Note des sociétés adhérentes** et.... des délégués (au 3ᵐᵉ Congrès internat. de la paix à Rome). (Roma 1891.)

.... **Note** remise le 11 avril 1891 à S.S. Léon XIII. 4.ᵃ ed. (1891.)

.... **Organisation**. Dansk Fredsforening. 2. aendr. opl. København 1891.

.... **Osborne**, G., Peace or war. (dans :) **Contemporary Review**, oct. 1891.

.... **O'shea**, John A., Hans and Hamet. London 1891.

.... **Oxenden**, Bishop, Peace and its hindrances. London 1891.

.... **Pandolfi**, B., Discours prononcé à la Conférence interparl. Rome 1891.

.... **Pandolfi**, B., Résumé de l'histoire du mouvement interparl. Padoue 1891.

.... **Pankhurst**, R. M., Pax Homini under the reign of law. London 1891.

P.P. **Passy**, Fréd., La question de la paix. Guise 1891.

.... **Passy**, Fréd., Le congrès de Rome. (dans :) **Journal** des économistes, déc. 1891, p. 428—432.

.... **Passy**, Fréd., (Article sur le carnage de la guerre dans :) **Revue libérale** 1891.

.... **Paulovic**, A., Der entwaffnete Friede. Spalato (1891).

.... **Paulovic**, A., La paix désarmée. Naples 1891.

.... **Per la pace** : conferenza.... preparatoria al congresso internat. di Roma. Milano 1891.

.... **Prengel**, Th., Der Friedenskongresz und die interparl. Konferenz in Italiën. Königsberg 1891. (Extrait.)

.... **Prima lista** dei membri del Comitato parlam. ital. per l'arbitrato e la pace. Padova 1891.

.... **Pumphrey**, S. L., All men are brothers. (Tract of the *Peace Soc.*) 1891.

.... **Quincy**, Jos., The coming peace. Boston 1891.

.... **Reconciliation** the ground of peace (par J. G. **Gray**). London (1891).

.... **Relazione** del Comitato parlam. ital. per la
   pace. Roma 1891 (Extr. de **La Cultura**).
.... **Résumé** de l'histoire du mouvement interparl.
   pour l'arbitrage. Padoue 1891.
P.P. **Retortillo y Tornos**, A., Apuntes para un estu-
   dio sobre la guerra y la paz armada. Madrid
   1891.
.... **Rizzone**, G., La democrazia e la pace. Palermo
   1891.
.... **Robinson**, E., Is there not a better way ? 1891.
.... **Robinson**, W., The white feather of peace.
   (Tract of the *Peace Soc.*) 1891.
.... **Rohrer**, F., Le droit à la paix. 1891.
.... **Sessions**, F., A slave for many years. (Tract
   of the *Peace Soc.*) 1891.
.... **Sessions**, F. War and Christianity. (Tract
   of the *Peace Soc.*) 1891.
.... **Sessions**, F., Working men and war. (Tract
   of the *Peace Soc.*) 1891.
.... **Siccardi**, F.. Gli eserciti permanenti e la pace.
   Roma 1891.
.... **Spalikowski**, Ed., Au travail pour la paix.
   Rouen 1891.
   Standing court of arbitration. (par) **D. A. R.**
   (dans :) **Nation**, LIII, p. 213 (Sept. 17,
   1891).
.... **Statuten** der vereeniging Pax humanitate.
   (1891.)
.... **Stella**, Sab., La pace perpetua. Torino 1891.
.... **The Peace Society** and its auxiliaries. (Tract
   of the *Peace Soc.*) 1891.
.... **The praises of war.** (par) A. **Repplier**, (dans :)
   The Atlantic Monthly, LXVIII (Dec. 1891),
   p. 796—805.
.... **The proved practicability** of international
   arbitration. (Tract of the *Peace Soc.*) 1891.
.... **The wars** and war system of Europe, 1891.
   (Tract of the *Peace Soc.*) London 1891.
.... **The white Crown.** (dans :) **Century Magazine**,
   Aug. 1891.
.... **Tolstoï**, Leo, Krieg und Vernunft. Berlin 1891.
P.P. **Tripier**, J., Un oiseau de passage. Abbeville
   1891.
.... **Trueblood**, B. F., An das executive board der
   christl. Arbitrations- und Friedensgesell-
   schaft. Ostaloosa 1891.
.... **Umano** (= C. **Meale**), La guerra del prof. Car-
   ducci flagellata. Milano 1891.
.... **Umilta**, A., L'oeuvre de la Ligue internat. de
   la paix et de la liberté. Neuchâtel 1891.
.... **Umilta**, A., L'oeuvre de la Ligue internat.
   de la paix et de la liberté. (autre éd.)
   1891.
P.P. **Umilta**, A., Paix ou guerre. Saint-Imier 1891.
.... **Wilson**, J. J., The devilry of war. 1891.
.... **Witmeur**, Henri, La guerre. Liège 1891.
.... **Yoxhall**, J. H., The confessions of a soldier.
   (Tract of the *Peace Soc.*) 1891.
...., (on arbitration and peace dans :) City
   of London **School magazine**, Oct. 1891.

89

1892
.... **Address(es)** and **Annual Report(s,** of ....
   Peace Society(ies) 1892.
P.P. **Almanach de la paix.** Paris 1892.
.... **American Advocate** of peace and arbitration.
   Boston 1892.
....- **Annales de la paix.** Bruxelles 1892.
P.P. **Bulletin trimestriel** des jeunes amis de la paix.
   Nîmes 1892.
P.P. **Concord.** London 1892.
P.P. **Correspondance autographiée** (du) Bureau
   international de la paix. Berne 1892.
.... **Dansk Fredsforenings Medlemsblad.** Køben-
   havn 1892.
.... **Die Waffen nieder.** Berlin, Dresden, Wien 1892.
P.P. **Jaarboekje van het Nederlandsche Vredebond.**
   's-Gravenhage 1892.
.... **Jahresbericht** der Oesterreichischen Gesell-
   schaft der Friedensfreunde. Wien 1892
.... **Julebog for fredsvenner**, II. København 1892.
.... **L'Amico della pace.** Milano 1892.
.... **La Libertà** e la Pace. Palermo 1892.
.... **La Pace.** Torino 1892.
.... **Le courrier diplomatique.** Roma 1892.
P.P. **Le Devoir.** Guise (Aisne) 1892.
P.P. **Les Etats-Unis d'Europe.** Genève 1892.
.... **Mittheilungen** der Oesterreichischen Gesell-
   schaft der Friedensfreunde. Wien 1892.
.... **Pacific Banner.** Winthrop Centre, Maine 1892.
P.P. **Peace and Goodwill.** London-Wisbech 1892.
.... **Svenska freds- och skiljedomsföreningens**
   Årsbok. Stockholm 1892.
.... **The Arbitrator.** London 1892.
.... **The Christian Arbitrator and Messenger** of
   peace. Richmond, Ind. 1892.
P.P. **The Herald of peace.** London 1892.
.... **The Messiah's Kingdom.** London 1892.
P.P. **The Peacemaker and Court of Arbitration.**
   Philadelphia 1892.
.... **Wochenschrift für einheitliche Jugenderziehung**
   und Volksbildung. Sankt Gallen 1892.

.... **Actes du troisième Congrès** international de la
   paix, Rome 1891. Roma 1892.
.... **Addresses** to the electors, issued by the Com-
   mittee of the Peace Soc. 1892.
.... **Adler**, Moritz, Offenes Sendschreiben an Theo-
   dor Billroth. Berlin u. Leipzig 1892.
.... **Aguanno**, Gius. d', Il programma pratico dei
   fautori della pace. Palermo 1892.
.... **Anspach**, Lucien, La trêve de dix ans. Bruxelles 1892.
.... **Appel** aux instituteurs et institutrices. (Berne
   1892).
P.P. **Appleton**, Lewis, The foreign policy of Europe.
   London (1892).
.... **Appleton**, Lewis, The military and financial
   condition of Europe. 4th ed. London
   (1892).

90

.... **Armament** and disarmament. 1892 (Tract of the *Peace Soc.*).

P.P. **Arnoldson,** K. P., Pax mundi. London 1892.

.... **Aveling,** F. W., Arbitration or war. 1892 (Tract of the *Peace Soc.*).

.... **Avowals** of military waste. 1892 (Tract of the *Peace Soc.*)

.... **Bajer,** Fred., Statsforeninger med Verdensbureauer. (dans :) **Nationaløkonomisk Tidsskrift,** 1892.

.... **Bajer,** Fred., Verdensfredsmødernes meninger. København 1892 (*Dansk fredsforenings smaaskr.* 3).

.... **Bergen,** A., Die Friedensära und das Wehrsystem der Zukunft. Basel 1892.

P.P. **Björklund,** G., Der bewaffnete Friede. Stockholm 1892.

P.P. **Björklund,** G., La paix armée. Stockholm 1892.

P.P. **Björklund,** G., Om den beväpnade freden. Stockholm (1892).

.... **Björklund,** G., The armed peace. Stockholm 1892.

.... **Björklund,** G., Om utvecklings-anarki. Stockholm 1892.

.... **Björnson,** B., Fred. Oratorium. Köbenhavn 1892. (*Dansk fredsforenings smaaskrifter* 5).

P.P. **Boguslawski,** (A.) von, Der Krieg in seiner wahren Bedeutung. Berlin 1892.

P.P. **Bremond d'Ars,** Guy de. Les temps prochains. La guerre etc. Paris 1892.

.... **Brown,** A. W., Vasile Verestchagin. London 1892.

.... **Brown,** A. W., War scenes in word pictures. London 1892.

P.P. **Bulletin du IVe Congrès universel de la Paix.** Berne 1892.

.... **Burroughs,** S. M., A strange dream. London 1892.

.... **Burrows, J.,** Is war compatible with the Christian religion? (1892) (Tract of the *Peace Soc.*).

P.P. **Carlsen,** V., Krigen, som den er. Kjøbenhavn 1892.

.... **Carlsen,** W., War as it is. London 1892.

.... **Castro,** José de, Pour l'arbitrage international. Lisbonne 1892.

.... **Charles Dickens** on a great battle. London 1892.

.... **Clark,** W. S., Arbitration a practical means of settling national disputes. (1892).

.... **Courtépée,** P. F., La paix partout et toujours. Nantes 1892.

.... **Dalla vera pace** la vera gloria. Berne 1892. (Extr. de Il Secolo XXIV, 8457, 20-21 ott. 1889).

.... **Darby,** W. E., Arbitrato internazionale. Milano 1892.

.... **Darby,** W. E., Declarations of war. 1892.

.... **Darby,** W. E., L'arbitrage international. Londres 1892.

.... **Darby,** W. E., Les plus récents progrès de l'arbitrage international. Londres 1892.

.... **Darby,** W. E., Popular responsability in declaring war. 1892.

.... **Darby,** W. E., The more recent progress of international arbitration. London 1892.

.... **Darby,** W. E., The value of the principle : Si vis pacem para bellum. London 1892.

P.P. **De permanente internationale Raad van opvoeding** (par A. H. **Gerhard).** Amsterdam 1892.

.... **Deliberazioni** prese dai tre primi Congressi universali della pace. Milano 1892.

.... **Desjardins,** A., L'arbitrage international. Paris 1892.

.... **Douay,** M., Les bienfaits de la paix. Paris 1892.

P.P. **Dreyfus,** F., L'arbitrage international. Paris 1892.

.... **Durham,** Bishop of (= B. F. **Westcott),** Peace address. 1892.

.... **Dymond,** Jon., An inquiry into the accordancy of war. Philadelphia 1892.

.... **Elsdale,** H., Is war inevitable ? (dans :) **United service magazine,** 127, p. 337—449.

P.P. **„Es müssen doch schöne Erinnerungen sein."** Wien 1892.

.... **Eschenauer,** A., La guerre devant la civilisation. (dans :) **Bulletin de la Soc. d'études philosophiques,** Paris (1892 ?).

.... **Fischer-Lette,** Marie, Friede sei in diesem Hause. Bern 1892.

P.P. **Fischer-Lette,** Marie, L'amour de la patrie. Berne 1892.

.... **Fischer-Lette,** Marie, True patriotism. 1892.

.... **Forster,** A., The Citizen reader, London 1892.

.... **Friedberg,** E., Der ewige Friede. (dans :) **Universum,** 21, 1892.

.... **Friede** und Abrüstung. Dresden 1892.

.... **Frohschammer,** J., Der Religionsfanatismus und der Krieg. (dans :) **Deutsche Revue,** XVII (April 1892).

.... **Garié,** Jean, L'arbitrage international en matière financière. Paris (1892).

.... **Gill,** J. J., A soldier's story. 1892.

.... **Gillett,** Georges, War loans. London 1892.

.... **Grimbert,** Ed., La guerre. Dijon 1892.

.... **Haaf,** Fanny, Vortrag über „Die Waffen nieder". Sankt Gallen 1892.

.... **Håkansson,** Maria, Rödt eller hvitt ? 1892.

.... **Hale,** E. E., Peace on earth. (dans :) **Cosmopolitan,** XII, p. 379.

.... **Hertz,** Fanny, A palm of peace from german soil. (dans :) **Internat. Journal of ethics,** II, p. 201.

.... **Huberti,** L., Gottesfrieden und Landfrieden. Ansbach 1892.

.... **Hughes,** H. P., The philantrhopy of God. London 1892.

.... **Il plebiscito** internazionale per l'arbitrato. Faenza 1892.

122   *1892*

.... **Indberetning** fra de norske delegerede .... til fredskongressen i Rom. (Kristiania 1892). (*Stortingsdokument* 118, 1892).

.... **Jones**, W., Addresses on peace and arbitration. London 1892.

.... **Jones**, W.. Peace and war. London (1892).

.... **King**, Alex, Pax vobiscum. 1892.

.... **Lagneau**, G., Conséquences démographiques pour la France.... (des) guerres. (Paris, Orleans 1892).

.... **Lalatta Costerbosa**, G., Codicillo della pace economica. Parma 1892.

P.P. **Les contes** de l'oncle Georges. Jette, Bruxelles 1892.

.... **Letter** from the Secretary of State (James G. Blaine) relative to a peace conference of the governments of the world. (Washington) 1892.

.... **Levi**, Eliphas, Le catéchisme de la paix. Paris 1892.

.... **Lewakowski**, Ch., Discours prononcé.... (au) congrès de la paix à Berne. Paris 1892.

.... **Liebknecht**, W.. Die Emser Depesche. Nürnberg 1892.

.... **Lockwood**, Belva A., Discours sur la proposition de M. Fr. Bajer. Berne 1892.

.... **Lockwood**, Belva A., Fourth interparl. conference of peace at Berne. (dans :) Amer. journal of politics, I, p. 506.

.... **Logan**, W. S., International tribunals with jurisdiction. (dans :) **Lend a Hand**, VIII, p. 20—25, 1892.

.... **Lopez**, J., Das internationale Friedensgericht. Hamburg—Altona 1892.

.... **Love**, Alfred H., The modern peace movement. (dans :) **Amer. journal of politics**, I, p. 607.

.... **Lugnet**, Marcel, Le monde militaire. Paris 1892.

.... **Mac Dargus**, J., Who are the disturbers of the peace in Europe ? London 1892.

.... **Maineri**, B. E., Le plébiscite international pour l'arbitrage. Roma 1892.

.... **Manfredi**, C., Conferenze interparlementari. Roma (1892).

.... **Marcus(s)en**, W., Die Friedensidee und der vierte Weltfriedenskongresz. (Extrait de : **Schweizerische Rundschau** 1892 ?).

.... **Mariner**, F., Der internat. Friedensrath und die Friedensliga. (dans :) **Oesterreichische Schulzeitung**, 1892, 4—5.

.... **Mazzoleni**, A., La guerre, est-elle nécessaire ? Berne 1892.

.... **Mazzoleni**, A., Nécessité de combler la lacune .... dans la législation des divers états. Rapport. (1892).

P.P. **Melander** (H.) Försvarskriget ifrån biblisk synpunkt. Stockholm 1892.

.... **Mirabelli**, R., Discorso e conferenze. Napoli 1892.

.... **Molkenboer**, H., Geschichtsunterricht in Volksschulen. Leipzig 1892.

.... **Moscheles**, F., Pictures with a purpose. 1892.

.... **Müller**, Ed., Der Friedensvereine Heil und Haken. Berlin 1892.

P.P. **Musset**, E. St. B., Le droit de guerre devant le congrès de Berne. Paris 1892.

.... **Norgelmüller**, Ed., Bismarck und der neue Cours. Zürich 1892.

.... **Oeuvre** de la paix. (par) **A. M.** (dans :) **Revue du 20me siècle**, 1892, p. 47—58.

.... **Pandolfi**, B., La fédération et la paix. Rapport. Rome 1892.

.... **Pandolfi**, B., La federazione e la pace. Venezia 1892.

.... **Pareto**, V., (Sur les dépenses militaires ; en italien) 1892.

.... **Passy**, Fréd., La paix internationale. Paris 1892.

.... **Passy**, Fred., La question de la paix à la conférence de Berne. (dans :) **Compte-rendu** de l'Acad. des sciences mor. et pol., novembre 1892, p. 588—597.

.... **Passy**, Fred., Le congrès de Berne. (dans :) **Revue libérale** 25 sept. 1892, p. 2—8.

.... **Petersen**, N., Gladstone som Fredsven. København 1892. (*Dansk Fredsforening Smaaskrifter* 4).

.... **Pifferi**, Erc., Per la guerra. Torino 1892.

.... **Pisani**, G. C., I funesti effetti della guerra. Firenze 1892.

.... **Pompery**, Ed. de, La guerre tuera la guerre. (dans :) **Revue socialiste**, 15 août 1892.

.... **Procès-verbaux** (du) IV. conférence interparlamentaire. (Berne 1892).

.... **Question** des Roumains.... au congrès de paix. Berne 1892.

.... **Rami d'oliva** o peana ? Firenze 1892.

.... **Résolutions textuelles** des congrès universels de la paix. Berne 1892.

P.P. **Revon**, M., L'arbitrage international. Paris 1892.

.... **Ritter**, Nationalität und Humanität. Dessau 1892.

.... **Robinson**, E., Anti-war manuel. 1892.

P.P. **Rouard de Card**, E., Les destinées de l'arbitrage international. Paris 1892.

P.P. **Rühl**, F., Kant über den ewigen Frieden. Königsberg 1892.

P.P. **Saint-Lanne**, E., et **Ner**, H., La paix pour la vie. 1892.

.... **Sandford**, Arbitration. 1892 (Pamphlet of the *Peace Soc.*).

P.P. **Schlief**, E., Der Friede in Europa. Leipzig 1892.

.... **Seraffini**, G. G., Le due supreme necessità. Roma 1892.

.... **Sessions**, Fred., Moral evils inherent in the war system. London 1892.

P.P. **Sève**, A., Peace and war. London, Glasgow (1892 ?)

93   94

P.P. Spengler, F. de, La guerre et l'arbitrage inter-nat. Genève 1892.
.... Sundblad, C., og J. M. Omberg, Fridens Härold. Köping 1892.
.... Suttner, B. von, Ground arms. Chicago 1892.
.... Suttner, B. von, Lay down your arms. London 1892.
.... Thorp, Fielden, (A report of President Bonghi's opening and concluding addresses) (dans :) Friends' Quarterly Examiner 1892.
.... Thoulet, Scientific warfare. 1892. (Pamphlet of the *Peace Soc.*).
.... Tripier, J., Discours prononcé au congrès de la paix. Berne 1892.
.... Troisième congrès international de la paix. Roma 1892.
.... Vasseur, M., Quelques mots de réponse aux avocats de la guerre. (Poème). Paris 1892.
.... Vidari, Il congresso per la pace in Roma. (dans:) Rendiconti del R. Istituto lombardo di scienze e lettere 24, p. 1125.
P.P. Wie man den Krieg abschafft. Berlin 1892.
.... West, L. H., International quarrels. (dans :) Internat. Journal of Ethics 1892.

1893
.... Address(es) and Annual Report(s) of.... Peace Society(ies) 1893.
P.P. Almanach de la paix. Paris 1893.
.... American Advocate of peace and arbitration. Boston 1893.
.... Annales de la paix. Bruxelles 1893.
P.P. Bulletin du IVe congrès universel de la paix. Berne 1893.
P.P. Concord. London 1893.
P.P. Correspondance autographiée (du) Bureau international de la paix. Berne 1893.
.... Dansk Fredsforenings Medlemsblad. København 1893.
.... Der Friede. Zürich 1893.
.... Die Waffen nieder! Berlin, Dresden, Wien 1893.
.... Giù le armi! Almanacco. Milano 1893.
P.P. Jaarboekje van het Nederlandsche Vredebond. 's-Gravenhage 1893.
.... La Conférence interparlementaire. Berne 1893.
.... La Libertà e la Pace. Palermo 1893.
P.P. La paix par le droit. Nîmes 1893.
P.P. Le Devoir. Guise (Aisne) 1893.
P.P. Les Etats-Unis d'Europe. Genève 1893.
P.P. Monatliche Friedenskorrespondenz. Bern, Berlin 1893.
P.P. Ned med Vapnen. Stockholm 1893.
.... Pacific Banner. Winthrop Centre (Maine) 1893.
P.P. Pax humanitate. Amsterdam 1893.
P.P. Peace and Goodwill. London-Wisbech 1893.
.... Rapport du Bureau internat. de la paix. Berne 1893.
.... Svenska freds- och skiljedomsföreningens Årsbok. Stockholm 1893.

.... The Arbitrator. London 1893.
.... The Christian Arbitrator and Messenger of peace. Richmond (Indiana) 1893.
P.P. The Herald of peace. London 1893.
.... The Messiah's Kingdom. London 1893.
P.P. The Peacemaker and Court of Arbitration. Philadelphia 1893.

.... Arminius, Volksstimmen und Posaunenklänge vom ewigen Frieden. Berlin 1893.
.... Bajer, Fred., Internationale Brücken. (Dresden 1893).
.... Bebel und Liebknecht, Gegen den militarismus. Berlin 1893.
P.P. Becker, W. C., „Patriotismus" contra Civilisation ! Zürich 1893.
.... Bericht die Nationalitäten betreffend. Bern 1893.
.... Beschlüsse der fünf ersten Weltfriedenskongresse. Bern 1893.
.... Birkedahl, U., Til det danske folk om fredssagen. (1893). (*Dansk Fredsfor. Smaaskr.* 7).
.... Boardman, D.G., Nationalism and internationalism. Boston 1893.
.... Brasch, M., Die Ziele der ethischen Bewegung. Leipzig 1893.
.... Brugnoli, B., La pace e il disarmo. Perugia 1893.
.... Burrows, J., Is war compatible with the Christian religion ? London 1893.
.... Butterworth, H., White city by the Inland sea. Boston 1893.
.... Carl (= Erzherzog v. Oesterreich), Aphorismen. Wien 1893.
.... Carrier, F., La triple réforme et la fraternité. Paris 1893.
.... Ciuflea, I., Darea de seama asupra lucrarilor congresului Pacei. Bucuresci 1893.
.... Conemeno, N., Ladri e omicidi. Corfu 1893.
.... Corre, A., Militarisme. Bruxelles 1893.
P.P. Corsi, A., Arbitrati internazionali. Pisa 1893.
.... Darby, W. E., Armed peace. (London 1893).
.... Darby, W. E., The continuing progress of international arbitration. London 1893.
P.P. Darby, W. E., The origin of peace societies. London 1893.
.... De mellan folkliga riksdags mannamötena. Stockholm 1893.
.... Der erste Mai und der Militarismus. (dans :) Neue Zeit, II. p. 100—103.
P.P. Der Militarismus im heutigen deutschen Reich. Stuttgart 1893.
.... Desfontaines, J., La paix. Paris 1893.
P.P. Ducommun, E., Discours sur l'oeuvre de la paix. Berne 1893.
P.P. Ducommun, E., Vortrag über das Friedenswerk. Bern 1893.
.... Engels, F., Kann Europa abrüsten ? Nürnberg 1893.

.... **Ernst,** Otto, Soldaten oder Menschen. Hamburg 1893.
.... **Ferrero,** G., Militarism. N.Y. 1893.
.... **Field,** D. D., Karnak and Carthage. Chicago 1893.
.... **Gaggiano,** G., Soldato rebelle. Napoli 1893.
.... **Gallo,** O., Umanità e fratellanza. 1a ed. Milano 1893.
.... **Gareis,** Carl., Die Friedensbestrebungen unserer Zeit. (dans :) **Nord und Süd,** Okt. 1893.
P.P. **Getaz,** S., Rapport sur l'oeuvre de la propagation de la paix. Bienne 1893.
P.P. **Gizycki,** H. von, Der Krieg. Ethische Betrachtungen. Berlin 1893.
P.P. **Griess-Traut,** Arguments en faveur de la transformation des armées guerrières-destructives. Paris 1893.
.... **Guidotti,** G., I tre papi, ossia la pace tra le chiese christiane. Palermo 1893.
.... **Harmening,** E., Der Krieg und seine Lorbeeren. (dans :) **Ethische Kultur,** 40.
.... **Harmening,** E., Sedanfeier. (dans :) **Ethische Kultur,** 39.
P.P. **Heilberg,** (A.), Die Idee des allgemeinen Völkerfriedens. Breslau 1893.
P.P. **Hilty,** Carl., Ueber Krieg und Frieden.... (dans :) **Politisches Jahrbuch** der Schweiz. Eidgenossenschaft VIII p. 197—273.
.... **Holm,** J., Fredssagen belyst fra et faedrelandsk og bibelsk-kristeligt synspunkt. Aalborg 1893.
.... **Hornby,** Edm., Essay on a permanent court of arbitration. London 1893.
.... **Jacobi,** E., Der Völkermord. Neuwied a.R. 1893.
.... **Jacobi,** E., Der Völkermord. 2. Auflage. Dresden (1893 ?).
P.P. **Jähns,** M., Ueber Krieg, Frieden und Kultur. 2. Auflage. Berlin 1893.
P.P. **Janes,** L. G., War and progress. New York 1893.
.... **Jorrand,** L., Conférence sur la paix. Limoges 1893.
.... **Kamarowsky,** L., L'idée de la paix et le militarisme. (dans :) **Recueil du droit** et des sciences sociales, 1893.
.... **Kapitalismus** und Militarismus. (dans :) **Neue Zeit,** II, p. 193.
P.P. **Krause,** K. C. F., Der Erdrechtsbund an sich selbst. Leipzig 1893.
P.P. **Kükelhaus,** Th., Der Ursprung des Planes vom ewigen Frieden. Berlin 1893.
.... **Landi,** L., Au Congrès de la Paix. Faenza, Berne 1893.
.... **Leeds,** J. W., Ought Christians to engage in war ? 1893.
.... **Leeds,** J. W., The dress parade at West Point. Philadelphia 1893.
P.P. **Leroux,** J., Vos nationalités et vos patries. Paris 1893.
.... **Leverson,** Le nuage de la guerre. Baltimore (1893).

.... **Leverson,** M. R., War clouds. New York 1893.
.... **Loewenthal,** Ed., Offener Brief. (dans :) **Die Neue Standarten,** 6 Mai 1893.
.... **Milkowski,** La morale dans la politique. Genève—Paris (1893).
.... **Molard,** J., Puissance militaire des états de l'Europe. Paris 1893.
.... **Mole,** Ricc. dalle, Tra lauri ed olivi. Vicenza 1893.
.... **Morley,** J., On war and peace. Newcastle (1893 ?).
.... **Moxom,** P. S., The social and moral aspects of war. Boston 1893.
P.P. **Nicolet,** J., Plus de guerre. Bourg-en-Bresse. 1893.
.... **Novicow,** J., Les luttes entre sociétés humaines. Paris 1893.
.... **Ormsby,** M. F., Peace congresses and the peace flag. (dans :) **Home and country,** 1893, p. 615—621.
.... **Pacific settlements.** 1893 (Tract of the *Peace Soc.*).
.... **Pandolfi,** Sul bilancio degli esteri. Roma 1893.
.... **Passy,** F., L'arbitrage international et ses récents progrès. (dans :) **La Réforme sociale,** 1 mars 1893, p. 369—382.
.... **Passy,** F., L'oeuvre de la paix en Amérique, etc. (dans :) **Journal des écon.,** oct. 1893.
.... **Passy,** F., Le prix de la gloire. Orléans 1893.
.... **Petersen,** N., Militarismen og Historieundervisningen. København 1893.
.... **Petition** der Schweizerischen Friedensfreunde an den hohen Bundesrat. Bern 1893.
.... **Pichot,** L., Le désarmement, la paix et l'arbitrage. Tours 1893.
.... **Pisani,** G. C., Les funestes effets de la guerre. Florence 1893.
.... **Pitt,** G., English history with its wars left out ! 2nd ed. Mitcham (Surrey) 1893.
.... **Politique internationale.** 1893 Guerre ou paix. Blois 1893.
.... **Potonié-Pierre,** E., Un peu plus tard. Paris 1893.
.... **Procès-verbal** de la première assemblée générale (de la Commission du Bureau internat. de la paix). 1893.
.... **Quelques traits** d'histoire rétrospective (par Paul Passy). (Orléans 1893).
.... **Rapport** sur les questions se rapportant aux nationalités (du Bureau internat. de la paix). (Berne 1893).
.... **Règlement** pour les assemblées générales (de la Commission du Bureau internat. de la paix). (Berne 1893).
.... **Reichert,** A., Richard Wahrlieb und die Insel Friedland. Dresden u. Leipzig 1893.
.... **Report** on questions relating to nationalities. Berne 1893.
.... **Résolutions prises** dans les cinq premiers Congrès universels de la paix. Berne 1893.

P.P.   Reuter, R., Was will das Volk ? Leipzig 1893.
....   Robinson, E., A word to the working classes. 3d ed. Leominster 1893.
....   Rosegger, P. K., Krig eller fred. Kristiania 1893.
....   Rossel, V., Louis Ruchonnet. 2me éd. Lausanne 1893.
P.P.   Roszkowski, G., Ueber das Wesen und die Organisation der internationalen Staatengemeinschaft. Erlangen 1893. (aussi dans :) Zeitschrift für internat. Privat- und Strafrecht III (1893). p. 253.
....   Schippel, Max, Die Parteien und die Militärfrage. (dans :) Neue Zeit, II, p. 207.
....   Schneider, S., Lösung der sozialen Frage. München 1893.
....   Scholl, C., Krieg dem Kriege ! Bamberg 1893.
....   Sessions, F., The duties of ministers of religion. (Tract of the *Peace Soc.*). 1893.
....   Suttner, B. von, Bas les armes ! Berne 1893.
....   Suttner, B. von, Ned med vapnen ! Stockholm (1893).
....   Suttner, B. de, Le mouvement pacifique en Europe. (dans :) Vie contemporaine, 1893, p. 554.
....   Sveistrup, P., Fredsvennernes Katekismus. 1893 (*Dansk Fredsfor. Smaaskr.* 1).
....   The armed peace of Europe. (Tract of the *Peace Soc.*) (1893).
P.P.   The general programme of the world's congresses of 1893. 1893.
....   The growth of European militarism. (Tract of the *Peace Soc.*). (1893 ?)
....   The proved practicability of international arbitration. London 1893 (Tract of the *Peace Soc.*).
....   Thiebauld, G., L'Europe délivrée. (dans :) Le Figaro, 11 nov. 1893.
....   Thomas, Reuen, The war system. London 1893.
....   Tolstoï, L. Le salut est en vous. Paris 1893.
....   Tolstoï, L., The kingdom of God is within you. New-York (1893 ?).
....   Touchet, La justice internat. dans la guerre et la paix. (dans :) Annales franco-comtoises, juillet/août 1893.
....   Traube, Ludw., Der Militarismus und seine moralische Wirkung. (dans :) Ethische Kultur, 19.
....   Trueblood, (B. F.), (On the Boys' Brigade). (1893 ?).
....   Villari, P., Dove andiamo ? Roma 1893.
P.P.   Wicksell, A. B., Fredsrörelsen. Stockholm (1893). (*Studentföreningen Verdandis Småskrifter*, 49).
....   Williams, F. P., A true son of liberty. New-York (1893). (*The Waldorf series* 7).
....   Wisbech illustrated peace leaflets. New series 1—8. 1893.

1894
....   Address(es) and Annual Report(s) of .... Peace Society(ies) 1894.
....   Almanacco Umbro della pace. Perugia 1894.
P.P.   Almanach de la paix. Paris 1894.
....   Annales de la paix. Bruxelles 1894.
....   Concord. London 1894.
P.P.   Correspondance autographiée (du) Bureau international de la paix. Berne 1894.
....   Der Friede. Zürich 1894.
....   Det Norske Fredsblad. Flekkefjord 1894.
P.P.   Die Waffen nieder. Berlin, Dresden, Wien 1894.
....   Fredsbladet. København 1894.
P.P.   Giù le armi ! Milano 1894.
P.P.   Jaarboekje van het Nederlandsche Vredebond. 's-Gravenhage 1894.
....   L'Amico della pace. Milano 1894.
....   L'Etranger. Paris 1894.
....   L'Europe nouvelle. Paris 1894.
....   La Conférence interparlementaire. Berne 1894.
....   La Libertà e la Pace. Palermo 1894.
P.P.   La paix par le droit. Nîmes et Paris 1894.
....   La Revue pacifique et littéraire. Sainte Colombe 1894.
P.P.   Le Devoir. Guise (Aisne) 1894.
P.P.   Les Etats-Unis d'Europe. Genève 1894.
....   Mittheilungen der Deutschen Friedensgesellschaft. 1894.
....   Monatliche Friedenskorrespondenz. Bern, Berlin 1894.
....   Ned med Vapnen. Stockholm 1894.
....   Pacific Banner. Winthrop Centre (Maine) 1894.
P.P.   Pax humanitate. Amsterdam 1894.
P.P.   Peace and Goodwill. London-Wisbech 1894.
....   Rapport du Bureau internat. de la paix. Berne 1894.
....   Rivista mensile della Società.... „I Pionieri della Pace". Torino 1894.
....   The Advocate of peace. Boston 1894.
....   The Arbitrator. London 1894.
....   The Christian Arbitrator and messenger of peace. Richmond (Indiana) 1894.
P.P.   The Herald of peace. London 1894.
....   The Messiah's Kingdom. London 1894.
P.P.   The Peacemaker and Court of Arbitration. Philadelphia 1894.

....   Again the Panic-Mongers ! (1894 ?) (Tract of The *Peace Soc.*).
....   Aguanno, G. d', L'ideale scientifico della pace. (Estr. dalla Rivista di sociologica I : 4). Roma 1894.
....   Angelis, G. de, La pace e la guerra. Roma 1894.
....   Bajer, F., Dansk fredsforenings historie. København 1894.
....   Beschlüsse der internationalen Friedenskongresse. Bern 1894.

.... **Billard,** E., Léon XIII et le désarmement. Paris 1894.

.... **Birkedahl,** U., Til det danske folk om fredssagen. København (1894). (*Dansk fredsforenings smaaskrifter*).

.... **Charles,** Alb., Pendant la guerre. (dans :) **Société nouvelle,** X, 2.

.... **Code** d'arbitrage. (Rapport du) Bureau int. de la paix. Berne 1894.

.... **Courtépée,** P. F., La paix partout et toujours. Nantes 1894.

.... **Darby,** W. E., The arbitration alliance. London 1894.

.... **Darby,** W. E., L'alliance d'arbitrage. London 1894.

.... **Darby,** W. E. Sermon notes on peace topics. London 1894.

.... **Darby,** W. E., The peace society and what it has accomplished. (dans :) **Pall Mall magazine,** Oct. 1894.

.... **Davis,** H. A., Eighty years of arbitration. (dans :) **Harvard Law review,** VIII, p. 107—110.

.... **Déclaration** de principes. 1890. Statuts (de la Ligue internation. de la paix et de la liberté). 1894.

.... **Desjardins,** A., Bienheureux les pacifiques. Paris 1894. (*Ligue contre l'Athéisme. Conférences*, 13).

.... **Dollfus,** Ch., Les problèmes. Paris 1894.

.... **Ducommun,** E., Aux sociétés de la paix. Berne 1894.

.... **Ducommun,** E., L'oeuvre de la paix. (dans :) **Revue socialiste,** 15 oct. et 15 nov. 1894.

.... **Dymond,** Jon., Essays on the principles of morality. Ninth ed. Dublin, London 1894.

.... **Erasmus** redivivus. Der Moloch des Militarismus. Zürich 1894.

.... **Forbes,** Arch., Vae vulneratis ! (dans :) **Revue des revues,** 15 juin 1894.

.... **Friedensgesellschaften.** (par) **H.** (dans :) **Die Kritik,** 1894, p. 34.

.... **Gewaltpolitik** und Völkerfriede. (dans :) **Freidenker,** Dez. 1894.

.... **Goldbeck,** Ed., Friede auf Erden. (dans :) **Zukunft,** Dez. 1894.

P.P. **Grasserie,** R. de la. Des moyens pratiques pour parvenir à la suppression de la paix armée. Paris 1894.

.... **Grelling,** R., Quousque tandem. Dresden u. Leipzig 1894.

P.P. **Griess—Traut,** Argumente zu Gunsten der Umwandlung der zerstörenden Kriegsarmeen. 3. Ausgabe. Wien 1894.

.... **Griess—Traut,** Fredsvenlig haerreform. København 1894.

.... **Griess—Traut,** Grunde for omdannelsen af ødelaeggende krigshaere. København 1894.

.... **Griess—Traut,** La transformazione delle armate guerriere. Roma 1894.

.... **Griess—Traut,** Transformacion de los ejercitos bélico. Madrid 1894.

P.P. **Griess—Traut,** Transformation des armées guerrières. Paris 1894.

.... **Hamon,** A., Psychologie du militaire professionel. Bruxelles, Paris 1894.

.... **Haury,** S. S., Die Wehrlosigkeit in der Sonntagschule. Dayton, Ohio (1894).

.... **Hofgaard,** H. J., Den seirende verdensopinion. Drammen 1894.

.... **Hornby,** Edmond, Report on the necessity of a perm. Court of arbitration. 1894.

.... **Il padiglione** della pace. Milano 1894.

P.P. **Kamarovsky,** L., Glavnye momenty idei mira v istorii (= moments décisifs de l'idée du pacifisme dans l'histoire). (1894).

.... **Katscher,** Leop., Die Friedensbewegung. (dans :) **West-oestl. Rundschau,** Juli 1894.

.... **Koht,** Halvdan, Union og Freden. 1894.

P.P. **La Ligue** de la paix (par **Picard d'Estelan**). (1894).

.... **La parola** di Leone XIII e la pace armata. (dans :) **Civilta cattol.,** agosto 1894.

.... **Lacaze,** F., Lernen wir uns kennen. (dans :) **Deutsche Wochenschrift,** 1894, 1.

.... **L(e) M(archand),** (G.), La question du désarmement. (dans :) **Revue scientifique,** juillet 1894.

P.P. **Linker,** E., Der Friedenseid. 3. vermehrte Auflage der „Begründung des europäischen Friedens". Dresden, Leipzig 1894.

.... **Linker,** E., Erlauschte Mädchengespräche. Dresden 1894.

.... **Lutte** ou accord pour la vie. (dans :) **Revue socialiste,** mai et juin 1894.

P.P. **Manuel** des lois de la paix. Bruxelles 1894.

P.P. **Martens,** F. de, La question du désarmement dans les relations entre la Russie et l'Angleterre. (dans :) **Revue de droit internat.** XXVI, p. 573—585.

.... **Nieuwenhuis,** F. Domela, Le militarisme. (dans :) **Almanach** de la question sociale pour 1894.

P.P. **Novicow,** J., La guerre et ses prétendus bienfaits. Paris 1894.

.... **On the threshold** of universal peace (dans :) **Review of Reviews,** X (Dec. 1894), p. 635.

.... **Pandolfi,** (B.), Sul bilancio degli affari esteri. Roma 1894.

.... **Passy,** F., La question de la paix. (dans :) **Journal des économistes,** XX (1894), p. 73—79.

P.P. **Passy,** F., La question de la paix. Paris 1894.

.... **Passy,** F., Vérités et paradoxes. Paris 1894.

.... **Patiens** (= G. Moch), L'Alsace—Lorraine devant l'Europe. 2me éd. Paris 1894.

.... **Pax,** ricordo del convegno internazionale per la pace. Perugia 1894.

P.P. **Praechter—Haaf,** F., Eine Stunde im internazionalen Friedensbureau. St. Gallen 1894.

.... **Quartier-la-Tente,** La guerre jugée au point de vue de la morale chrétienne. Neuchâtel 1894.
P.P. **Quartus,** Völkerbund, nicht Völkerkrieg. (Basel 1894).
.... **Rapport** sur les réponses.... au questionnaire relatif à l'idée d'une trève entre les nations européennes. (Berne 1894).
.... **Renooz,** Cél., Les femmes au congrès internat. d'Anvers. (dans :) **Nouv. revue internationale,** Oct. 1894.
P.P. **Report** of the 5th Universal Peace Congress, Chicago. Boston (1894).
.... **Resolutions** of the universal peace congresses. Berne 1894.
.... **Résolutions** prises dans les six premiers congrès universels de la paix. Berne 1894.
.... **Samson—Himmelstjerna,** H. von, Zollkrieg und Weltfrieden. Freiburg i. Br. 1894.
.... **Sarrazin,** E., Mémoire sur la propagande générale. Laon 1894.
.... **Scalvanti,** O., Alberigo Gentile e la pace. Perugia 1894.
.... **Schacht,** Hans, Worte des Friedens aus Frankreich. (dans :) **Gegenwart,** 28.
.... **Sette anni d'esistenza** etc. (*Unione Lombarda per la pace e l'arbitrato*). Milano 1894.
.... **Sève,** A., La guerre et la paix. Bourg 1894.
.... **Sève,** A., Peace and war. London 1894.
.... **Simon,** J., Disarmament (dans :) **Contemporary Review,** LXV (May 1894). p. 609—615.
.... **Sixième anniversaire** de la mort de J.-B.-A. Godin. Laon 1894.
.... **Sixième Congrès** universel de la paix. Clermont-Ferrand (1894).
.... **Statuto** (e Regolamento. *Unione Lombarda per la pace e l'arbitrato*). Milano (1894).
.... **Stobert,** W. L., Plea for peace (dans :) **Westminster Review,** 142 (July 1894), p. 135—141.
P.P. **Suttner,** B. von, Die Waffen nieder! Dresden, Leipzig 1894.
.... **The 6th Universal Peace Congress :** 1894. Berne 1894.
.... **Tolstoï,** L. N., Das Reich Gottes ist in euch. Stuttgart 1894.
.... **Tolstoï,** L., The Kingdom of God is within you. London 1894.
.... **Tolstoï,** L., Christentum und Vaterlandsliebe. Berlin (1894).
.... **Tolstoï,** L., L'esprit chrétien et le patriotisme. Paris 1894.
.... **Tolstoï,** L., Patriotism och Kristendom. Stockholm 1894.
.·.. **Tolstoï,** L., Patriotismus und Christentum. Berlin 1894.
.... **Trarieux,** L., L'arbitrage international. Paris 1894. (*Ligue contre l'athéisme. Conféren·e 9*).
P.P. **Tripier,** J., Discours prononcé au congrès universel de la paix. Bruxelles 1894.

P.P. **Trudjen,** M., Friede! Amsterdam (1894).
.... **Trueblood,** B. F., International arbitration. Address, Ocean Grove, N. J. 1894.
.... **Ueberschär,** M., Im Frieden ruht das Glück. Magdeburg (1894).
.... **Umfrid,** O., Welt- und Zeitartikel (dans :) Grüss Gott, 1894 (etc.).
.... **Una festa** della pace a Roma. Roma 1894.
.... **Urechia,** V. A., Discours. Bucarest 1894.
P.P. **Valbert,** G. (= V. **Cherbuliez),** La guerre et la paix perpétuelle. Paris 1894.
.... **Vrooman and Will,** Abolition of war. (dans :) Arena II, p. 118—144 (Dec. 1894).
P.P. **Zimmerman,** A. R., Internationale arbitrage. Leiden 1894.
.... **Zollinger,** E., Schule und Friedensbestrebungen. Dresden 1894.

1895

.... **Address(es)** and **Annual Report(s)** of.... Peace Society(ies). 1895.
P.P. **Almanach de la paix.** Paris 1895.
P.P. **Concord.** London 1895.
P.P. **Correspondance autographiée** (du) Bureau international de la paix. Berne 1895.
.... **Der Friede.** Zürich 1895.
.... **Det Norske Fredsblad.** Flekkefjord 1895.
P.P. **Die Waffen nieder.** Berlin, Dresden, Wien 1895.
.... **Fredsbladet.** København 1895.
.... **Fredstidende.** Korrespondance redigeret af Fredrik Bajer. (København) 1895.
.... **Giù le armi!** Milano 1895.
P.P. **Jaarboekje van het Nederlandsche Vredebond.** 's-Gravenhage 1895.
.... **Jahresbericht der Oesterr. Gesellschaft der Friedensfreunde.** Wien 1895
.... **L'Etranger.** Paris 1895.
.... **L'Europe nouvelle.** Paris 1895.
.... **La Conférence interparlementaire.** Berne 1895.
.... **La Libertà e la pace.** Palermo 1895.
P.P. **La paix par le droit.** Nîmes, Paris 1895.
P.P. **La Revue pacifique.** Sainte-Colombe 1895.
P.P. **La Revue pacifique et littéraire.** Sainte-Colombe 1895.
P.P. **Le Devoir.** Guise (Aisne) 1895.
P.P. **Les Etats-Unis d'Europe.** Genève 1895.
P.P. **Monatliche Friedenskorrespondenz.** Bern, Berlin 1895.
.... **Ned med Vapnen.** Stockholm 1895.
.... **Pacific Banner.** Winthrop Centre, Maine 1895.
P.P. **Pax humanitate.** Amsterdam 1895.
P.P. **Peace and Goodwill.** London—Wisbech 1895.
.... **Rapport du Bureau internat. de la paix.** Berne 1895.
P.P. **Report** of the 1st annual meeting of the Lake Mohonk conference on internat. arbitration. 1895.

.... Rivista mensile della Società.... „I Pionier: della Pace". Torino 1895.
.... The Advocate of peace. Boston 1895.
.... The Arbitrator. London 1895.
P.P. The Herald of peace. London 1895.
P.P. The Peacemaker and Court of Arbitration. Philadelphia 1895.
.... War or brotherhood. Organ of the Christian Union for promoting international Concord. London 1895. (In continuation of the Messiah's Kingdom).

.... A. F. Åkersberg minne. Stockholm 1895.
.... Aguanno, G. d', L' ideale scientifico della pace internazionale. Roma 1895.
.... Aicard, Jean, Quel fut le vainqueur de 1870 ? (dans :) Le Figaro, 12 sept. 1895.
.... An die Kaiser, Könige und Potentaten. Dresden (etc.) 1895. (Supplément de „Die Waffen nieder".)
P.P. Arnaud, Em., Les traités d'arbitrage. Genève — Paris 1895.
.... Ashe, rev., Sermon against the crime of war. London 1895.
.... Babut, H., A propos du congrès de Berne. (dans :) L'Emancipation, 15 sept. 1895.
.... Bajer, Fred., Statistique des dépenses militaires. Copenhague 1895.
.... Barber, Ida, Die Friedensidee und die Schule. (dans :) Westöstliche Rundschau, Dez. 1895.
.... Benham, Will., The Christmas song a reality. Sermon, 1889. London 1895.
P.P. Björklund, G., Freds- och afväpningsfrågan. Stockholm (1895).
P.P. Björklund, G., Friede und Abrüstung. Berlin 1895.
P.P. Björklund, G., Paix et désarmement. Berne 1895.
.... Björklund, G., Pokoj i rozbrojenie. Poznan 1895.
.... Björklund, G., War and armaments. London 1895.
.... Bleibtreu, Karl, Ewiger Frieden. (dans :) Neue Revue, Jan. 1895.
.... Bowker, R. R., Peace between kin. New York 1895.
P.P. Brunet, Ch., La mission individuelle des pacifiques. Nîmes 1895.
P.P. Bulletin du 6me congrès univ. de la paix, Anvers 1894. Anvers 1895.
P.P. Burrows, Jos., Is war compatible with the Christian religion ? London 1895.
P.P. Cartland, F. G., Southern heroes or the Friends in war time. Cambridge 1895.
.... Chadwick, John W., Peace and war. A sermon. Boston 1895 (?).
P.P. Corsi, Al., Rapport sur les conclusions.... *Assoc. pour la réforme et la codif. du droit des gens*, 17me conférence. Turin 1895.
.... Darby, W. E., Europe in 1895. London 1895.

.... Darby, W. E., The place of internat. law in the evolution of peace. London 1895.
.... Descamps, Dés., A bas les frontières ! Roubaix 1895. (*Bibliothèque du peuple*.)
.... Desclozeaux, J., La guerre. Conférence. Paris 1895.
.... Diggs, L. A., Past and future. War. Peace. (dans :) Arena, XII, p. 275.
.... Dollfus, Ch., Les problèmes. 2e éd. Paris 1895.
.... Douglas, A. M., How to interest children in the subject of peace. 1895.
.... Ducommun, E., La guerre. La croix rouge. La paix. (Berne 1895.)
P.P. Ducommun, E., Le programme pratique des amis de la paix. Berne 1895.
.... Feldhaus, Rich., Die Kunst und die Friedensbewegung. (dans :) Deutsche Bühnengenossenschaft, 1895, 6.
.... Fried, A. H., Die moderne Friedensbewegung. (dans :) Deutsche Hausfrauenzeitung, 1895, 4—5.
.... Fried, A. H., Elsass-Lothringen und der Krieg. Leipzig 1895.
.... Fried, A. H., Friedens-Katechismus. Dresden (etc.) 1895.
.... Friedens- und Kriegsmoral der deutschen Heere. (par) C. v. B. K. Wien 1895.
.... Gillet (George), The old testament on war. Boston 1895.
.... Gori, Gugl., La donna e la pace. Milano 1895.
.... Hubbard, La conférence interparl. de la paix. (dans :) Revue libérale, 11 août 1895.
.... Indberetning angaaende den 5te internat. parlam. fredskonference. (Kristiania 1895. *Stortingsdokument* 153.)
.... Jannum, Kr., Krigens ofre. Aarhus 1895.
P.P. Kamarovsky, L., Ob ideë mira. (dans :) Rousskaia mysl, VII, p. 120—135.
.... Kamarovsky, L., Voina ili mir. Odessa 1895.
.... Katscher, L., War and peace. London 1895. (Extr. de : Free Review.)
.... Krieg und Frieden. (Publié par) L. Katscher. 1895.
.... Lefaivre, A., La propagande pour la paix universelle. (dans :) La quinzaine, 14.
.... Livres de lecture et manuels d'histoire. Copenhague 1895.
.... Lockwood, Belva A., The growth of peace principles. Washington 1895.
.... Magalhaes Lima, S. de, O livro da paz. Lisboa 1895.
.... Mandes, H. P., Solution of war. (dans :) North Amer. Review, 161 (1895), p. 161—168.
.... Marmaduke, emperor of Europe. (par) X (= F. A. Fawkes). Chelmsford 1895.
.... May, Jos., The wicedkness of recklessly invoking war. Philadelphia (1895).
.... Mayer, E. M., Der ewige Friede. Trauerspiel. Mannheim 1895.

.... **Middleton,** Thom., A southerner's plea for peace. (dans:) **Arena,** XII, p. 205—208.

.... **Moch,** Gaston, Autour de la conférence interparl. Paris 1895. (*Questions du temps présent.*)

.... **Morice,** Ch., Le désarmement européen. (Extrait de ?) **Revue libérale** internat., 1895.

.... **Müller,** Gustav, Mehr Licht in unsere Welt. Leipzig (1895 ?).

.... **Novicow,** G., La federazione europea. Milano 1895. (Extrait de :) **Idea liberale,** 1895.

.... **Novikow,** J., La question de l'Alsace-Lorraine. Paris 1895.

.... **Ossmund** (= C. **Sturzenegger),** Friede auf Erden. Bern (etc.) 1895.

.... **Pa Bryon,** Auf der Schwelle des univ. Friedens. (dans :) **Review of reviews** (New York), Dec. 1895.

.... **Passy,** Fréd., L'arbitrage international. (1895).

P.P. **Passy,** Fréd., L'avenir de l'Europe. Paris (1895).

.... **Passy,** Fréd., La question de la paix. Paris 1895. (Extrait de :) **Revue des revues,** 1895.

P.P. **Passy,** Fréd., Les armements de l'avenir. Paris 1895.

.... **Patiens** (= G. **Moch),** Alsace-Lorraine. Paris 1895. (*Etudes sur la paix armée,* 1.)

.... **Peace** and disarmament. (Essais de **Björklund, Reuter et Reiffel.**) London 1895.

.... **Per l'inaugurazione** di una scuola femm. per la pace. Palermo 1895.

.... **Pro pace.** (par) **D. A. B.** Pavia 1895.

P.P. **Rapport** om förhandlingarna vid femte interparl. fredskonferensen i Haag. (Stockholm 1895).

.... **Reiffel,** A., France and peace. Wisbech 1895.

.... **Reuter,** Rich., German prize essay.... Wisbech 1895.

.... **Ricordo** agli amici di Angelo Mazzoleni. Milano 1895.

P.P. **Robinson,** E., Is there not a better way ? Leominster (1895 ?).

.... **Rouanet,** G., Les unions de la paix et le socialisme. (dans :) **Revue socialiste** 1895, p. 708—714.

.... **Solidarietà** latina. Bucuresci 1895.

.... **Souscription** générale pour l'oeuvre pacifique. (Copenhague 1895 ?).

.... **Speech** (by B. F. **Westcott**) at the annual meeting (of the Arbitration alliance). London (1895).

.... **Statistique** des dépenses militaires. Copenhague 1895.

.... **Sundblad,** Carl, Hvarför bilda vi fredsföreningar ? 3e uppl. Stockholm 1895.

.... **Suttner,** A. G. von, Was die Kriegsfreunde sagen (dans :) **Heimgarten,** Juli 1895.

.... **Suttner,** Bertha von, Ned med vapnen. Stockholm 1895.

.... **Tolstoï,** L. N., Patriotisme en Christendom. Dalfsen 1895.

P.P. **Trueblood,** B. F., International arbitration. Boston 1895.

.... **Trueblood,** B. F., The nation's responsibility for peace. Delivered Boston, Febr. 1895.

.... **Trueblood,** B. F., William Penn's holy experiment. Boston 1895.

.... **Vrooman,** Harry C., The ethics of peace. (dans :) **Arena,** XI, p. 118—127.

.... **Walcker,** Die Friedensbewegung. (dans :) **Gegenwart,** Jan. 1895.

P.P. **Walcker,** Karl, Die Notwendigkeit einer europ. Abrüstung. Sondershausen 1895.

.... **Weltcongress** und Weltarmee oder der Weltfrieden. Von N. Wien 1895.

.... **Will,** Th. E., The abolition of war. (dans :) **Arena,** 1895, p. 127—144.

.... **Zook,** J. K., War, its evils and blessings. (1895 ?).

1896

.... **Address(es)** and **Annual Report(s)** of.... Peace Society(ies). 1896.

P.P. **Almanach de la paix.** Paris 1896.

P.P. **Concord.** London 1896.

P.P. **Correspondance bimensuelle.** Berne 1896.

.... **Der Friede.** Zürich 1896.

.... **Det Norske Fredsblad.** Flekkefjord 1896.

P.P. **Die Waffen nieder.** Berlin, Dresden, Wien 1896.

.... **Fredsbladet.** København 1896.

.... **Fredstidende.** København 1896.

P.P. **Giù le armi !** Milano 1896.

P.P. **Jaarboekje van het algemeen Nederlandsch Vredebond.** 's-Gravenhage 1896.

.... **Jahresbericht der Oesterr. Gesellschaft der Friedensfreunde.** Wien 1896.

P.P. **L'Etranger.** Paris 1896.

.... **L'Europe nouvelle.** Paris 1896.

.... **La Conférence interparlementaire.** Berne 1896.

.... **La Libertà e la pace.** Palermo 1896.

.... **La paix.** Genève 1896.

P.P. **La paix par le droit.** Nîmes, Paris 1896.

P.P. **Le Devoir.** Paris 1896.

P.P. **Les Etats-Unis d'Europe.** Genève 1896.

.... **Monatliche Extrablätter über die Friedensbestrebungen im In- und Auslande.** Bern 1896.

P.P. **Monatliche Friedenskorrespondenz.** Bern, Berlin 1896.

.... **Ned med Vapnen.** Stockholm 1896.

P.P. **Peace and Goodwill.** London—Wisbech 1896.

.... **Rapport du Bureau internat. de la paix.** Berne 1896.

P.P. **Report** of the 2d annual meeting of the **Lake Mohonk conference** on internat. arbitration. 1896.

.... **Rivista mensile della Società....** „I Pionieri della Pace". Torino 1896.

.... **The Advocate of peace.** Boston 1896.

.... **The Arbitrator.** London 1896.

P.P.　The Herald of peace. London 1896.
....　The Peacemaker and Court of Arbitration. Philadelphia 1896.
....　War or brotherhood. London 1896.

....　Abbott, Lyman, Christ's law for the settlement of internat. controversies. (dans :) Christianity and social problems. Boston 1896.
....　Annual meetings (of the) Arbitration alliance. London 1896.
P.P.　Arnoldson, K. P., Pax mundi. Uebersetzung von J. Müller. Stuttgart 1896.
....　Ashe, R. P., Sermon against the crime of war. London 1896.
....　Atkinson, E., Cost of an Anglo-American war. (dans :) Forum, XXI, p. 74—88.
P.P.　Aux congrès univ. de la paix (par Fréd. Bajer). Copenhague 1896.
P.P.　Azzeo, R. d', I 'etnarchia o corte arbitrale internazionale. Roma 1896.
....　Bajer, Fred., Aarsager til krig og voldgift i Europa siden aar 1800. Flekkefjord 1896.
....　Bajer, Fred., Armées et flottes productives. Paris 1896.
....　Bajer, Fred., Rapport sur.... une statistique comparative des dépenses militaires. (Budapest 1896).
....　Bajer, Fred. og N. J. Sørensen, Inlet eller alt. Flekkefjord (1896).
P.P.　Balch, Thomas, International courts of arbitration, 1874. Philadelphia 1896.
....　Ballou, Adin, Autobiography, edited by W. S. Heywood. Lowell, Mass. 1896.
....　Bauer, Ach., Kritik der Friedensbewegung. Fiume 1896.
P.P.　Bilder vom Friedenskongress (par G.). (dans :) Neues Pester Journal, 19 Sept. 1896.
....　Breitung, Max, Der Sonnenkaiser. Leipzig 1896.
P.P.　Breukelman, J. B., Redevoering.... bij gelegenheid van het 25-jarig bestaan (van het) Algemeen Nederlandsch Vredebond. 's-Gravenhage 1896.
P.P.　Bulletin du VIIme Congrès universel de la paix, Budapest. Berne 1896.
....　Catellani. La propaganda della pace. Venezia 1896.
....　Code international. Rapport prés. au VIIe congrès de la paix de Budapest. (1896).
....　Crane, Stephen, The red badge of courage. London 1896.
P.P.　Darby, W. E., Sermon notes on peace topics. 1st series. London 1896.
P.P.　Das Buch des Friedens. Bern 1896.
....　Deane, Bishop, Follies and horrors of war. (dans :) North Amer. Review, 162, p. 190—194.
P.P.　Der Friedenskongress. (dans :) Neues Pester Journal, 19 Sept. 1896.
P.P.　Descamps, E., Essai sur l'organisation de l'arbitrage internat. (dans :) Revue de droit internat., XXVIII, p. 5—74.

P.P.　Descamps, E., Essái sur l'organisation de l'arbitrage internat. Bruxelles 1896.
P.P.　Descamps, E., The organisation of internat. arbitration. London 1896.
....　Ducommun, E., Aux sociétés de la paix. (Berne 1896).
....　Ducommun, E., Le congrès de la paix. (dans :) Revue socialiste, 1896. p. 714—723.
....　Ducommun, E., Rapport sur une réforme des manuels scolaires au point de vue des idées pacifiques. (Berne 1896).
....　Dymond, Jon., War, its causes, consequences (etc.). Leominster 1896.
....　Empire, trade and armaments. London 1896.
....　Epheyre, Charles (= Ch. Richet), La douleur des autres. Paris 1896.
P.P.　Fiore, Pasq., Settlement of the internat. question. (dans :) Internat. journal of ethics, VII, 1, p. 20—32.
....　Fleuriaux, J., L'esprit chrétien et le patriotisme. (dans :) Revue de Belgique, 1896, p. 91—100.
....　Fontana, F., Nabuco, Dramatisches Gedicht. Deutsch von B. v. Suttner. Dresden 1896.
....　Fox-Bourne, H. R., European rivalries. London 1896.
....　Fox-Bourne, H. R., Les rivalités européennes. Berne 1896.
....　Fredsvennernes Sanghaefte. Kjøbenhavn 1896.
....　Frei, M. H., Dschingis-Khan mit Telegraphen. 3. Aufl. Leipzig 1896.
....　Fried, A. H., Friedens-Katechismus. 3. Aufl. Dresden 1896.
P.P.　Friede. Von einem Optimisten. (dans :) Nord und Süd, 1896, p. 50—71.
....　Friederici, B., Sedansgedanken. Leipzig 1896.
....　Frollo, Jean, (Article sur la folie des armements dans :) Le petit Parisien, juin 1896.
P.P.　Gates, M. E., Why should we have a permanent system of internat. arbitration ? Boston 1896.
P.P.　Gennadius, J., International arbitration. (dans:) Cosmopolis I, p. 400—415.
....　Giretti, Ed. La cooperazione e la pace internazionale. Caserta 1896.
....　Giretti, Ed., La donna e l'opera internaz. per la pace. Torre Pellice 1896.
....　Gohier, U., Sur la guerre. Propos d'un jeune homme et de François Coppée. Paris 1896.
　　　Gray, J. G., Peacemakers, the sons of God. London 1896.
P.P.　Griess—Traut, Urgence d'une langue internat. Paris 1896.
....　Guétant, L., L'Italie devant l'Europe. Lyon 1896.
....　Hale, E. E., High court of nations. (dans :) Lend a hand, XVII, p. 176—188.
....　Hale, E. E., Permanent tribunal. (dans :) Lend a hand, XVII, p. 33—39.

... **Hamon, A.,** Patrie et internationalisme. Paris 1896.

... **Indberetning** angaaende den 6te internat. parlam. fredskonference. Kristiania 1896. (*Stortingsdokument* 121).

... **Internat. arbitration.** Nat. conference at Washington, April 1896. 1896.

... **Internat. arbitration.** The nat. conference at Washington. London 1896.

... **Jordy,** Über das Leben und Wirken von H. Dunant. Bern 1896.

P.P. **Jung,** Théod.. De la paix. Paris (1896).

.... **Katscher, L.,** Krieg und Frieden. Aus den schriften von B. v. **Suttner.** Berlin 1896.

.... **Le Sueur,** W. D., War and civilisation. (dans :) **Pop. Science monthly,** XLVIII, p. 758—771.

.... **Leeds,** Jos. W.. Against the teaching of war in history text-books. Philadelphia 1896.

.... **Les massacres** d'Arménie. Réponse du sultan, trad. par **U Gohier.** Paris 1896.

.... **Lewakowski,** Karl, Rede.... über die Völkerverbrüderung. Lemberg 1896.

.... **Liste** des membres de la 7me conférence interparlementaire, Budapest 1896.

... **Lockwood,** B. A., A resume of internat. arbitration. Parkesburg, Pa. 1896.

... **Loewenthal,** Ed., Der wahre Weg zum bleibenden Frieden. Berlin 1896.

P.P. **Loewenthal,** Ed.. Der wahre Weg zum bleibenden Frieden. 2. Aufl. Berlin 1896.

P.P. **Loewenthal,** Ed., Ein Welt-Staatenbund. Berlin 1896.

P.P. **Logan,** W. S., A working plan for a permanent internat. tribunal. (1896 ?) (Reprinted from the **Report** of the Lake Mohonk arbitration conference, 1896).

P.P. **Maier,** Gust., Die Schiedsgerichtsfrage und die schweiz. Friedensvereine. Bern 1896.

P.P. **Mead,** E. D., Kant's „eternal peace". Reprinted from editor's table of **New England Magazine,** June 1896. (Boston) 1896.

P.P. **Memorial** of the New York state bar assoc..... recommending the creation of an internat. court of arbitration. (1896).

P.P. **Moore,** J. B., The United States and internat. arbitration. Boston 1896.

P.P. **Morven,** Kalo, The garden of the earth. Suggestion, 1895. (1896).

.... **Müller,** H., Friede auf Erden. Gotha 1896.

.... **Müller,** Rud., Henry Dunant. Stuttgart 1896.

P.P. **Novicow,** J., Der Krieg und seine angeblichen Wohltaten. Leipzig 1896.

P.P. **Novicow,** J., Les luttes entre sociétés humaines. 2e éd. revue. Paris 1896.

.... **Øvergaard,** A., Lov — ikke krig! Flekkefjord (1896).

.... **Ollivier,** R. P., La guerre. Paris 1896.

.... **Opinions.** Arbitration conference, Washington 1896.

... **Ordre du jour** définitif du 7me congrès univ. de la paix. Berne 1896.

.... **Ossmund** (= C. **Sturzenegger),** Paix sur la terre. Berne 1896.

.... **Ouvrages** en dépot. Bureau internat. perm. de la paix. Berne 1896.

.... **Paiva,** João de, Relatorio ácerca das conferencias interparlamentares. Lisboa 1896.

P.P. **Palfray,** L., Contre la guerre. Paris 1896.

.... **Passy,** Fréd., Echos de Budapest. Paris (1896 ?)

.... **Passy,** Fréd., Le congrès des religions à Chicago en 1893. (dans :) **Le Monde économique,** 8 février 1896.

.... **Passy,** Fréd., Le congrès des religions à Chicago en 1893. Paris 1896.

.... **Passy,** Fréd., Le mouvement de la paix en Europe. (dans :) **Revue des revues,** 1 mars 1896.

.... **Passy,** Fréd., Le mouvement pacifique. (dans :) **Bibliothèque universelle** et revue suisse, déc. 1896.

.... **Passy,** Fréd., Peace movement in Europe. (dans :) **American journal of sociology,** II, (July 1896), p. 1—12.

.... **Phelps,** E. J., Arbitration and our relations with England. (dans :) **Atlantic,** LXXVIII (July 1896), p. 26—34.

.... **Pollaroli,** Rob., La guerre. Commedia. Milano 1896.

Posodoff, A letter to Thomas Edison. (A Russian opinion of war.) London (1896).

.... **Prato,** Gius, La teoria della pace perpetua. Torino 1896.

P.P. **Précis** sur le comité permanent franco-italien de propagande conciliatrice. Rome 1896.

.... **Report....** of the conference of members of the Soc. of Friends, held.... in Manchester, 1895. London 1896.

.... **Résultats** de la manifestation des groupes de la paix. Berne 1896.

.... **Résumé** du 1er annuaire (de la) Soc. hongroise de la paix. (1896).

P.P. **Réveillère,** P.-E.-M., L'Europe-Unie. Paris, Nancy 1896.

.... **Revision** des Frankfurter Friedens. (par) Gaston **Moch.** (1896).

P.P. **Revon,** Mich., Philosophie de la guerre. Saint-Quentin 1896.

.... **Revon,** Mich., Die Philosophie des Krieges. München—Leipzig 1896.

.... **Ritchie,** Arthur, Peace with the sword. Philadelphia 1896.

P.P. **Schurz,** Carl, Arbitration in internat. disputes. (dans :) *America and Europe,* a study of internat. relat. New York—London 1896.

.... **Seghers,** Ad., L'illusion de la paix. (dans :) **Philosophie de l'avenir,** avril 1896.

P.P. **Siebenter** internat. **Friedenskongress.** (dans :) **Politisches Volksblatt,** XXII, 259 (Budapest, 20 Sept. 1896).

.... **Smith,** E. G., Our educators for war or peace—
which? Amherst, Mass. 1896.

.... **Sørensen,** N. J., Fred paa jorden. Første
fredsbog. Kristiania (1896).

.... **Sørensen,** N. J., Fremtidens muligheter. Anden
fredsbog. Kristiania (1896).

.... **Statuto** (della) Soc. internaz. per la pace, comitato di Torre Pellice. 1896.

P.P. **Stein,** Ludw., Das Ideal des „ewigen Friedens"
und die soziale Frage. Berlin 1896.

.... **Stourm,** René, Le trésor de guerre. (dans :)
Revue de Paris, 1er mars 1896.

.... **Substitutes** for war. (par) **J. B. W. G.** (dans :)
Westminster Review, 146 (Dec. 1896),
p. 676—680.

.... **Sul** momento attuale (par E. T. **Moneta).**
Milano 1896.

.... **Suttner,** B. von, Die Waffen nieder. Volksaus-
gabe. Dresden 1896.

.... **Suttner,** B. von, Odzbrojte. Praha 1896. (Traduction tchèque de „Die Waffen nieder".)

.... **Suttner,** B. von, Krieg und Frieden. Berlin
1896.

.... **Suttner,** B. von, Wohin? Die Etappen des
Jahres 1895. Berlin 1896.

P.P. **Tableau** synoptique de la création.... des
soc. de la paix, dressé par le Bureau internat.
de la paix. Berne 1896.

P.P. **The American conference** on internat. arbitration held in Washington, April 1896.
New-York (1896).

.... **The wars** and war system of Europe. London
1896.

.... **Thiaudière,** Edm., Etat actuel du mouvement
pacifique en Europe. (dans :) **La Coopéra-
tion des idées,** 1896, p. 25—31.

.... **Thiaudière,** Edm., Un colloque de rois sur l'union
européenne. Paris 1896.

.... **Tolstoï,** L. N. (L'esprit chrétien et le patriotisme. En russe.) Berlin 1896.

.... **Tolstoï,** L. N., La guerre et le service obliga-
toire. Bruxelles 1896.

.... **Tolstoï,** L. N., Le commencement de la fin.
(dans :) **Magazine international,** 1896.

.... **Tolstoï,** L. N. (Le patriotisme ou la paix?
En russe. Berlin 1896.

.... **Tolstoï,** L. N., Patriotismus oder Frieden?
Berlin 1896.

P.P. **Triac,** Jean de, Guerre et Christianisme. Paris
1896.

.... **Triac,** Jean de, Réponse au père Ollivier.
Paris 1896.

.... **Trueblood,** B. F., The coming of peace. (dans :)
The Christian register, Dec. 26, 1896.

P.P. **Umano** (= C. **Meale),** La fine delle guerre.
3ª ed. Milano 1896.

.... **Umfrid,** O., Die verbündeten Staaten Europas.
1896.

.... **Vasseur,** Mich., (Articles sur la folie des armements dans :) **L'Epoque,** juin 1896.

.... **Vetter,** Ferd., Friede auf Erden. Sonetten-
kranz. Bern 1896. *Friede-Freiheit-Men-
schenwürde,* 1.

.... **Weltcongress** und Weltarmee oder der Welt-
friede. Von N. I. Militarismus. 2. Aufl. 1896.

P.P. **Westlake,** John, Internat. arbitration. (dans :)
Internat. journal of ethics, VII, 1 (Oct. 1896),
p. 1—20.

.... **Widmer,** C., Unser Lebensgesetz. Frauenfeld
1896.

Wolff, Julius, Aus dem Felde. 3. Aufl. Berlin 1896.

1897

.... **Address(es)** and Annual Report(s) of.... Peace
Society(ies). 1897.

P.P. **Almanach de la paix.** Paris 1897.

P.P. **Concord.** London 1897.

P.P. **Correspondance bimensuelle.** Berne 1897.

.... **Der Friede.** Zürich 1897.

.... **Det Norske Fredsblad.** Flekkefjord 1897.

P.P. **Die Waffen nieder.** Berlin-Dresden-Wien
1897.

.... **Fredsbladet.** København 1897.

.... **Fredstidende.** København. 1897.

.... **Giù le armi!** Milano 1897.

P.P. **Jaarboekje van den algemeenen Nederlandschen
Vredebond.** 's-Gravenhage 1897.

.... **Jahresbericht der Oesterr. Gesellschaft der
Friedensfreunde.** Wien 1897.

P.P. **L'Arbitrage entre nations.** Paris 1897.

P.P. **L'Etranger.** Paris 1897.

.... **L'Europe nouvelle.** Paris 1897.

P.P. **La Conférence interparlementaire.** Berne 1897.

.... **La Libertà e la pace.** Palermo 1897.

.... **La paix.** Genève 1897.

P.P. **La paix par le droit.** Nîmes, Paris 1897.

P.P. **Le Devoir.** Paris 1897.

P.P. **Les Etats-Unis d'Europe.** Genève 1897.

.... **Monatliche Extrablätter für Friede, Freiheit
und Fortschritt.** Bern 1897.

P.P. **Monatliche Friedenskorrespondenz.** Bern-Berlin
1897.

.... **Ned med Vapnen.** Stockholm 1897.

P.P. **Peace and Goodwill.** London-Wisbech 1897.

.... **Rapport du Bureau internat. de la paix.** Berne
1897.

P.P. **Report** of the 3rd annual meeting of the **Lake
Mohonk conference** on internat. arbitration.
1897.

.... **Rivista mensile della Società....** „I Pionieri
della Pace". Torino 1897.

.... **Svenska freds- och skiljedoms föreningens
Årsbok.** Stockholm 1897.

.... **The Advocate of peace.** Boston 1897.

.... **The Arbitrator.** London 1897.

P.P. **The Herald of peace.** London 1897.

.... **The Peacemaker and Court of Arbitration.**
Philadelphia 1897.

.... **Vrede.** 's-Gravenhage 1897.
.... **War or brotherhood.** London 1897.

.... **Afhold og fred.** Kristiania 1897.
.... **Amo.** Le congrès de l'humanité. Articles groupés par M. **Decrespe.** Paris 1897.
P.P. **Appel** adressé aux étudiants pour fonder la „Corda fratres". Torino 1897.
.... **Appel aux nations.** Mémoire aux gouvernements. Berne 1897.
.... **Arbitration** or war ? 1897.
P.P. **Arbitration** the American principle. New-York 1897.
.... **Aux sociétés de la paix.** Berne 1897.
.... **Bajer,** Fredr., Om Aarsager til Krig og Voldgift i Europa siden Aaret 1800. København 1897.
.... **Beschlüsse** der 8 ersten internat. Friedenscongresse, 1889—1897. (Bern 1897).
.... **Bilz,** F. E., Bessere Zeiten ! Die wahre Lösung der sozialen Frage. Leipzig 1897.
P.P. **Bulletin** du VIIIe congrès univ. de la paix, Hamburg 1897. Berne 1897.
P.P. **Cabane,** E., Pour la paix. Drame en vers. Cahors 1897.
.... **Cappellini,** A., Guerra e pace. Lendinara 1897.
.... **Christian Martyrdom** in Russia. Containing a concluding chapter and letter by Leo **Tolstoï.** London 1897.
.... **Ciccotti,** E., La pace e la guerra nell'antica Atene. (dans :) **Rivista Ital. di sociologia,** 1897, p. 151—177.
.... **Circulaire** aux sociétés et aux amis de la paix. Programme.... du VIIIe congrès. Berne 1897.
.... **Compte rendu** de la VIIe conférence interparl. de Budapest. Budapest 1897.
.... **Compte-rendu** du Bureau français de la paix. Paris 1897.
.... **Conseils** de conciliation internationale. (Signé : Hodgson **Pratt.**) Berne (1897).
.... **Coudert,** Fred. R., Internat. arbitration. (dans:) **American Law Review,** XXXI.
.... **Councils of internat. concord.** (Signé: Hodgson **Pratt.**) London (1897).
.... **Darby,** W. E., International arbitration. A supplement to „ *International Tribunals".* London 1897.
P.P. **Darby,** W. E., Sermon notes on peace topics. 3rd series. London 1897.
.... **Das Buch** des Friedens. 2. revidiertes Tausend. Bern 1897.
.... **De la clause arbitrale....** comme fondement des traités d'alliance défensive (signé : Gaston **Moch)** (1897).
P.P. **De vervolgingen** der Duchoboren in Rusland. Slotbeschouwingen door Leo **Tolstoy.** (1897).
P.P. **Deluns—Montaud,** La guerre et la paix. (dans :) **Questions diplom. et coloniales,** I, p. 129 (etc.).

P.P. **Descamps** (Éd.), Die Organisation des internat. Schiedsgerichtes. Leipzig (1897).
.... **Drew,** Charles H., Internat. arbitration. (dans :) **New-church review** IV, p. 161—174.
.... **Ducommun,** E., Un fil conducteur à travers les délibérations des congrès annuels de la paix. (Berne) 1897.
.... **Ducommun,** E., A key to the deliberations of the annual peace congresses. (Berne) 1897.
.... **Ducommun,** E., Leitfaden zu den Beschlüssen der allg. jährl. Friedenskongresse. Bern 1897.
.... **Ducommun,** E., Aux sociétés de la paix. (Berne 1897).
.... **Ducommun,** E., Le 8me congrès de la paix. (dans :) **Revue socialiste,** 1897, p. 713—720.
P.P. **Ducommun,** E., Le programme pratique des amis de la paix. 2me éd. Berne 1897.
.... **Dunant,** Henry et B. v. **Suttner,** Adresse aux nations de l'Extrême-Orient. 1897.
.... **Egidy,** (M.) von, Die Friedensaera. (dans :) **Versöhnung,** Sept. 1897.
.... **Egidy,** M. von, Die Krieglose Zeit. (dans:) **Versöhnung,** 1897, p. 81—92.
.... **Engel,** A., Der Friedens-Onkel. Wiesbaden 1897.
.... **Ernst,** Otto, Buch der Hoffnung. Hamburg 1897.
.... **Farquharson,** Ch. D., The federation of the powers. London-New York 1897.
.... „**Felicia".** A peace anthem. London 1897.
.... **Fierens-Gevaert,** H., La guerre et la littérature. (dans:) **Journal des débats,** mai 1897.
.... **Fisichella,** S. F., Lotta ed etica. Discorso. Messina 1897.
.... **Ger Ger,** Les femmes et la paix. (dans :) **Revue libérale,** juin 1897.
.... **Godkin,** E. L., Absurdity of war. (dans :) **Century,** XXXI, p. 468—479.
.... **Gohier,** U., Vertus de la guerre. (dans :) **Le Soleil,** 17 février 1897.
.... **Gramont,** Louis de, Les forgerons de la paix. (dans :) **L'Eclair,** oct. 1897.
P.P. **Grasserie,** R. de la, De la transformation des armées. Paris 1897.
.... **Gray,** A., The ghost of war and the potentates of peace. London 1897.
.... **Hampelmann,** Settche, Fridde uff Erde. Frankfurt a. M. 1897.
.... **Held,** Friedensbestrebungen und Friedensvereine. Schweinfurt 1897.
.... **Hottinger,** R., Henri Dunant. Zürich 1897.
.... **Huitième congrès** univ. de la paix. Questions soulevés.... en vue d'un tribunal d'arbitrage permanent. (Signé : Hodgson **Pratt.)** (1897).
.... **Indberetning** om den 7de interparl. fredskonference i Budapest, 1896. (Christiania 1897. *Stortingsdokument* 121.)
P.P. **International tribunals.** A collection by W. E. **Darby.** London 1897.

.... **Jacques** (Frère), Réflexions d'un solitaire. Nantes 1897.
.... **Jahresbericht,** Statuten (etc. der) Oesterr. Gesellschaft der Friedensfreunde. Wien 1897.
P.P. **Kant,** Imm., Perpetual peace. Transl. by B. F. **Trueblood.** Boston 1897.
.... **Kate,** J. J. L. ten, De vredetempel. Epe 1897.
.... **Kate,** J. J. L. ten, Der Friedenstempel. Epe 1897.
.... **Kate,** J. J. L. ten, The temple of peace. Epe 1897.
P.P. **Kate,** J. J. L. ten, New propositions for the internat. peace association. Epe 1897.
.... **Katscher,** Bertha Soldatenkinder. Stuttgart 1897
P.P. **Kazansky,** Pierre, Les premiers éléments de l'organisation univ. (dans :) **Revue de droit int.** et de législ. comp., XXIX, p. 238—247.
.... **Kitchin,** G. W., Ethical considerations. An address. London 1897.
.... **Kofod,** R., Fredssagen. Rönne 1897.
.... **La conquête** de la paix. Montluçon 1897.
.... **Laffite,** J. G., Comment assurer la paix. (dans :) **Revue bleue,** 27 février 1897.
.... **Le congrès** de la paix. (dans :) **Belgique militaire,** 1897, p 200—204.
.... **Legrand,** Louis, L'idée de patrie. Paris 1897.
P.P. **Legrand,** Louis, L'internationalisme et l'idée de patrie. (dans :) **Revue polit.** et parlem., XII, 245.
P.P. **Lewal,** Jules, La chimère du désarmement. Paris 1897.
.... **Lindström,** Johan Kriget utan svärdsslag. Stockholm 1897.
.... **Lockwood,** B. A., Arbitration and the treaties. Washington 1897.
P.P. **Loewenthal,** Ed., Obligatorische Friedensjustiz, nicht Schiedsgericht. Berlin 1897.
.... **Lopez,** José, Das internat. Friedensgericht. Hamburg—Altona 1897.
.... **Love,** A. H., Compliments of a brief synopsis of works.... by the Universal peace union, 1866—1896. (Philadelphia 1897.)
.... **Magalhães Lima,** S. de, L'oeuvre internationale. Paris 1897.
.... **Magelhães Lima,** S. de, Paz e arbitragem. Lisboa 1897.
.... **Mantegazza,** Paolo, L'anno 3000. Milano 1897.
.... **Martha's Tagebuch.** Nach „Die Waffen nieder" (von B. v. **Suttner)** bearbeitet. Dresden (etc.) 1897.
P.P. **May,** R. E., Die Kanone als Industriehebel nach national-sozialem Rezept. Zürich-Leipzig 1897.
.... **Mazel,** Henri, La guerre. (dans :) **Revue de Belgique,** 1897.
P.P. **Melander,** Henning, Värnplikt och samvetstvång. Stockholm (1897).

.... **Melville,** R. D., The prospects of internat. arbitration. (dans :) **Westminster Review,** 147, p. 367—377. (et dans :) **Eclectic magazine,** 128, p. 759—766.
P.P. **Moch,** Gaston, Comment se fera le désarmement. Berne (1897).
.... **Møller,** Dikka, Julehilsen fra Thorsnaes fredsforening. Kristiania 1897.
.... **Müller,** H. Friede auf Erden. Gotha 1897. (Voir aussi ci-dessus: 1896 ?)
.... **Newesely,** Karl, und A. **Renk,** Pax vobiscum ! München—Leipzig 1897.
P.P. **Nosce te ipsum.** Vier Aufsatze von einem Optimisten (p. 153—206 : **Friede).** Breslau 1897.
.... **Parent,** Marie, La guerre ou l'arbitrage. (dans :) **La Ligue,** V. p. 126—130.
.... **Passy,** Fréd., Le mouvement de la paix dans le monde. (dans :) **Revue des revues,** 15 déc. 1897.
P.P. **Passy,** Fréd., L'utopie de la paix. Paris (1897).
.... **Penn,** Will., An essay towards the present and future peace of Europe. (1693/94). Boston 1897.
.... **Per la giustizia** e la pace. Milano 1897.
P.P. **Physsenzidès,** N., L'arbitrage internat. et l'établissement d'un empire grec. Thèse Louvain 1897.
.... **Praechter-Haaf,** F., Eine Friedensplauderei. Vortrag in Huttwyl. 1897.
P.P. **Prato,** Gius, La teoria della pace perpetua. Torino 1897.
.... **Pratt,** Hodgson, Arbitration versus war. London 1897.
.... **Rapport** et proposition touchant la manifestation du 22 février. Berne 1897.
.... **Rapport** om förhandlingarna vid 6te och 7de interparl. fredskonferenserna.... Stockholm 1897.
.... **Rapport** sur la question de la langue internationale. (Signé : G. **Moch.** 1897.)
.... **Rapport** sur l'exécution des résolutions prises par le 7me congrès univ. de la paix. Berne 1897.
.... **Résolutions** textuelles des 8 premiers congrès univ. de la paix, 1889—1897. (Berne) 1897.
.... **Résultats** de la manifestation des groupes de la paix. Berne 1897.
.... **Résumé** des résolutions des 7 premiers congrès univ. de la paix. Berne 1897.
P.P. **Rieninger,** Carl, Eine Posaune zur Friedensbewegung. Schwäb. Hall 1897.
.... **Ryan,** Ch., Adventures of an English surgeon with the Turkish army, 1877—1878. London 1897.
.... **Schindelhauer,** Emma, Sozialismus und ewiger Frieden. Leipzig (1897).
.... **Schmidt,** (G.), Taschenbuch für Freunde des Friedens. Zürich 1897.

P.P.   Besson, E., L'arbitrage internat. (dans :) Revue polit. et parlem., XVII, p. 465-515.
....   Bloch, Is., La paix. Nancy 1898.
....   Bouet, H., Guerre et Christianisme. (dans :) Journal des écon., déc. 1898.
....   Bresca, G. N., La Unione interparl. per la pace. Potenza 1898.
P.P.   Breukelman, J. B., Het ontwapeningsvoorstel van den Tsaar. (dans :) Vragen van den dag, XIII, 10.
....   Bridges, J. H., Democracy and war. (dans :) Positivist review, VI, p. 164.
....   Brown, Ch. R., The outlook for univ. and perm. peace. 1898.
....   Cabot, R., Belligerent discussion. (dans :) Internat. journal of ethics, Oct. 1898.
....   Capper, S. J., The peace congress of Turin. London 1898. (Extr. de) Friends quarterly examiner, Oct. 1898.
....   Clarke, G. S., Tsar's conference. (dans :) Nineteenth century, LIV, p. 697-706.
....   Compte rendu de la 8me conférence (interparl.), Bruxelles 1897. Braine-le-Comte 1898.
....   Compte rendu du Bureau français de la paix (par G. Moch). Paris 1898.
....   Cooke, M. L., Forces making for war. A paper read 1898. London (1898 ?).
....   Crane, Internat. disarmament. 1898/99.
....   Crosby, E. H., The Czar's rescript. 1898.
....   Czar's disarmament. (dans :) The Nation, LXVII, p. 160.
....   Darby, W. E., A political blunder. London 1898.
P.P.   Darby, W. E., Armed peace, or the value of.... si vis pacem para bellum. London (1898 ?). (*The tzar's rescript.*)
....   Darby, W. E., Peace and national prosperity. London 1898.
....   Darby, W. E., Reactionary ethics. London 1898.
....   Die moderne Friedensbewegung und die Jugenderziehung (par R. Meyer, dans :) Schulblatt der Prov. Sachsen, 7 Sept. 1898.
....   Dillon, E. J., Tsar's eirenicon. (dans :) Contemporary review, LXXIV, p. 609-642.
P.P.   Durch die Fluth. Ein Beitrag zur Abrüstungsfrage von A. v. B. Berlin 1898.
P.P.   Egidy, M. v., Die Friedensbotschaft des Zaren. Vortrag. (Danzig 1898.)
P.P.   Eisler, (Rud.), Zur ethischen Bewegung. Leipzig 1898.
....   Fabris, C. Psychology of war. (dans :) Chatauquan, XXVIII, p. 68.
....   Farningham, Mar., A window in Paris. London 1898.
P.P.   Ferrero, G., Il militarismo. Dieci conferenze. Milano 1898.
....   Förer paa Werestchagin. Udstillingen. (1898.)
....   Fontana, G. (e) D. Bartocci, Il Vaticano e la pace. (dans :) Armi e progresso, nov. 1898, p. 122-140.

P.P.   Friedensstimmen. Herausgeg. von L. Katscher. Esslingen 1898.
....   Galassi, L. M., Lo Czar e la pace. Firenze 1898.
P.P.   Garien, V., Un cri d'alarme ! Paris 1898.
....   Gaulke, Joh., Ueber die Grenzen des Nationalismus und Internationalismus. Berlin 1898.
....   Goes, F. van der, Tegen den vrede van den Tzaar. (dans :) De nieuwe tijd, III, p. 656.
....   Gsell, Rud., Die sittliche Weltordnung und der Krieg. (dans :) Schweiz. Protestantenblatt, 1898.
....   Hamon, A., A propos du désarmement (dans :) L'Humanité nouvelle, 2me année, III p. 427-445.
....   Harrison, Fred., Peace and war. (dans :) Positivist review, VI. p. 201.
....   Heilberg, A., Die Erziehung zum Frieden. Breslau 1898.
....   Heilberg, A., Völkerfrieden. (dans :) Der kleine Wanderer, 1898.
P.P.   Incessant armaments. London (1898 ?).
....   Indberetning angaaende det.... bestyrelsesmøde i det Interparl. forbund.... ved John Lund. (Christiania 1898. *Stortingsdokument* 15.)
....   Ingegnieros, José, La mentira patriotica, el militarismo y la guerra. Buenos Aires 1898.
....   Kamarowski, L. (?), (Les progrès de l'idée de la paix. En russe.) Moscou 1898.
....   Karski, J., Völkerrecht und Militarismus. (dans :) Neue Zeit, XVII (1898/99).
....   L'idée de la paix chez les économistes. (dans :) Economiste français, 15 oct. 1898.
....   L'iniziativa dello Czar e la sua attuazione practica. (dans :) Nuova antologia 161 p. 334-346.
....   La cooperazione militare e la pace. (par F. Ranzi. dans :) Armi e progresso, nov. 1898, p. 89-121.
....   La femme et la paix. Appel aux mères portugaises par Caïel (= Alice Pestana). Lisboa 1898.
P.P.   La question du désarmement et la note du Tsar. (dans :) Revue Gén. de droit internat. public, V, p. 687-743.
....   Le Foyer, L., La patrie pacifique. Conférence faite 1898. Paris—Nîmes (1898).
....   Lecomte, L., Thomas de Saint-Georges d'Armstrong. Sa vie et ses oeuvres. Paris (1898).
P.P.   Les grands artisans de l'arbitrage et de la paix. (Tableau de A. Labbé, notice par G. Quesnel.) (Paris) 1898.
....   Lettre aux membres des sociétés françaises de la paix, déc. 1898. Londres (1898).
P.P.   Loewenthal, Ed., Grundzüge zur Reform und Codification des Völkerrechts. (En allemand et en français.) Berlin 1898.
....   Looker on, Russian circular. (dans :) Blackwood, 164 (Oct. 1898), p. 582-588.

.... Lorimer, G. C., Christianity and the social state (chap. XII). Philadelphia 1898.

.... Louis, Paul, Désarmement ? (dans :) **La Revue socialiste**, XXVIII, p. 257-262.

.... Low, Sydney, Should Europe disarm ? (dans :) **Nineteenth Century**, XLIV, p. 521-530.

P.P. Mahy, Fr. de, Le désarmement. (dans :) **Questions diplom.** et colon., V, p. 65-70.

.... Massarani, T. Diporti e veglie. (L'utopia della pace, p. 29-122.) Milano 1898.

P.P. Mead, E. D., Charles Sumner's more excellent way. Boston (1898 ?). (Repr. from **New England Magazine**, Oct. 1898.)

P.P. Mead, E. D., Kant's „Eternal peace". Boston (1898 ?). (Repr. from **New England Magazine**, June 1896.)

P.P. Mead, E. D.. Organize the world! Boston (1898?). (Repr. from **(New England Magazine**, Dec. 1898.)

.... Molinari, G. de, Grandeur et décadence de la guerre. Paris 1898.

.... Muret, M.. Henry Dunant. (dans :) **Revue chrétienne**, 1898, 3, p. 161-178.

.... Murray, D. Chr., The truth about war. Newcastle 1898.

P.P. Nicolas II, Proposition à tous les représentants étrangers. London 1898.

.... Novicow, J., Désespérance et militarisme. (dans :) **Revue des revues**, sept. 1898, p. 470.

.... Olchowik, Pierre, Lettres de —, paysan.... qui a refusé de faire son service militaire en 1895. Genève (1898).

.... Opitz, Hermann, Wider den Krieg, für den Frieden. Frankfurt a. M. 1898.

.... Ossip—Lourié, Pensées de Tolstoï. Paris 1898.

.... Paiva, João de, Arbitrage international. Résolutions (des) conférences interparl. Lisbonne 1898.

P.P. Passy, Fréd., Le mouvement de la paix en 1898. Paris 1898 (Extr. de) **Revue des Revues,** déc. 1898.

.... Passy, Fréd.. The advance of the peace movement. (dans: American) **Review of rexiews,** XVII, p. 183—188.

.... Passy, Fréd., Une fête de la paix. (dans :) **Le monde économique,** 15 oct. 1898.

P.P. Pratt, Hodgson, Internat. arbitration, its necessity and its practicability. London 1898 (*Humanitarian league's* publications, n.s., 1.)

P.P. Proces-verbal de l'assemblée générale des délégués des sociétés de la paix, Turin 1898. Berne 1898.

.... Rapport sur les manifestations du 22 février 1898. Berne (1898).

P.P. Reduction of armaments. London (1898 ?). (*The tzar's rescript.*)

.... Resolutions of the 8 universal peace congresses. 1889-1897. Berne 1898.

.... Résolutions textuelles des 8 premiers congrès univ. de la paix. Berne 1898.

.... Robinson, H. P., La dernière guerre. (dans :) **Revue des revues,** 1 et 15 août 1898.

.... Rogers, J. G., The Tsar's proposed conference and our foreign affairs. (dans :) **Nineteenth Century,** LIV, p. 706-717.

.... Ross, J. H., War and peace in hymnology. (dans :) **Homiletic review,** XXXV, p. 555.

.... Sandberg, S. Ø. og Johan Houen, Oliegrenen. Fredssangbog. Fredrikshald 1898.

.... Sørensen, N. J., Enden er naer ! Kristiania 1898.

.... Strauss, Dav. Fr., Kleine Schriften. 3. Aufl. Bonn 1898. (Voir aussi ci-dessus 1870).

.... Suttner, B. von, Gio las armas. Samaden 1898.

.... Tchertkoff, V., Ou est ton frère? Purleigh 1898.

.... Tchertkoff, V., The league of peace in relations to the Nazarenes. (dans :) **The new order,** 1898, p. 1—4.

.... The Czar's manifesto on disarmament. Great town's meeting. Harrogate (1898).

P.P. The European disease of militarism. London (1898 ?). (*The tzar's rescript.*)

.... Thomas, Reuen, The war system. 3d ed. Boston 1898.

.... Tiberi, Leop., La teoria della pace perpetua. (dans :) **La Favilla,** genn.—febbr. 1898.

.... Triebel, E., Was kann die Schule zur Förderung der Friedensbewegung beitragen ? Bonn 1898. (*Samml. pädag. Vorträge.* X, 11.)

.... Tsar's appeal for peace. By a soldier. (dans :) **Contemporary review,** LXXIV, p. 498-504.

.... Umfrid, O., Der Krieg auf der Anklagebank. Esslingen 1898.

.... Umfrid, O., Der russische Abrüstungsvorschlag. (dans :) **Gegenwart,** 1898.

P.P. Umfrid, O., Friede auf Erden ! 2. Aufl. Esslingen 1898.

.... Umfrid, O., Völkerevangelium. Heilbronn (1898 ?).

.... Una spiegazione necessaria. (Signé : Ed. Giretti.) Torini 1898.

P.P. Valmigère, P., De l'arbitrage international. Thèse. Paris 1898.

.... Walker, Th. A., Sursum corda. A sermon. London 1898.

.... War : the Shepherd's sorrow. (By Eliz. **Hanbury,** when El. **Sanderson** about 1812.) London 1898.

.... Ward, E. S. P., Russia as a missionary. (dans :) **Independent,** L, p. 1656-58.

.... Welsh, Herb., The ethics of the war. 1898.

.... Wheeler, B. I., Russia's peace proposition. (dans :) **Independent,** L, p. 669-672.

INDEX, 1776–1898

INDEX ALPHABETIQUE DES NOMS PROPRES

Les nombres indiquent les années. Quelquefois, pour faciliter la recherche, l'année est suivie entre parenthèses du numéro de la colonne.

ALPHABETICAL INDEX OF NAMES

The numbers refer to the years. Occasionally, to facilitate the looking up, the number of the column is added in brackets.

About the Editor

PETER VAN DEN DUNGEN is lecturer in Peace Studies at the University of Bradford. Among his publications are bibliographical studies of two seventeenth century peace classics, Emeric Crucé's *The New Cyneas* (1623) and William Penn's *Essay towards the Present and Future Peace of Europe* (1693), as well as *A Bibliography of the Pacifist Writings of Jean de Bloch* (1977). He also contributed the introductory essay "Peace Encyclopedias of the Past and Present" to the *World Encyclopedia of Peace* (1986).

JACOB TER MEULEN (1884-1962) was director of the library of the Peace Palace in The Hague from 1924-1952. He is the author of a standard three-volume history of the idea of international organization and peace, and of the definitive bibliography of Hugo Grotius, the founder of modern international law.

ARTHUR EYFFINGER was deputy director of the Peace Palace library from 1985-1988 and since Spring 1988 is librarian of the International Court of Justice. He is secretary of the Grotius Institute, The Hague, and executive editor of *Grotiana*. Most recently he has published, commemorating its 75th anniversary, *The Peace Palace: Residence for Justice, Domicile of Learning* (1988).